Health Education and Administration

Health Education and Administration

Rashmi Soni

ATLANTIC

PUBLISHERS & DISTRIBUTORS (P) LTD

Published by

ATLANTIC

PUBLISHERS & DISTRIBUTORS (P) LTD

7/22, Ansari Road, Darya Ganj,
New Delhi-110002
Phones : +91-11-40775252, 23273880, 23275880, 23280451
Fax : +91-11-23285873
Web : www.atlanticbooks.com
E-mail : orders@atlanticbooks.com

Branch Office
5, Nallathambi Street, Wallajah Road,
Chennai-600002
Phones : +91-44-64611085, 32413319
E-mail : chennai@atlanticbooks.com

Printed in India at Glorious Printers, A-13, D.S.I.D.C., Jhilmil Industrial Area, Delhi-11009

Dedicated to

My late grandparents
Who knew the real meaning of health and remained
Always healthy till they left for their final abode

Foreword

The concept of health has undergone a revolutionary change in modern times. To be successful in life one has to be mentally and physically healthy. In old days people used to have little knowledge about health related issues, but in present era there is more emphasis on health, diet, nutrition, regular exercise, etc. To make people aware of the merits of health and well being, health education has been started worldwide which broadens the thinking of the people in society. Until recently, the processes which emanate from those presumed boundaries between physical factors and physical illnesses had not been adequately described. They essentially remained hypotheses. Some scientists are of the opinion that there is so little proof of relation between these two that it is useless to continue research in this direction, especially within these hypothetical boundaries where so complex a mechanism as the immunity system is involved.

According to World Health Organisation (WHO), "Health is a state of physical, mental and social well being and not merely an absence of disease or infirmity." This definition takes a holistic view of health. With the advent of many lifestyle diseases like hypertension, diabetes and psycho-somatic disorders, the ill effects of environmental pollution on the health of a person have taken a central place. Besides this, the pressure of competition and over-ambition along with parental pressure is driving many students to commit suicide or take other extreme steps. Thus, the teachers and students need to be sensitized first of all for making themselves aware of the factors mentioned above. The students need to be taught how to cope up with the pressures.

It has been suggested that proper management and use of information within health care systems will determine the effectiveness of systems in detecting health problems, defining priorities, identifying innovative solutions and allocating resources to improve health outcome.

Thus, a book analysing all the factors affecting the health of people is the need of the hour. *Health Education and Administration* is one such book. It has a wide coverage and includes all the important aspects of health education, personal hygiene, sanitation, physical exercise, balanced diet, nutrition, immunization, mental health, childhood needs, among other pertinent topics. The syllabi of various educational institutions including medical colleges on the subject of health is vast. There are few books among those available which deal with all the important topices. This book fulfills the needs of students pursuing various courses on health education. It covers a wide area, including the science of health, health education in schools and understanding adolescents, which are issues of recent origin. Teachers and health administrators can use this book as a reference manual. To those who wish to know about health education it will offer a richly rewarding reading.

The author of this book, Dr. Rashmi Soni is a reputed academician. At a young age she has acquired immense knowledge in the field of health, psychology and education. She has written this book in a simple yet effective language, which makes it readable and interesting. I wish her all the success in life.

Dr. N.L. Srivastava
Professor, Education and Training
State Institute of Health and Family Welfare, U.P.

Preface

> Health is a large word. It embraces not the body only, but the mind and spirit as well... and not today's pain or pleasure alone, but the whole being and outlook of a man.
>
> —*James H. West*

Health is rightly described as the greatest of our possessions, one of the most essential to the enjoyment of all our other faculties and blessings; hence it should be highly prized and carefully guarded. However, the predicament is that people in general give little attention to health until it is destroyed. Man's natural aim in life is happiness which is largely an attitude of the mind. While the laws of physical health have been disseminated in different ways, the question of mental health is sadly neglected, as a result of which, people in general are not aware of the right concept of health, particularly mental health.

The aim of the book *Health Education and Administration* is not to claim that all illnesses can be avoided by following the fundamental rules of nature. It only says that many, if not most, can be avoided since they are the result of the breaking of the rules that determine nature's harmony. We are living in a world full of physical and mental stress and strife because of the uncontrolled forces released by the new science and technology which leads to insatiable human greed and pressures for our present generation. This book sheds light on the basic concepts and related aspects of health and disease and tells us how to develop a more natural and holistic approach to life, not only to achieve physical and mental health but also to restore the harmony which alone can ensure human happiness if not the very survival.

The book aims to provide information for understanding and implementing the basic principles of physical, mental and spiritual wellness. Overall there are three aspects that have been emphasized in this book. Firstly, being responsible for one's behaviour, for example not smoking cigarette or overusing alcohol or taking drugs, maintaining healthy body weight, getting sufficient exercise, consuming nutritious food, managing stress and living in harmony with oneself. Secondly, contributing to the health of one's social and physical environment, for example supporting laws that enhance the health and safety of children, ensure safe food and medicine, and making the air, water and land healthy and safe for everyone. Last but not least, realizing that health and wellness encompass one's entire being—body, mind and spirit and relationship with the environment—rather than the medical management of illness and the repair of diseased and broken body parts.

The book was conceived as a result of my experiences as a teacher educator, and as a counselor and trainer helping families, couples, individual adults, adolescents and children who are troubled. I have experienced that parents are always eager to provide the best for their children but sometimes they are not aware of the roadblocks to acchieving this, and neither do they know how to overcome them. I hope that the book will assist the parents to some extent in overcoming such roadblocks and in better understanding the psychological and physical needs of their children and teenagers.

During my experience as a teacher educator for the last many years, I felt a great need to make the prospective teachers aware about the physical and mental health of children and adolescents with whom they are going to be concerned in near future as secondary school teachers, about many behavioural and personality problems and emotional disorders of children and adolescents, about the laws that govern a good physical and mental health and about a comprehensive school health education programme. I felt a dearth of one complete and comprehensive book covering both physical and mental aspects of health together. There is a need for a book which not only serves as a textbook for the B.Ed, M.Ed and M.A. (Education) courses in universities and colleges but is also informative and helpful to in-service school teachers nurturing the innocent and sensitive minds of children and adolescents. The students who are pursuing teacher training courses from different universities and colleges can be benefitted by this book as a handbook with the help of which they will be able to easily identify the underlying intricacies of behavioural maladjustment of children and adolescents and at the same time understand the basic principles of a healthy life and physical and psychological health needs of children.

The book has been conceptualized in three sections. Section-I contains three chapters with topics related to health and health education in general. It throws light on the basic concepts of health and disease, difference between health, hygiene and wellness, laws of health and about the importance of education for health at secondary school level.

Section-II covers twelve chapters dealing with areas like school health education programmes, personal hygiene, importance of correct postures and physical exercises, immunization, infectious diseases and medical inspection. It also provides information on the current status of Mid-day Meal Scheme in Indian schools, importance of first aid and safety education at secondary school level and last but not least, the role of teachers in health education and administration.

Mental health has been taken for granted too much and for too long in our country. This is in sharp contrast to how it is treated in developed countries. To most people, mental health at best is a nebulous concept full of mystery and disdain. To an average person, the thought or suggestion of 'mental health' is instantly followed by the image of an insane patient whom they have seen wandering in the streets. Consequently, the immediate response is one of fear, repulsion and rejection. However, such a response is born out of ignorance on the part of the individual as well as socially conditioned prejudice.

There is a wide gap between the actual need and the available mental health facilities both in the urban as well as in the rural areas in our country. The main reason for this is lack of awareness about mental health among people in general and the policymakers in particular.

Under Section-III of the book, I have endeavored to explain the nature and scope of mental health and hygiene with the intelligent and curious layman in mind. The difference between normal and abnormal behaviour has been explained in an exclusive chapter. Comman man's misconceptions about abnormality have been shattered. Other chapters under this section will help the teachers and parents in general to understand the developmental and emotional needs of children and adolescents in today's fast changing technological world. It will also enlighten them with the common mental health problems of these specific stages of life, and the signs and symptoms discussed in detail will help them to easily identify those children who need help and counselling.

The main idea running through Section-III of the book is that the skills necessary for survival are present in our children; and though by overprotection and unconscious fear, we are in danger of extinguishing these skills, we have the resources within us to foster and develop these skills. It becomes important for the present and prospective teachers to be aware of the present status of mental health disorders existing in children and adolescents. The increasing suicide rate among adolescents today makes it all the more necessary for the parents, teachers and all those around them to understand the stress, pressures and anxieties that an adolescent faces and thus empower him/her to overcome and manage emotional trauma. If the book helps in achieving this aim and satisfies the intellectual curiosity of the reader, I shall consider my effort really worthwhile. I will feel contented if the book conveys a sense of dynamism and dialogue in the area of health to the readers. Comments by the readers are most welcome and will help me to be closer to their requirements.

The images and the relevant tables, boxes and data graphs used in the book with up-to-date information will help in sustaining interest of the readers. This book is neither a guide nor an encyclopedia; it provides a discussion of the central and key concepts related to health in general and mental health in particular, rather than having a more superficial but broader coverage. I am aware of the omissions in the book but further editions of the same in near future including experiences of discussions of case studies and counseling sessions with children and adolescents on various kinds of problems will provide a deeper insight in understanding and handling the emotions and behaviour of this age group and will make the readers aware of more specific areas related to the subject.

My best wishes to all the prospective teachers who are the nation builders and parents of future generation.

Rashmi Soni

Acknowledgements

My deepest gratitude and humble bow to my grandparents who although are no more physically with me, yet I can feel their presence every moment of my life. They lived a healthy and happy life till their last breath. They were staunch followers of naturopathy and had a positive approach to life which kept them mentally alert and healthy throughout their lives. This book is a tribute to my late grandparents.

I want to thank my B.Ed. students, the prospective teachers who inspired me to write this book by their queries regarding mental health, how to understand and deal with the behavioural and emotional problems of children and adolescents and their own personal problems.

I have drawn insights and ideas from many sources including magazines, books, seminars, lectures, workshops and internet. I am grateful to them. I have many people to thank for their significant contribution in my understanding of the concept of mental health. I thank most respected Prof. H.S. Asthana, Dr. Pallavi Bhatnagar, Dr. Rajendra Misra and Prof. N.L. Srivastava, renowned psychologists in their fields, and Prof. Anthony Williams, trainer in personality development, for their blessings.

My acknowledgement will be incomplete without making a mention of those people who have been a constant source of inspiration throughout my career and have always motivated me to contribute something worthwhile in the field of education and psychology. I owe my deep and sincere gratitude to Padamshree Prof. M.S. Sodha and Prof. M. Varma, Department of Education, Lucknow University.

I am grateful to my cousin Mr. Prashant Soni for always being with me in giving colours and wings to my ideas. I thank him for his contribution in editing the third section of the book. I want to make a special mention to my friends and my most near and dear ones who have always been there with me. Their constructive criticism has pushed me forward to identify my potential and come out with something new. I am grateful for their generous encouragement and never-ending support.

I express my deep and humble gratitude to Prof. N.L. Srivastava, Professor Education and Training, State Institute of Health and Family Welfare, Uttar Pradesh, for writing the Foreword for this book.

Last but not least, my parents, without whose blessings and support I would not have achieved all that I have today. It is because of them that I feel myself responsible towards the larger society with a willingness and ability to make a little contribution towards its growth and well being. I thank God who is always there beside me in all my work.

Rashmi Soni

Contents

SECTION—III

Mental Health, Hygiene and Education

Section–I

Understanding Health and Health Education

The Science of Health

1

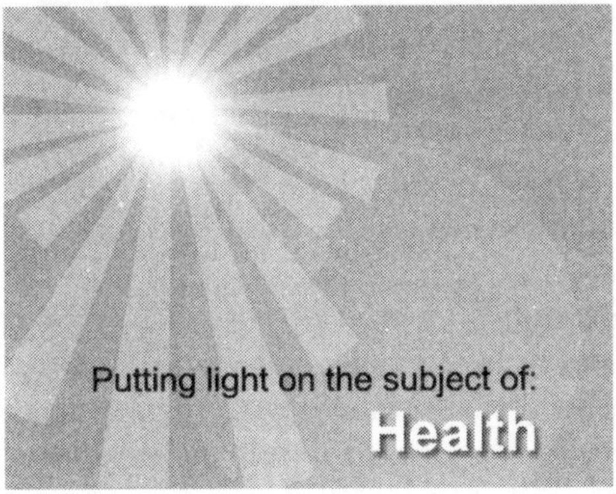

To live is not sufficient. We need also the joy of living; and the joy of life requires health. Above all we need that health which embraces body, mind and soul.

—Alexic Carrel

Good health, longevity and happiness—these have been the aspirations and dreams of mankind. However, we always seem to be talking of disease, getting more and more disease conscious rather than health conscious. Medical journals and medical literature abound in material on disease. It is rare on the other hand, to find any constructive writings on preserving or improving health (both physical and mental) by preventive health measures. We cannot hope to achieve health by studying disease alone as it does not tell us how to be healthy; it is far more expensive to be sick than it is to get well and stay well. Our so-called civilization has performed so many wonderful achievements, but it is certainly lagging far behind in educating the future generation in health principles and living habits.

Meaning and Concept of Health

The word health is derived from the old English word 'hoelth' meaning a condition of being safe and sound and denotes wholeness. Terms such as 'whole', 'sound' and 'vigorous' were formerly used to define health in a positive sense. Then 'health' came to be visualized more in a negative way as freedom from disease, defect and disability. Today, in the minds of most people, health still has this historical meaning and was until the end of the Second World War considered merely as 'freedom from disease'. Finally, we have made the crucial rediscovery that health is a dynamic process involving the whole person and his unique style of living. Defined in this modern sense we can say, "Health is optimal personal fitness for full, fruitful creative living."

In 1947, WHO defined health as "a state of complete physical, mental, and social well-being and not merely the absence of disease or infirmity". Although this is the most accepted definition of health today, it is also probably the least meaningful and the least effective from the percept viewpoint of stimulating positive health behaviours. Only a handful of publications have focused specifically on the definition of health and its evolution in the first six decades. Some of them highlight its lack of operational value and the problem created by use of the word 'complete'. Others declare the definition, which has not been modified since 1947, 'simply a bad one'. There is great difficulty in using it as a measurement criterion. What, for example, is social well-being? How do we measure it?

There is, in these definitions of health, no appreciation of the varying degrees of healthfulness or wellness among those usually classified as well. Although levels of health cannot as yet be reliably measured, one need be only a casual observer to recognize that a great number of people today are living below their best levels of attainment. Many persons believe themselves healthy because they are not sick. This lack of appreciation of health as a quality of life prevents the realization of a greatly superior type of life.

In 1986, the WHO, in the Ottawa Charter for Health Promotion, said that health is "a resource for everyday life, not the objective of living. Health is a positive concept emphasizing social and personal resources, as well as physical capacities." Classification systems such as the WHO Family of International Classifications (WHO-FIC), which is composed of the International Classification of Functioning, Disability, and Health (ICF) and the International Classification of Diseases (ICD) also define health.

The *ICD* is the *International Standard Diagnostic Classification* for all general epidemiological, many health management purposes and clinical use. These include the analysis of the general health situation of population groups and monitoring of the incidence and prevalence of diseases and other health problems in relation to other variables such as the characteristics and circumstances of the individuals affected, reimbursement, resource allocation, quality and guidelines. It is used to classify diseases and other health problems recorded on many types of health and vital records including death certificates and health records. In addition to enabling the storage and retrieval of diagnostic information for clinical, epidemiological and quality purposes, these records also provide the basis for the compilation of national mortality and morbidity statistics by WHO Member States.

The *International Classification of Functioning, Disability and Health*, known more commonly as *ICF*, is a classification of health and health-related domains. These domains are classified from body, individual and societal perspectives by means of two lists: a list of body functions and structure, and a list of domains of activity and participation. Since an individual's functioning and disability occurs in a context, the ICF also includes a list of environmental factors. The ICF puts the notions of 'health' and 'disability' in a new light. It acknowledges that every human being can experience a decrement in health and thereby experience some degree of disability. Disability is not something that only happens to a minority of humanity. The ICF thus 'mainstreams' the experience of disability and recognizes it as a universal human experience. (http://www.who.int/classifications/icf/en/)

Other Definitions

The dictionary defines health as freedom from disease or pain. The physician views health as a normal functioning of the body organs and systems.

J.F. Williams defined health as "that quality of life which enables the individual to live most and to serve best".

Anderson and Ereswell stated, "Health is that quality of physical, emotional and mental well-being that enables one to live effectively and enjoyably."

Romano's definition, "Health consists in the capacity of the organism to maintain a balance in which it may be reasonably free of undue pain, discomfort, disability or limitation of action including social capacity."

Jonas Salk, who developed a vaccine for polio, believed "health should be viewed not merely as being free from disease but as activity growing and developing".

Hoyman (1970) stated that the concept of health has several dimensions, each having its own continuum. Each continuum ranges from desirable to undesirable. The individual's ability to make decisions and interact socially, psychologically and physically with society determines wellness.

Dunn also reflected this viewpoint when he stated that optimal health or high-level wellness is "an integrated method of functioning which is oriented toward maximizing the potential of which the individual is capable. It requires that the individual maintain a continuum of balance and purposeful direction within the environment where he or she is functioning."

Finally, Sigerist's (1960) statement and definition: "We all live in a specific rhythm, determined by nature, culture and habit. Day and night alternate in an unebbing flow, and we ourselves conform to this rhythm with waking and sleeping...with work and rest.... An undisturbed rhythm means health.... Disease then strikes abruptly into this structure."

Patrick and Bush (1971) at the University of California Medical School at San Diego did some interesting work in the area of definitions. These researchers postulated that "health can be defined as a composite of an individual's level of function at a point in time and his expected transition to other levels, more or less favourable at future times". They developed various categories of functional status and prognosis which, when combined, define a given health level at a given time. They attempted to delineate in a quantitative manner "what states of being are healthier than others" by getting judges to classify 29 different function levels into a scale of perfect health to death.

Inference from Definitions

Thus, health has positive as well as negative aspects. It is a dynamic process, not a static condition, which can be quantified, measured and appraised. Health has both qualitative and quantitative dimensions. There are various levels of health, and a well person can become healthier. Health depends upon multiple factors, not upon a single cause. Health and disease are ecologic resultants, indicating the need for an epidemiology of health, as well as disease.

Theoretically, modern man's health potential ranges from zero health (death) at one end of a continuum to optimal health at the other end. Man's health status can be divided into five levels: (i) health-ranging from a sub-optimal level to optimal health—a theoretical level at which an individual's living approaches his full desirable potentialities; (ii) wellness—a sub-health level ranging from low level to high level wellness; (iii) minor illness incipient or sub-clinical to manifest milder illnesses and disabilities; (iv) major illness—incipient or sub-clinical to manifest diseases and disabilities of a more serious nature; and (v) critical illness—grave illness to approaching death.

A man wants health as a means of living the kind of life and striving toward the kinds of goals that he sets for himself and by means of which he measures the success and failure of his life. A full human life is built on cornerstones such as work, family life, citizenship, recreation, esthetic experiences, love and faith. At its best a healthy human life is an adventurous struggle for freedom, truth, goodness, beauty, harmony, excellence, peace, joy and happiness. As Emerson put it, "man is the dwarf of himself", and he needs to grow up into healthy civilized maturity, using acceptable means to achieve noble ends.

Health, Hygiene and Wellness

Source: @2005-www.CaptainFit.Com

All methods of biologic living are natural living and common sense methods, making right use of the agents of life such as food, air, water, exercise, physical and mental relaxation, sleep, etc. Instruction in the art of living should always begin in early life, when the principles can be grasped more easily than in adulthood when we have already formed rather fixed habits and follow certain patterns of living detrimental to our health. When we are talking of health, we are not just talking about good physical health but also about sound mental health. Thus, total health is a combination of the physical, emotional, social and spiritual components of life, balanced in a way that produces satisfaction and happiness for the individual. To accomplish this goal, each individual must engage in wellness and hygiene activities.

Hygiene

The term 'hygiene' is derived from *Hygei*, the Greek goddess of health, cleanliness and sanitation. *Hygiene* is also the name of a branch of science that deals with the promotion and preservation of health, also called *hygienics*. Initially, worshipped in her own right, by the fifth century BC in Athens Hygeia was instead depicted as a demi-god, the daughter or wife of the god of healing, Asclepius. While worship of Asclepius aimed at curing disease through divine intercession, worship of Hygeia emphasized obtaining health by living wisely in accordance with her laws. In contemporary Western society, the concept of hygiene has become associated with standards of personal grooming which often have little effect on individual health. The eleventh edition of the *Encyclopedia Britannica* asserts that hygiene embraces "all the agencies which affect the physical and mental well-being of man".

Hygiene is an old concept related to medicine, as well as to personal and professional care practices related to most aspects of living. In medicine and in home (domestic) and everyday life settings, hygiene practices are employed as preventative measures to reduce the incidence and spreading of disease. In the manufacture of food, pharmaceutical, cosmetic and other products, good hygiene is a key part of quality assurance, i.e. ensuring that the product complies with microbial specifications appropriate to its use. The terms cleanliness (or cleaning) and hygiene are often used interchangeably, which can cause confusion. In general, hygiene mostly means practices that prevent spread of disease causing organizms. Hygiene practices vary widely, and what is considered acceptable in one culture might not be acceptable in another. Since cleaning processes (e.g., hand washing) remove infectious microbes as well as dirt and soil, they are often the means to achieve hygiene. Other uses of the term appear in phrases including: body hygiene, personal hygiene, mental hygiene, dental hygiene, and occupational hygiene, used in connection with public health. (Hygiene, both mental and physical in detail have been explained in Section II and III of this book.)

Wellness

Wellness is a fairly recent concept that combines conventional ideas of physical health with larger issues of emotional stability, psychological and emotional comfort, and sometimes even spiritual or mental fulfillment. It is one of the leading areas of interest for parents planning the best for their child. The majority of people attribute wellness to not being sick or ill. This is a misconception. Illness occurs when one or more body parts are not functioning properly or sometimes not at all. We begin to feel "not well" or uncomfortable and go to the doctor for help. Through the use of pharmaceuticals, drugs and therapy, we can return to feeling well as opposed to feeling sick. But the question is whether the drugs and medical materials actually cure the malady or do they simply make one more comfortable while the body naturally takes care of its own needs? While one treatment may work exceptionally for one person, it may have absolutely no effect on another. This raises the previous question again. For instance, medical science cannot cure the flu, rather all they are able to do is relieve the symptoms while the virus runs its course.

Wellness is the state of keeping our body healthy so that we are able to keep away illness when it tries to invade our comfort zone. There are many ways to achieve a level of wellness, including: eating healthy, regular exercise, regular physical exams, quitting bad habits like smoking or excessive drinking and by following a healthy personal lifestyle. Just as important as physical wellness is mental wellness. Each person must foster attitudes that improve the quality of life and expand the human potential. It is extremely important to have the right frame of mind. It is believed that if our mind is in a good state, the body will follow suit. This is sometimes called the power of suggestion or positive thinking. In this way, wellness can be stated as a continuous forward motion towards comfortable living. It is not the absence of illness as much as living in a state of mind that keeps the body operating comfortably and properly.

Health Determines Wellness

Since the 1970s, many experts believe that lifestyle choices, environment, health care awareness and access to health care choices greatly influence the quality of someone's wellness. A scientific explanation of health is also helpful in determining wellness. Many biologists describe health as an organism's ability to resist and recover from stress-inducing influences in their environment, achieving a state of balance called homeostasis. Wellness can also be simply described as the ability to feel "fine"—to feel comfortable and well given an individual's surroundings and circumstances. The relationship between health and wellness can be understood through following indexes:

Physical health and illness prevention

Current medical research indicates a low-fat, high fruits and vegetable diet works best for helping children achieve their maximum growth potential. Many minerals found in vegetables are shown to encourage development of a child's immune system and mental faculties, while at the same time resisting susceptibility to certain diseases. Routine physical exercise stimulates the body and provides powerful emotional comfort in the form of endorphins, or chemicals, which send messages of well-being to the brain.

Emotional health and psychological well-being

A child's emotional health depends to a great extent on his ability to function within his environment. Stressors such as problems at school, unrecognized learning disabilities, and strife at home can seriously impair emotional comfort and present psychological challenges later in life. If the child is responding to events in a different manner, such behaviour is commonly a sign of an emotional maladjustment and could indicate a need for guidance. Psychological problems also sometimes become apparent during childhood, and might include any number of issues that can be resolved either with medication or through therapy.

Spiritual and mental fulfillment

In most countries, spiritual development is a matter left to the parents to determine and guide. Mental fulfillment and cultivation remain the responsibility not just of the schools a child attends but also to an even greater degree on parents. Children crave mental stimulation and interaction, possibly almost as much as parental affection. Giving them "something to think about" will go a long way in making them happy and well.

Importance of Health

Good health can be described as the condition where both our body and our mind is functioning properly. The main causes behind ill health are various types of illnesses, improper diet, injury, mental stress, poor hygiene, unhealthy lifestyle, etc. Over the past few years, our attitude towards health has changed and we are unaware why health is important for all of us. Good health is recognized as a critical pillar in ensuring individual, household, and community and country prosperity. The pursuit of this good health has been a critical focus area for all persons. Individuals seek to maximize their health to ensure they are able to carry out the activities that will improve their overall welfare. Communities and countries, in the same manner, seek to ensure services, and activities that maximize the health of the individuals that contribute to the overall improvements in societal welfare.

There are several advantages of a healthy life. The body will be free from various forms of health problems and thus one will get a longer life. One can live a life without suffering from aches, pains and discomfort. The person will be able to perform in every sphere of one's life to the best of his ability. Apart from this, it makes one looks good and attractive and one starts feeling good about himself. A healthy person can lead a physically active life even after growing old. The body will be able to heal faster, thought regular wear and tear associated with ageing. In short, good health brings about a drastic improvement in the overall quality of one's life.

Why is Health Important for Children

Health is important for proper growth and development of the mind and body of the child. The younger that child begins the lifelong process of becoming healthy, the greater the possibility that he will be successful in life. They require enough energy to spend the entire day in school. They should be able to focus in the classroom and fully participate in the activities on the field. For this, they need proper nutrition, which includes carbohydrates, proteins, calcium, minerals, etc. Today, most parents have a basic knowledge of food and health related issues. However, they often fail to understand why health care is important for their children. Regular health check up with a health care provider is a must for every child. This helps to learn from the experts whether the child's development in terms of height and weight is right or not. Other aspects of health that have to be monitored are their behaviour, oral health and eye check up which are equally important. This will also prevent any health problems in future.

Teachers must recognize that children bring to schools many values and behaviours. These values represent both the beneficial and the negative aspects of a child's living practices. At the same time, teachers should be aware of the powerful influence they exert on the lives of their students. Nowhere in the entire educational spectrum can a teacher make such an impression as at the elementary level. Consequently, the teacher who exemplifies a lifestyle conducive to high-level wellness, who exhibits a style of living that is physically, socially and psychologically healthy, enhances the probability that his/her students will attempt to incorporate those beneficial aspects in their own lives.

Dimensions of health

Overall good health and wellness are interdependent on five dimensions, namely physical, intellectual, emotional, social and spiritual. The World Health Organization (WHO) has set these good health parameters in 1948. Our body and mind are tuned to send us signals for any non-functional activity, generally called as symptoms. It is important to understand these parameters in time, to ensure balance of mind, spirit and body.

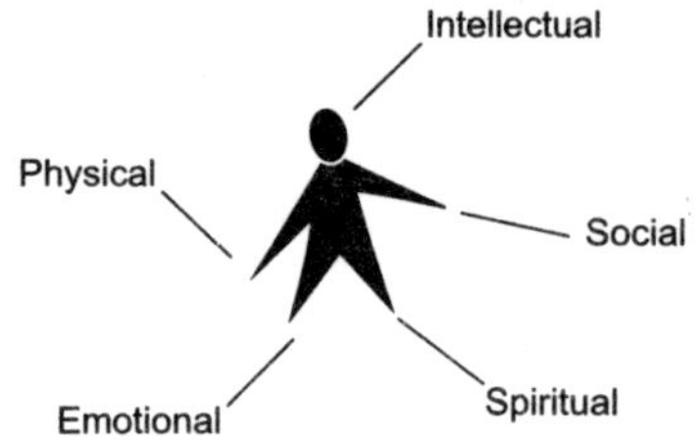

1. *Physical*

Physical health refers to the state of the body: its compositions, development, functions and maintenance. Few ways to ensure good physical health are as follows:

- Eating nutritious food to keep the body and mind energized.
- Never skipping meals or overeating.
- Water is essential for cleansing the body.
- Fitness through exercise will increase immunity and endurance levels of the body.
- Regular medical checkups can help in arresting an illness, in its early stages.
- Sleeping at least for seven uninterrupted hours daily.
- Avoiding addictive substances.

2. *Intellectual*

This is a cognitive ability to develop skills and knowledge to enhance one's life. Our intellectual capacity helps to stimulate our creativity and insight in decision-making. For this the basic requirements are:

- Setting realistic goals will go a long way in life planning.
- Exploring every opportunity with an open mind.
- Being aware of the demands and expectations from oneself.
- A positive outlook, especially when dealing with conflicts.

3. *Emotional*

Our ability to accept and cope with our own and others feelings is defined as emotional well-being. Emotions contribute to almost all aspects of our life, at times, even setting course of actions. Symptoms of emotional problems as hopelessness, depression, anxiety and even suicidal tendencies are not always easily detectable, but can lead to dire consequences. Thus:

- Awareness and acceptance of our strength and shortcoming is essential for our emotional well-being.
- Ability to handle stress and seek help, if needed.
- Building strong communication networks among family, friends and peers.

4. *Social*

To build and maintain satisfying relationships comes naturally to us, as we are social animals. Being socially accepted is also connected to our emotional well-being. For this we should:

- Increase our ability to interact with people and their ideas.
- Accept and understand diverse cultural norms.
- Build networks among different kinds of people.
- Adapt a positive self-image.
- Enhance our interpersonal communication skills.

5. *Spiritual*

Our good health is incomplete without being spiritually healthy. To seek meaning and purpose of life is termed as being spiritual. Spiritual health dimension refers to our personal belief and value, our own acceptance or rejection of the creation. There are no prescribed ways, to attain spiritual well-being; it is more a matter of looking inwards, at our own depth of understanding, our existence and creation.

Life as we know is a puzzle; health dimensions are like separate pieces that need to be fitted together to make meaning. Though we all seek a harmonious balance between the mind, body and spirit to lead an optimal fulfilled life, it is rarely attained in totality. Perfect health is a myth. Optimum health is that condition which every individual can attain. Our own feelings of weakness and non-acceptance of life's events, causes much distress in our daily life. Understanding the roles these dimensions play will perhaps lead us to what we seek the most, viz. health and happiness.

Conclusion

Thus, overall health is achieved through a combination of physical, mental, and social well-being, which, together is commonly referred to as the 'Health Triangle'. Health is a positive state of well-being, where every part of the organ of the body and mind is in harmony and in proper functioning balance with every other organ. In other words, when every organ of the body is functioning normally the state of physical well-being known as health exists. So functional balance is health and functional imbalance is disease. Positive health, which has the ability to resist disease, is entirely different from artificial health. By positive health we mean natural health obtained by following the laws of health and biological living—that is quite different from artificial health obtained through the use of vaccinations, inoculations, antitoxins, chemicals or potent drugs. To build and maintain health, it is necessary to see that one's habits are correct and the laws of life observed in the best possible manner, taking into consideration the environment, circumstances, the type of work, and how one is placed in life. In short, it requires treating and recycling the complete man. In other words, to live biologically means to live rightly.

The Laws of Health

2

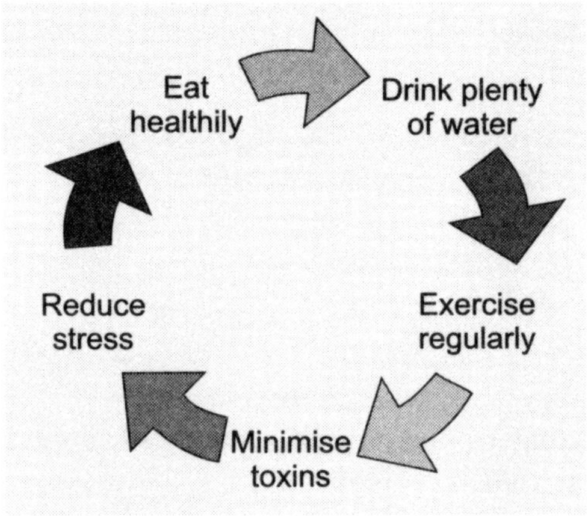

There is an alarming increase in degenerative diseases and failing health. The reason why most people suffer from various ailments and maladies is simply because they are ignorant of the laws of life. They fail to realize that they are working with a human machine. Often they do not want to know the facts, or are too skeptical or indifferent to investigate them, and those who do investigate and specialize in the human machinery, are trained to think and concentrate in terms of disease and drugs only. Instead of emphasizing the value of personal hygiene, sanitation, the laws of health and stressing the right methods and principles of living by avoiding illness and maintaining good health, these specialists issue warning against cancer, heart diseases and other allied ailments and now very much AIDS. This approach to health or disease is suicidal as it works very dangerously on the mind however intelligent it may be.

To assert that the average man cannot be expected to know about his body, under the false illusion that this is exclusively the work of a doctor, is simply absurd. The blame may lie with our system of education that devotes itself mainly to the teaching of purely academic interests. It is true that some physiology and hygiene is taught in schools, but considering the great importance of the subjects, physiology and hygiene should be taken up in a more thorough manner and the practice of those habits conducive to health and energy should be insisted upon. Health must be made a habit through education.

Health is the blending of the ingredients of physical, mental and spiritual. There are certain basic guidelines for healthy living. These guidelines should not be taken as rules but as principles to be adapted to one's circumstances and physical condition mixed with common sense.

- In order to build and maintain positive health, it is necessary to have an organized balanced programme consisting of a balanced diet, fresh air and sunshine, regular physical exercises, games, sports or walks, systematic rest, relaxation, sleep, personal hygiene and cleanliness—external and internal, a positive mental attitude, social hygiene and above all, harmonious development of physical, mental and spiritual powers. In short, for gaining positive health, we must lead a balanced life for which we need a balanced body, a balanced mind, balanced emotions, a balanced diet and a balanced faith in oneself within and beyond.
- The conditions and surroundings of the home and work life should be analyzed and a careful thought should be given to personal habits and practices with special reference to bearing on health.
- The principle causes of ill health are errors in diet, impure food, and an excess of stimulants, insufficient exercise, loss of sleep, physical and mental fatigue, wasting of vital force and wrong or shallow breathing.

Pure air and proper sunlight, pure water, wholesome food, do contribute to health and life but we can never obtain good health unless we lead a clean and hygienic life.

- Personal hygiene does not mean merely washing the skin, or putting on clean clothes. Cleanliness involves the teeth, the nose, the eyes, the mouth, hands and feet, food, clothes and above all, internal cleanliness, which is a matter of regular and thorough elimination through the bowels, lungs and skin, since on the condition of the internal organs depends the health of the body.
- Public hygiene may be enforced, but personal and domestic hygiene has to be taught by educating the public as humanity suffers from their lack of knowledge of individual hygiene.

Through good heredity, we do inherit health to a great extent, but we create to a greater extent by living within the immutable laws of health and life. The best heredity may be dissipated through the unwise management of our bodily powers and exceeding our bodily capabilities, or neglecting to replenish fully our body's own losses. Life demands intelligent direction and therefore we must thoroughly understand the principles essential to health and thereby a full life. The creation of health, as well as its maintenance is wholly a matter of keeping up normal bodily functions and following and observing the fundamental principles and laws of health can definitely make this happen.

Good health and wellness are not a luxury but an essential for people everywhere to reach their life's potential. The secrets to health and wellness are simple: good lifestyle and wholesome diet choices; sufficient rest, exercise, and good water; conscientiously practicing one's faith; and spending time with friends and family who love and support one in healthy ways.

A Healthy Living

The general belief among most people today is that health comes to us in the natural course of events; that it requires no special knowledge, and that if one goes on in an ordinary way, adhering to the conventional habits of life, one will naturally acquire health as one acquires full growth. The main fault with modern life is that ambitious people fail to realize that they are working with a human machine, made of flesh and blood. Nearly everybody neglects the human machine with which we work everyday of our lives. Much of the attention essential to keep it in repair is ignored, so failure, in nearly all cases, is due to this neglect.

Health is the result of living in accordance with the natural laws that operate in the mind, emotions and body of a man. To build and maintain maximum health, it is necessary to see that every habit is correct and every law of life observed, as far as it is possible to do so. These laws may be grouped under the following heads:

Fresh air and sunshine

Fresh air and sunshine are as necessary for good health as food and water and bathing. Oxygen, received into the body from the air, is necessary for every function of the organs, as it has the very important task in the body of burning up "waste material". It is impossible to have pure blood, good nerves, and proper functioning if fresh air is denied. The direct contact of the air with the innumerable nerves and organs located in the skin has a most refreshing influence. Every person should favour those styles of clothing, which make for exposure of the body to sun and air. Fresh air is needed day and night.

The sun is the greatest aid to health, a source of energy and vitality. The sun has always been considered as an aid to restoration of health and as a means of maintaining and increasing it. Without the beneficial influence of sunlight, there can be no life on this planet, neither animal nor vegetable. It is only natural therefore, that sunbaths should have a profound influence upon the body. There is no doubt about the fact that sunlight is a fundamental biological need, ranking with oxygen, water and food in importance. The contact of sunlight with the skin produces effects identical with those caused by certain food constituents thus actually taking the place of food. It is found that food when exposed to the action of light acquires nutritive properties, which it did not possess before. Not being in direct contact with sunlight is responsible for much of our ill-health today–not only because of possible deprivation of vitamins, but because of many other values of sunlight that we are denied when it is shut out from our bodies. There are some rays in sunlight that cannot be seen, viz. ultraviolet rays, which are effective in preventing and curing rickets.

It is the duty of all educated persons to have knowledge about the importance of sunlight and fresh air as an essential means of preventing disease, and ensuring normal development and to take advantage of those elements provided by nature. The importance of sunlight as an essential means of preventing disease and ensuring normal development is well established.

Deep breathing, exercise and correct posture

Life is absolutely dependent upon the act of breathing. By taking a full breath we inhale a large quantity of oxygen and by retaining it a while, we stir and purify the air which always remains in the lungs. On exhaling, we expel the carbon dioxide and other poisonous gases. Nature intends that a certain amount of oxygen must come from the air we breathe. In a natural and outdoor life, one can breathe freely an abundance of this oxygen, but artificial habits of life, and especially despondency and work that requires much stooping or bending over, are apt to produce an apathy of the nerves and muscles that control breathing, resulting in an insufficient supply of health-giving oxygen.

Not only does the physical health depend very materially upon correct breathing, but mental power, happiness, self-control, clear-sightedness, moral and even spiritual growth may be increased by correct forms of breathing known as *pranayam*. The proper method of breathing is to take the breath through the nostrils as the organs of respiration have their only protective apparatus filter or dust catcher in the nostrils, which contain numerous tiny hairs adjusted to this purpose.

Breathing has the most profound influence upon every part of the body, including the brain. It uses the muscles, stimulates the action of the heart, increases the circulation, improves elimination, washes out the carbon dioxide from the blood, and has almost all the good effect of more general muscular activity. In fact, breathing and exercise so often go hand in hand, and are so inextricably bound up with each other that it is hardly possible to consider either by itself. If sufficient exercise is taken, the breathing is inclined to become very shallow. Improper posture makes it impossible to breathe correctly. Depressing emotions also inhibit normal breathing.

Exercise is as much of vital necessity for maintaining health as air, water and food. The ordinary daily work of the individual develops some parts of the body and neglects others. If the brain alone is worked, the body suffers and *vice versa*. Manual labour is often "one-sided", the postures adopted bring into play some parts of the body more than others and the range of movement is frequently very limited. The result of this is inharmonious development. Exercises ensure harmonious development of the whole body and at the same time correct the faults engendered by lop-sided work and so put the body in a better state to perform any other work that may be required of it. Exercises are not only for the maintenance of health and the building of a shapely and capable body, but are meant to develop weak muscles, improve coordination of movement, increase the mobility of joints, improve respiration, remedy defective postures and correct bodily deformation, improve circulation and develop weak hearty muscles, improve digestion and assimilation, and increase the process of elimination.

Walking is the greatest of all exercises. It is an exercise that can be taken by everybody, costs nothing and rewards in terms of physical well-being. No matter what form of muscular activity is employed, walking should be included.

There are physiological results of maintaining an erect spine. The mechanical arrangement of the spine itself is such that if it is held erect the important nerves that radiate to all the parts of the body from this central bureau are able more perfectly to perform their functions. When there is a pressure on these nerves there is bound to be imperfect functioning. The affected organs will not work normally. When the body is held erect the chest is full, round and somewhat expanded affording plenty of room for the heart and lungs to function. The stomach, liver, intestines all tend to drop or sag below their normal position when the body bends forward and the functioning of these organs is very much impaired.

There are various causes, which lead to faulty posture and consequent deformity of the body. Bones mature fully between the ages 20 and 25. During the years of development, the soft bones may be easily bent out of shape by bad posture while sleeping or by improper clothing. Careless habits might result in deformities of the body in early life and it clearly indicates the importance of training the body to correct and symmetrical development. Lack of well-balanced diet is responsible for muscular fatigue leading to faulty posture. Mental depression and a gloomy outlook on life too, are usually reflected in a slouched appearance. Foot trouble plays a major part in bad posture.

Apart from corrective measures, the best way to improve the posture is to follow the ordinary rules of health—proper and adequate meals, regular exercise, walks and games, enough rest and sleep, in short, anything which improves the tone of the muscles is called for. The use of properly constructed chairs not only prevents a flat chest and round shoulders but is helpful in preventing other deformities. School seats and desks, house chairs, office and automobile seats should be constructed to help maintain good posture. Thus, correct posture in sitting, standing and walking must be assiduously cultivated for keeping well and preventing illness. The essential thing is to keep the chest high and to the front, while the hips are held well back. This draws in the abdominal muscles, lifts the liver and stomach into place. The spine should be erect, keeping the head in the right position, chin inward and downward.

Rest, recreation, relaxation and sleep

Rest means the absence of effort. It is to counterbalance work in a physiological sense, whereas recreation is a change of effort. The latter equalizes the output of energy by exercising physical or mental forces that have been unengaged while other physical or mental energies have been at work. Recreation recreates by a change of activity. Relaxation is muscular limpness. Sleep is conditional or partial rest of human machine. One cannot be constantly active. Nature has provided for alternate activity and rest. Repair is accomplished during rest and relaxation. One cannot really rest unless there has been created a demand for rest by activity. During exercise, the muscles are not built; it is only when they are at rest or during muscular relaxation that the building process takes place.

The idea of providing rest and recreation for the whole machine is applicable with most beneficial result to any and every part and organ of the body. It is important to learn how to relax physically and mentally because in relaxation the muscles work more efficiently and secondly fatigue is completely relieved in a short time as the venous blood circulation is promoted throughout the body.

Sleep, air, water and food are universally recognized as essential for life but very few people understand and still fewer appreciate the importance of sound, healthy, regular, timely and refreshing sleep. The supply of oxygen is replenished during sleep and thus the body is refreshed and recuperated. The purpose of sleep therefore is to repair the losses and damage caused while working. Every nerve center, every cell in fact is a storage battery. Work discharges the battery while during sleep the battery is recharged. Sleep is not only the tissue builder, but also the force giver. Strength, whether of mind or body, depends upon the perfection of the body with which we pursue them. The sleep required for health is in proportion to the physical and mental strength of the individual. As a rule, an average man requires eight hours sleep. A high degree of mental activity cannot be maintained continuously without giving the brain an opportunity for storing energy, which can only be done by complete rest and repose for several hours.

Proper food and regular diet

The body is in many respects comparable to an engine. Like a piece of mechanism, it requires fuel to supply the muscles, etc. with energizing power for the various bodily activities and it likewise needs building materials to repair loss from wear and tear. The human food must be capable of supplying the body with the material needed for the repair of its tissues and for maintaining its various functions. Wholesome food is a normal and useful cell stimulant. The chief purpose of wholesome food therefore is to provide the elements necessary for the growth and repair of the body, to provide those with which the body generates energy and heat; and these two purposes serve one great end, the maintenance of the vital force within us at the highest level of perfection.

We should select and eat food, therefore, not only that helps us to exist but that helps us to live well and enjoy good health. We must intake only those elements that build the body, for we know that as soon the diet is confined to these elements, the most powerful curative process begins and is maintained. The normal and healthy development of the organism depends primarily upon the adequate supply of the organic salts, which truly may be called "the building stones of the body". The real secret of health, vitality, mental and physical efficiency, youthfulness and long-life therefore is well-balanced body chemistry. Fruits and vegetables together with nuts and cereals are very rich in organic salts and should be the bulk of the daily diet.

The amount of food needed depends on climatic conditions, age, size and activity of the individual. Natural and vitalized foods, therefore, judiciously selected and administered, have true value in maintaining good health and vitality by supplying the proper mineral and vitamin elements in their organic forms.

Right mental attitude

The right mental attitude is of great importance. Attitude is the way we look at our life, or future, people around us and ourselves. The notion of the hygiene of the body is familiar to most, but few people are alive to the necessity of the hygiene of the mind. The kind of ideas that form the content of the mind is not a matter of indifference to health of either body or mind. Agreeable thoughts and pleasant emotions influence bodily conditions, which favour health and efficiency; whereas fear, anger, worry induce morbid states and generate poisons, which create disease.

A person, who lives under fear, or under the shadow of any depressing emotions, seems to shrivel up, growing old prematurely. Constant fear of disease tends to set the forces of the body towards developing abnormal conditions. Worry, pessimism, jealousy, envy, fear, anxiety or any other depressing mental state, lowers the vitality, depresses bodily functions, fills the body with toxins and paves the way for disease. Cheerfulness, optimism, magnanimity, tolerance and all other elevating emotions and mental states promote health. Fear is both a cause and a result of disease. We may not be able to control voluntarily mental fears but with proper understanding and following the laws of health, the body can be kept healthy and strong, and in this way we can prevent fears.

We should, therefore, not lose sight of the mental influence on the physical, and *vice versa*. When the body and mind are in harmony, only then will there be opportunity for proper health and spiritual development. It may be said here that the cultivation of the right mental attitude either through religion, metaphysics, prayers or yoga, helps in controlling fear, worry and other emotions leading to gain in health and peace of mind.

Strict cleanliness and proper elimination

Cleanliness is a primary condition of health and a great panacea of all disease. Filth breeds disease. It should be noted that cleanliness is one of the main defenses against disease, whether commercial or self-generated. Cleanliness involves our internal bodies, our teeth and mouth, our hands and feet, our clothing, our food, everything with which we come in contact. It should not therefore only be observed at home, in streets and with regard to clothes and habits but also, and above all, within the human body as on the condition of the internal organs depends the health of the body.

Six Stage Handwashing Techniques

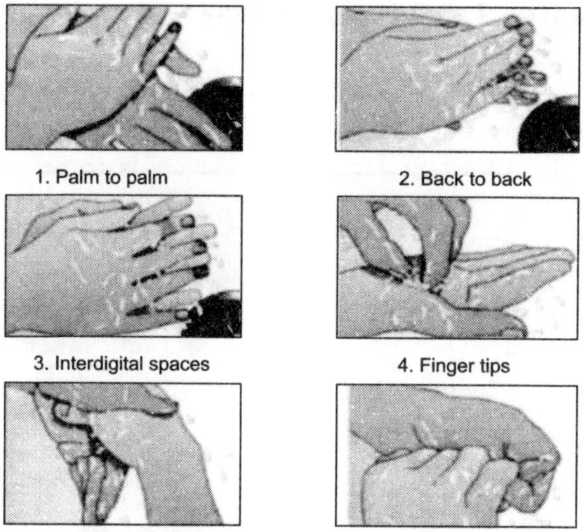

1. Palm to palm
2. Back to back
3. Interdigital spaces
4. Finger tips
5. Thumbs and wrists
6. Nails

Source: Reproduced with Kind Permission of the Nursing Standard

Disease exists with the accumulation of diseased soil, toxaemia that is the battleground for disease germs to thrive and attack the body. Intestinal sub-infection takes in its range practically every organ and tissue of the human body and a great many disease conditions have their origin in the intestinal tract. The refuse matter of the bowels contains violent toxins. Constipation is very rightly called the mother of nearly all diseases and should, therefore, be avoided, of course, not by a strong purgatives and pills but by regulating the diet and taking systematic exercise, in short, by observing the principles of health.

Health Education in Schools: Learning for Life

3

Health is a multidimensional concept because it is shaped by biological, social, economic and cultural factors. Health is not merely the absence of disease but is influenced and shaped by the access to basic needs like food security, safe water supply, housing, and sanitation and health services. Within this broader definition of health, individual health is intrinsically interrelated with social factors. Therefore, while individual health is important it is necessary to delineate its linkages with the physical, social and economic environment in which people live.

During the latter part of the 19th century, epidemics were taking a drastic toll among the school population of the United States. Children who survived these epidemic diseases often had a diminished capacity to learn as a result of their illness. Unsanitary conditions in the school played a part in the spread of disease. Alarmed school physicians instructed teachers to become more involved with the health of their students. At that time, health education was not yet part of the school curriculum. In fact, there was no such thing as health education as we know it today. The first efforts in this direction were more crises oriented than preventive. Teachers were instructed to make daily health inspections of their students and report any inspected cases of serious disease.

Health education has come a long way since its early history. Formal health education first took the form of instruction in anatomy and physiology. Health was taught purely as a science and emphasis was placed on retention of facts. As health education evolved, teachers became more concerned with the attitudinal and behavioural aspects of students health as well. Today, the emphasis is on a preventive approach as opposed to the crises oriented approach of yesteryears. The challenge for teachers today is to motivate students to improve their own health status through positive self-direction. Health education offers students an opportunity for personal growth and enhancement that is not duplicated anywhere else in the school curriculum. Therefore, it is vital to the development of a total positive lifestyle.

Children's health is an important concern for all societies since it contributes to their overall development. Health, nutrition and education are important for the overall development of the child and these three inputs need to be addressed in a comprehensive manner. While the relationship between health and education is seen more in terms of the role that the latter plays in creating health awareness and health status improvements, what is not adequately represented in the debates is the reciprocal relationship between health and education, especially when it comes to children. Studies have shown that poor health and nutritional status of children is a barrier to attendance and educational attainment and therefore plays a crucial role in enrollment, retention and completion of school education (Rana, K. & Das, S., 2004; World Bank, 2004).

The concerns related to health, nutrition and other inputs that contribute to the overall development of the child, therefore need to be part of the curriculum on 'Health and Physical Education' at the primary, secondary and senior secondary schools. Given the interdisciplinary nature of the subject, it should not be just another 'text-book learning' exercise but requires integration and cross curriculum planning with other subjects and co-curricular areas. This kind of a conceptualization lends itself to a number of possibilities for applied learning related to the immediate lives and environments of children and their communities.

What is Health Education?

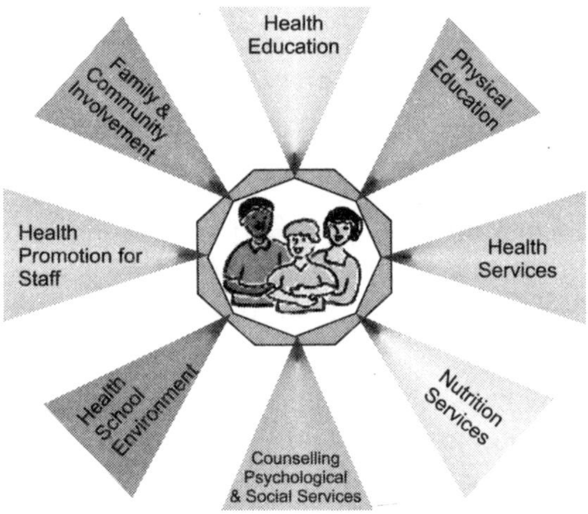

Health Education is a social science that draws from the biological, environmental, psychological, physical and medical sciences to promote health and prevent disease, disability and premature death through education-driven voluntary behaviour change activities. Health education is the development of individual, group, institutional, community and systematic strategies to improve health knowledge, attitudes, skills and behaviour. The purpose of health education is to positively influence the health behaviour of individuals and communities as well as the living and working conditions that influence their health. Thomas D. Wood said: "Health education is the sum of experiences, which favourably influence habits, attitudes and knowledge relating to individual, community and racial health." Ruth E. Grout opined, "Health education is the translation of what is known about health into desirable individual and community behaviour patterns by means of the education process."

From the elementary teacher's perspective, health education is the process of developing and providing planned learning experiences in such a way as to supply information, change attitudes and influence behaviour. In theory this process results in the child achieving individual responsibility for personal health, which leads to health enhancement, or high-level wellness. All this is accomplished through the teacher creating and facilitating learning experiences that develop the child's decision-making ability. With good decision-making skills, the child will make better choices about the personal, family, peer and social factors that influence his quality of life. An effective school health programme must have a direct influence on children's lives and behaviour.

Health education is a lifelong process. As a person develops awareness of the many components of health and incorporates them into his own life, he:

1. Assumes responsibility for his health and health care and participates in the decision-making.
2. Respects the benefits of medical technology but is not awe of medical equipment and tests.
3. Tries new behaviours and modifies others.
4. Is an active partner with the physician in the decision-making process.
5. Asks questions, seeks evidence and evaluates information.
6. Strives for self-reliance in personal health matters.
7. Voluntarily adopts practices consistent with a healthy lifestyle.

Health Education is integral to the primary mission of schools. It improves the health status of individuals, families, communities, states and the nation. Health education enhances the quality of life for all people and reduces premature deaths. By focusing on prevention, health education reduces the costs (both financial and human) that individuals, employers, families, insurance companies, medical facilities, communities, the state and the nation would spend on medical treatment. It provides young people with the knowledge and skills they need to become successful learners and healthy and productive adults.

Therefore, health education should contribute directly to a student's ability to successfully practice behaviours that protect and promote health and avoid or reduce health risks. Not only do schools provide critical outlets to reach millions of children and adolescents to promote lifelong healthy behaviours, they also provide a place for students to engage in these behaviours, such as eating healthy and participating in physical activity.

Difference between Physical Education and Health Education

Education about health is named as health education whereas education of the physique is called physical education. Health is a comprehensive term while physique carries a limited scope. Physical education can rightly be called one of the aspects of health education. Physical appearance, good physique and a sound body are the responsibility of physical education. But these constitute only an element of health education. Health education covers physical education also. Physical education fulfils a limited function of health education. Both aim at good health; whereas one is only a part, the other is a whole.

Good health is by far the most valuable asset, which any person can possess. The development of good health is a common cause with physical education and health education. Physical education employs for this purpose the medium of exercises, games, sports, dances, etc. Its main purpose lies on the skill of participation. Health education employs and develops the knowledge of rules of personal hygiene and ways of healthy living and immediate participation in healthful practices. The two are complementary forces leading to the total development of the individual, family, community and nation. J.B. Nash has very appropriately remarked, "Health and recreation are results while physical education activities are the means." There is no doubt, of course, that both aspire for a common goal, i.e. the development of the individual or that of a group.

When we look at the contents of these two areas we find that the scope of health education is very vast. Whereas physical education is the concern of physical instructors and directors of physical education, on the other hand health education necessitates team work on the part of teachers of hygiene and physiology, medical officers, P.T.I's, local bodies like municipality and panchayat, teachers in charge of various recreational activities and all other teachers.

Aims and Objectives of Health Education

Health education, as one facet of the school health programme and the total school curriculum is integral to "Education for All" and "Health for All". "Good health is essential for effective learning and education is a powerful means of enabling children and adults to attain and maintain good health" (*UNESCO/UNDP, 1995, Topic 11*). Not only does health education have a direct effect on the school pupil but through the pupils' examples, can benefit families, communities and environments. School health education should view health as more than the absence of disease, utilize all educational opportunities for health: formal and informal, traditional and alternative, inside and outside the school, harmonize all of the health messages, empower students to act for healthy living and to promote conditions supportive of health, establish a basis for lifelong learning and promotion of health, foster interaction between schools, the community, parents and local services and ensure a healthy school environment.

C.E. Turner has suggested the following aims and objectives of health education in order to bring the child upto his optimum level of health:

1. Providing healthful knowledge.
2. Protecting children against communicable and other preventable diseases.
3. Discovering physical defects and other abnormalities in the child and promoting their correction, if they are remediable.
4. Developing the knowledge and attitudes that will enable the individual to make intelligent health decisions.
5. Promoting desirable health habits.
6. Developing school, home and community cooperation in health promotion.

The aims of health education thus are basically three-fold:

(i) Preservation and improvement of physical health.

(ii) Preservation and improvement of mental health.

(iii) Preservation and improvement of emotional health of the pupils.

On this basis the objectives of health education can be classified under the following heads:

1. *Physical development*

Since the modern education aims at the growth and development of the learners' total personality, the physical aspect needs equal attention. The learner has to be enabled through health education to develop into a healthy, happy, strong, active, alert, skilful, charming and vitally alive personality.

2. *Improving human relations in matters of health*

It means establishing good relations between home, school and the community so that they cooperate for the health education of the child. In order to become a healthy nation, we must ensure that all agencies and individuals in the home, schools and the community understand and discharge their duties in this respect in a cordial manner.

3. *Developing a sense of civic responsibility*

People can be made conscious of unhealthy social behaviours and health education can help in eradicating such unhealthy practices and bad manners.

4. *Influencing and educating ignorant people*

Health education programme of a school is a fit aspect of its adult education programmes. The healthful, clean and disciplined way of life imparted to children in the school and adopted by them, indirectly influences and educates the ignorant parents and other people in the wider community.

5. *Making the students realize the necessity of having good health and providing information regarding health rules*

Health education programme should make the students understand the importance of keeping good health by making them aware about various aspects of health.

6. *Developing certain skills concerning health, e.g., training in first aid, etc.*

Thus, the aim of health education from kindergarten to grade 12 is to enable students to apply health knowledge in daily life in order to increase health-enhancing behaviours and decrease health-risking behaviours. Health education thus basically focuses on important behaviours and conditions that promote health or that put health at risk, skills needed to practice those behaviours or to address those conditions both personally and collectively, knowledge, attitudes, beliefs and values related to those behaviours and conditions and providing learning experiences that allow students to model and practice skills.

Why Health Education in School?

Schools lay a country's foundation for the future and have a major effect on a host of issues, including health. What is learnt at this impressionable stage of life in terms of knowledge, attitudes and behaviours has a lasting impact on the entire lifespan of the individual. Health is maintained and diseases most effectively controlled by knowledge—knowledge of prevention of disease and early recognition of signs of sickness. Ensuring that children have access to knowledge ensures that they are able to use it to mould not only their own attitude and behaviour, but that of their families and communities as well. This is the primary reason for health issues occupying the center stage in the school curriculum.

Perhaps the best argument for teaching health education is that health behaviours are the most important determinant of health status. Because health related behaviours are both learned and amenable to change, there is not better time to start formal health education than in the elementary school years, when the child is more flexible and more apt to accept positive health behaviours. In addition many of the negative aspects of life could be avoided. This avoidance becomes increasingly important with mounting evidence that most health problems are due to smoking, poor nutrition, excess weight, lack of exercise, stress, abuse of drugs and alcohol and unsafe personal behaviour.

Unfortunately, health education still suffers from a lack of importance in school curriculum and a lack of adequately trained teachers. If we wish to help prevent many of the conditions that are now the leading causes of death, then we must emphasize prevention in our educational efforts. Children receive nearly 12,000 hours of education in kindergarten through grade 12, yet less than 3 per cent of a child's total schooling is in health. A school can promote health if it constantly strengthens its capacity as a healthy setting for living, learning and working.

Increasing the number of schools that provide health education on key health problems facing young people is a critical health objective for improving our nation's health. Most states and districts in America have adopted a policy stating that schools will teach at least one of the following topics:

1. Alcohol or other drug-use prevention.
2. Asthma awareness.
3. Emotional and mental health.
4. Food borne illness prevention.
5. HIV prevention.
6. Injury prevention and safety.
7. Nutrition and Dietary behaviour.
8. Physical activity and fitness.
9. Suicide prevention.
10. Tobacco use prevention.
11. Violence prevention.

However, only 6.4 per cent of elementary schools, 20.6 per cent of middle schools and 35.8 per cent of high schools worked on all topics. The American Cancer Society, the American Diabetes Association, and the American Heart Association believe that school health education programmes can reduce health risks behaviours such as tobacco use, poor nutrition, lack of physical activity, drug and alcohol use, as well as actions that increase stress and risk of injury and violence. Because these behaviours are amenable to change, quality school health education taught by trained and certified health educators provides the best opportunity to promote positive health behaviour among children and adolescents.

Accomplishing Health Education

With the school day already so hectic and tight, many elementary and secondary teachers wonder how to find time to teach health education. Nevertheless time has to be taken out.

Health education can help ensure that the valuable resource of this generation is to be fit physically, psychologically and socially to assume the difficult tasks of adulthood. Still the question remains, when and how should health education be taught in the classroom? How can it be accomplished?

Health education that is relevant and motivating for the student requires careful planning. The quality of health instruction is reflected in the amount of planning and organization done by the teacher. There are many approaches to teaching health. However, the responsibility rests with each teacher to create and facilitate direct instruction in health and to correlate other health-related topics whenever the opportunity arises. A school can promote health by:

- Fostering health and learning with all the measures at its disposal.
- Engaging health and education officials, teachers, teachers' unions, students, parents, health providers and community leaders in efforts to make the school a healthy place.
- Striving to provide a healthy environment, school health education, and school health services along with school/community projects and outreach, health promotion programmes for staff, nutrition and food safety programmes, opportunities for physical education and recreation, and programmes for counselling, social support and mental health promotion.
- Implementing policies and practices that respect an individual's well-being and dignity, provide multiple opportunities for success, and acknowledge good efforts and intentions as well as personal achievements.
- Striving to improve the health of school personnel, families and community members as well as pupils; and works with community leaders to help them understand how the community contributes to, or undermines, health and education.

The American Medical Association has pointed out that efficient health instruction must be:

1. *Sequential*

Health should be taught from kindergarten through grade, in a sequence that introduces concepts at appropriate learning levels. The curriculum at each grade should build on what has been learned in previous years and should be the basis for curricula in future years.

2. *Planned*

Health instruction should have stated goals, objectives, activities and evaluation criteria. It should be given scheduled time within the total curriculum, not taught sporadically or used as a substitute for other subjects.

3. *Comprehensive*

Instruction in only one or several health topics is not adequate for an understanding of health. A comprehensive health curriculum includes instruction in growth and development, mental and emotional health, personal and family lifestyles, nutrition, disease prevention and control, safety, drug use and abuse, and consumer and community health. More important than the individual subjects, however, is a study of how all subjects are interrelated and how all affect the quality of life of an individual.

4. *Taught by qualified health teachers*

An elementary school teacher requires training to teach health concepts and to relate these to the wellness of the students. Junior and senior high school teachers and school health coordinators should be professionally prepared health educators. State departments of education have information regarding certification requirements in each state.

Health education plays a very important role in the promotion of health and also in the treatment of various diseases. Civilization, faulty educational methods and the generally complex life of today have all tended to degenerate the modern men and women. Nature has given way to "fashion". Since man has become "civilized" he has tried to improve on Nature in his ways of living, with the result that to please his palate, his food has become denatured, devitalized, overcooked and over-rich; he stimulates his nerves to get emotional enjoyment when his body wants rest; he neglects the need for fresh air and he is too enervated to take exercise. In time, under this perverted artificial mode of living even the strongest body tends to fail.

Scope of Health Education

In order to define the scope of this subject one needs to identify areas that are related to the needs of the overall development of the child. The access to basic needs in terms of food, clothing, and shelter is essential for the fulfillment of the psychosocial and higher needs. Given this broad understanding, this subject needs to address the fulfillment of these basic needs at various levels of schooling. Within this overall framework both yoga and physical education are seen as routes for achieving not merely physical fitness but for psychosocial development as well. There are broadly four areas that are related to health, yoga and physical education. These are:

1. Personal health, physical and psychosocial development,
2. Movement concepts and motor skills,
3. Relationships with significant others, and
4. Healthy communities and environments.

In order to address these four areas there is a need to identify topics that are covered in various school subjects, co-curricular subjects and also government programmes like the school health and mid-day meal initiatives. We recognize that the curriculum design for this subject is challenging both in terms of content and evaluation.

Health education includes all such instruction that enlightens a student about activities and functions contributing to preservation, promotion and restoration of health. By means of a health education programme the spread of disease in the school-going children can be checked and their eradication can also be attempted. A thorough knowledge of health rules underlines the needs of the study of anatomy and also the symptoms of common diseases of children. Practical knowledge of causes and diagnosis is equally essential. School health education also includes knowledge about the environment, equipments and routine of the school as well.

It is for the school health programme to contribute to the maintenance and improvement of the health of the pupils and school personnel including health services, healthful living and health education. Widely addressed topics in health education include:

- Personal growth, care and development,
- Effective relationships,
- Safety,
- Substance abuse,
- Common diseases,
- Sex education,
- Stress and mental health,
- Health policies and services, and
- Environmental health.

In the World Health Organization's Information Series on School Health, a decade of evaluation research indicates three important findings regarding quality school health education programmes:

1. Health education that concentrates on developing health-related skills and imparting health-related knowledge and attitudes are more likely to help youth practice health-enhancing behaviours.

2. Skill development is more likely to result in the desired healthy behaviour when practicing the skill tied to the content of a specific health behaviour or health decision.
3. The most effective method of skill development is learning by doing—involving students in active, participatory experiences, rather than passive ones.

In 1985 it was reported that the average fourth grader spends only 22 minutes a day in health instruction. Perhaps it is encouraging to think that the elementary school child is receiving at least 22 minutes per day. However, it is important to remember that in the last 20 years topics such as drug abuse, smoking, heart disease, prevention of teenage pregnancy, adolescent suicide, stress control, child abuse, AIDS have been added to nutrition, disease, mental health, sexuality, personal health, environmental health and first aid.

Health Needs of Children

While addressing the health needs of children it is important to examine the available data on causes of mortality and morbidity across the concerned age groups and also the variation it presents across caste/class; gender and regions. This is important for evolving a curriculum and syllabus that addresses the real life situations and experiences of school going children factoring in the variations across states, class/caste and gender. A review of available macro data and studies shows that the major cause of mortality and morbidity among children are a group of disease conditions like diarrhoea, pneumonia and fevers that are related to poor living conditions and lack of access to basic needs. An important cause for the above mentioned communicable diseases are the prevalence of under nutrition among children. The NFHS data show that 53 per cent of children in rural areas are underweight in India and this varies across states. In some states this figure is as high as 60 per cent who are underweight especially among the schedule tribes in poorer states. The extent of stunted growth of children is also of concern and has consequences for schooling.

The age specific data on major causes of mortality shows that low birth weight, respiratory infections and anemia are the major causes of mortality under five age group. Respiratory infections and anemia become the major causes for the age group 5-14. Respiratory infections especially tuberculosis becomes the major cause of mortality for females after the age of 15 (Shiva and Gopalan, 2000).

Since undernutrition and communicable diseases is a major problem among majority of school going children, the curriculum design has to address and integrate these concerns effectively. Even before independence, several Committees on education and health realized the need for a programme that would deal with both malnutrition and infectious diseases. Several countries including India have recognized the importance of a School Health programme.

School Health Programme in Other Countries: A Brief Review

In the United Kingdom school health services are provided through the Local Education Authorities with grants from the Ministry of Education. The National Health Service provides free medical care to all school children. In the former Soviet

Union, it was a part of the comprehensive scheme for children from birth until the child completes elementary education. Almost all schools with more than 800 children had full time doctors and nurses. In France there is a comprehensive programme for providing school health services until the university level with the required compliment of staff. After the World War II, as a part of its post-war reconstruction effort, Japan regarded school health services as an integral part of school education. The school health programme included regular medical check ups, school lunch programme and health education inputs. This programme was a cooperative effort between the school, Ministry of Education, Health Centers and other medical agencies. These countries represent examples where health input is an important constituent of the subject area of health and physical education.

Evolution of School Health Services in India

A framework for school health services was put forward in the Report on post-war Educational Development in India, which was issued by the Central Advisory Board in 1944. This report recommended that school health service should be under the administrative control of the education department. The Bhore Committee that provided the blueprint for health services development in independent India devoted a substantial section on the need and importance of school health programme for school going children. They recommended that the school health programme must be a part of the general health services and should not have a dual administrative control, viz. between the education and health departments, but should be under the control of the latter. They were of the opinion that a dual administration will result in the duplication of personnel and infrastructure (GOI, 1946: 111).

The Bhore Committee, which was set up around the time of independence, clearly spelt out the duties of a school health service and even today it represents the most comprehensive view of this programme. According to the committee, the duties of a school health service are:

"(1) Health measures, preventive and curative, which include: (a) the detection and treatment of defects and (b) the creation and maintenance of a hygienic environment in and around the school, and (2) measures for promoting positive health which should include: (a) the provision of supplementary food to improve the nutritional state of the child, (b) physical culture through games, sports and gymnastic exercises and through corporate recreational activities, and (c) health education through formal instruction and practice of the hygienic mode of life" (GOI, 1946: 112).

This comprehensive definition is valid even in the present context and therefore, the group recommends that it be adopted as a working definition for this subject area. Thus, the major components that have to be included in the school health programme are medical care, hygienic school environment, and school lunch, health, yoga and physical education. The School Health Programme has to be a coordinated effort between the education and health departments with the latter providing preventive, curative and promotive services at all levels of schooling.

The committee also recommended that the school health service must be introduced in phases whereby primary schools are covered first and then extended to secondary and high schools and colleges. As far as health education was concerned the Bhore Committee opined, "Formal classroom instruction in health matters should be reduced to the minimum. What is essential is that hygienic habits be inculcated." This recommendation is valid even today and therefore should be a guideline for evolving syllabus.

In 1958, the school health division was established in the Ministry of Health Welfare in order to strengthen health education programmes for young people. This division served as a resource center for the NCERT, the Department of Education and the Directorate of Adult Education. There have been efforts to integrate health education into school curricula with the Central Bureau of Health Education playing an important role in collaboration with the NCERT.

A review of the policy and curricular documents of the Ministry of Education shows that up to the late 1960's there was a comprehensive approach to the subject than during the later years where it gets fragmented into physical education and health education with little or no reference to the necessity of school lunch or medical check ups. An intensive pilot project was undertaken by the National Institute of Health and Family Welfare (NIHFW) and it came up with a number of suggestions. It stressed on the need for school health education to be intensified, sanitation in schools to be improved, nutritional programmes for the children and medical services to be provided.

Thus, the various components of the school health programme must be an integral part of 'Health and Physical Education'. In fact health and nutrition programmes should form the basis for health and nutrition education rather than just focusing on 'creating awareness' in children about what they should eat, especially when a large percentage of children do not have access to adequate food.

Conclusion

Knowledge, without action is as useless as a motorcar without petrol, neither can get one anywhere. Knowing what to do to acquire and maintain health is one thing, putting that knowledge into operation and persisting in doing so from day-to-day is quite another. It is the duty of every one of us to take care of his or her body and keep it in health. Primarily, of course, health is something to be lived with and not a subject merely to be taught. Children require to be initiated into a life of health. The study and practice of health must form, from the very beginning, a part of the daily curriculum of the school. But though it is by far the best thing to start this journey into the life of health while still a child, it is never too late to begin it even later in life. The healthy and rigorous life of its citizen is a nation's greatest asset. There is no need for one to accept mere existence for the joy of being alive. Health is the keynote of success.

Section–II

School Health Education and Programmes

School Health Programme

4

In a developing country like India, a substantial number of school going children suffer from various preventable diseases due to widespread poverty compounded by illiteracy and limited awareness. Many conditions can be prevented by appropriate health education and services, which must be adequately reinforced from time to time. The Government of India launched the School Health Scheme in the year 1996-97 but the enthusiasm in many states tapered off over time owing to competing priorities. Central Board of Secondary Education has communicated to all schools to carry out a comprehensive school health programme (beyond just health check up). The National Curriculum framework has also recommended that the health education should be incorporated as a part of the curriculum in schools.

Ensuring that children are healthy and able to learn is an essential component of an effective education system. Good health increases enrollment and reduces absenteeism. It also ensures attendance of the poorest and most disadvantaged children to school, many of whom are girls. It is these children who are often the least healthy and most malnourished and who have the most to gain educationally from improved health. Effective school health programmes that are developed as part of community partnerships provide one of the most cost-effective ways to reach school age children, adolescents and the broader community, and are a sustainable way to promote healthy practices.

The school health programme is defined as "the school procedures that contribute to the maintenance and improvement of the health of pupils and school personnel including health services, healthful living and health education". A comprehensive school health programme is designed to influence positively the knowledge, attitudes, and behaviours of students. Through the involvement of home, school, and community, a comprehensive school health programme relates to the emotional, intellectual, moral, physical, and social aspects of a student's life. A school health programme includes a wide range of school and community personnel collaborating to enhance the well-being of students. The health instruction component of the programme should be coordinated with health services, within a healthy school and community environment. The foundational pillars to comprehensive school health include instruction, support services, healthy school environment, and social support.

Eight-component Model

A coordinated school health program (CSHP) model consists of eight interactive components. Schools by themselves cannot, and should not be expected to, address the nation's most serious health and social problems. Families, health care workers, the media, religious organizations, community organizations that serve youth, and young people themselves also must be systematically involved. However, schools could provide a critical facility in which many agencies might work together to maintain the well-being of young people.

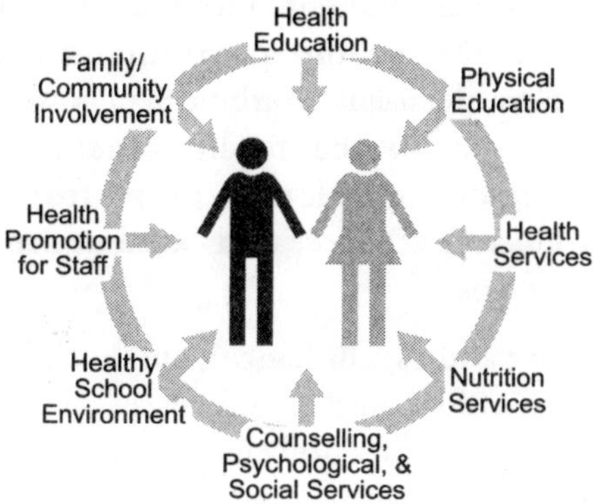

(Adapted from: *Healthy Youth: An Investment in Our Nation's Future*, 2004, Department of Health and Human Services, Centers of Disease Control and Prevention.)

1. Health Education: Classroom instruction that addresses the physical, emotional, mental and social aspects of health—designed to help students improve their health, prevent illness, and reduce risky behaviours.

2. Physical Education: A planned, sequential K-12 curriculum that promotes lifelong physical activity develops basic movement skills and sports skills. Physical education shall be the environment in which students learn, practice, and are assessed on developmentally appropriate motor skills, social skills, and knowledge.

3. Health Services: Preventive services, education, emergency care, referrals, and management of acute and chronic health problems—designed to prevent health problems and injuries and ensure care for students. Can include school nursing as well as dental services and school based/school linked health centers.

4. Nutrition Services: Integration of nutritious, affordable and appealing meals; nutrition education, and an environment that promotes healthy eating.

5. Health Promotion for Staff: Opportunities that encourage school staff to pursue a healthy lifestyle that contributes to their improved health status, improved morale, and a greater personal commitment to the school's overall coordinated health programme. This personal commitment often transfers into greater commitment to the health of students and creates positive role modeling. Health promotion activities have improved productivity, decreased absenteeism, and reduced health insurance costs.

6. Counseling and Psychological, and Social Services: Services that include individual and group assessments, interventions, and referrals—designed to prevent problems early and enhance healthy development.

7. Healthy School Environment: It includes the physical and aesthetic surroundings and the psychosocial climate and culture of the school. Factors that influence the physical environment include the school building and the area surrounding it, any biological or chemical agents that are detrimental to health, and physical conditions such as temperature, noise, and lighting. The psychological environment includes the physical, emotional, and social conditions that affect the well-being of students and staff.

8. Parent/Community Involvement: An integrated school, parent, and community approach for enhancing the health and well-being of students. School health advisory councils, coalitions, and broadly based constituencies for school health can build support for school health programme efforts.

Benefits Accruing from School Health Programme

An effective school health, hygiene and nutrition programme offers several benefits:

It responds to an increased need

The success of child survival programmes and the efforts of the government and communities to expand basic education coverage have resulted in a greater number of school-age children and in a greater proportion of these children attending school. Targeted education programmes have ensured that many of these new entrants are girls for whom good health is especially important since it has an intergenerational effect.

It increases the efficacy of other investments in child development

School health programmes are the essential sequel to and complement early childcare and development programmes. Continuing good health at school age is essential if children are to sustain the advantages of a healthy early childhood and make full use of what may be their only opportunity for formal learning.

It ensures good current and future health

It is estimated that the burden of disease for school-aged children of 5-14 years is 11 per cent of the total global burden of disease. School health activities contribute to prevention of health problems, their early detection and management as well as encourage healthy lifestyles and behaviours that secure future health. Good health practices promote reproductive health and help prevent HIV/AIDS as well.

It ensures better educational outcomes

Ensuring good health at school-age can boost school enrollment and attendance, reduce the need for repetition and increase educational attainment.

It improves social equity

As a result of improved education strategies, some of the most disadvantaged children—girls, poor, rural children and children with disabilities—have access to school for the first time. However, their ability to attend school and to learn is compromised at times by their poor health. These are the children who will benefit most from health interventions, since they are likely to show the greatest improvements in attendance and learning achievement.

It is a highly cost effective strategy

School health programmes help link resources for health, education, nutrition, and sanitation to an institutional body, the school—that is already in place and provides the network and foundation for young children. The school network is universal and coverage is often superior to health systems. At the same time, the school network has an extensive skilled workforce that already works closely with the community and hence ensures sustainability.

Desirable health related attitudes and health care practices learnt and adopted within the school also contribute to ensuring optimal health and education outcomes. An environment that is safe and healthy for children is imperative for the optimal development of children and adolescents.

Key Elements of School Health Programme

School Health Programmes succeed when health and education departments collaborate right from the planning stage along with community participation. School health programmes aim at providing a package of preventive, promotive and curative health services directed towards improving the current health status of the school-age children. School health programmes also facilitate promotion of healthy lifestyles, which include adequate physical activity, learning to respect each other, live in harmony and shun violence, as well as prevention of unhealthy practices like unsafe sex, alcohol and tobacco use. The schools may also choose to work towards addressing specific health problems in students, such as anaemia, asthma, thalassemia, obesity and infectious diseases depending on prevailing public health priorities and capacities of the local health and education systems.

Essential elements of school health are:

- *Health-related school policies* that include children of all communities, encourage healthy lifestyles, address priority public health problems and promote collaboration among teachers. It also enables students and their parents on one side and departments like health, education, women and child development on the other side to bring about convergence.

- ***Provision of safe (physically and psycho-socially) and supportive environment*** to ensure healthy development of students and provide a healthy learning environment. Provision of nutrition relieves the hunger of the child coming from deprived circumstances and provision of safe water and adequate sanitation reinforces hygienic behaviour. It is especially important to provide privacy and safety to promote participation of adolescent girls in education. Keeping the school free of violence and various forms of discrimination is also an important dimension.
- ***Health, hygiene and nutrition education*** that focuses upon the development of age appropriate knowledge, attitudes, values and life skills needed to establish lifelong healthy practices. Additionally, the school environment must provide opportunities to practice the acquired healthy behaviour in order to reduce the vulnerability of youth and teachers to common health risks. For example, mid-day school meal programmes cooked and served hygienically, sanitary toilets/latrines with running water supplies, soap and water for hand washing, adequate supply of potable water, provision of sanitary napkins for girls and kitchen garden to demonstrate feasibility of growing healthy food.
- ***School-based health and nutrition services*** that are equitable, simple, sustainable, safe and familiar and address problems that is prevalent and recognized as important within the community, e.g. mid-day school meals.

School age population is extremely vulnerable to health risks and illness. Illnesses and behaviour formed during this period can have a detrimental effect on health during the adult years of an individual's life. An effective school health programme provides the following key services:

Health screening and referral linkage with health services for remedial and preventive measures

Screening helps in early detection and the timely institution of treatment for the commonest causes of morbidity. Opthalmic and dental conditions, skin lesions and nutritional problems in particular are conditions where early identification can affect cure and prevent further progress and complications. By attending to some health determinants like anaemia and malnutrition it could play a preventive role in addressing these critical problems. It also helps identify children with refractive errors and hearing deficits, which are a major source of learning difficulties and by arranging to correct them, can dramatically improve school performance. Identification and support to children with disabilities is another major role that screening can play.

It is therefore, recommended to carry out health checkups of all students at least once in a year, but preferably twice a year. Much of the success of school health screening programmes lies in constructing effective post screening referral arrangements. This is needed to ensure that the roughly 1-1% of children who are identified during the screening process as having serious but correctable ailments receive the higher level of clinical care that they need.

Health education

This ensures the provision of age appropriate information on health, hygiene and nutrition, and to put it simply, education about the physical and mental aspects of growing up. It has great potential in promotion of healthy development and preventing risk behaviour.

There are four broad activity groups that constitute school health education. One is the form of incorporation of a better understanding of health issues in the formal curriculum. The second is the construct of a series of informal sessions for students on specific necessary health issues, which are not part of the formal learning system. This form of communication inculcates interest and enhances retention. It is effective for issues, which require interpersonal dialogue, like life skills education and menstrual hygiene or for issues, which require demonstrations, for instance, first aid education.

The third is the use of the school for behaviour change communication to disseminate health information and mould health related behaviours through extra curricular activities like poster making, plays, competitions, and quiz contests. Finally, it is also the health and hygiene related practices that the school consciously inculcates in its students; for example the use of toilets, hand washing before meals, the disposal of waste and the cleanliness of classrooms and school campus.

Addressing nutritional issues, particularly anaemia and malnutrition

Health department can assist in providing specific interventions in the school setting for the priority areas of micro and macronutrient deficiency. This includes identification and correction of anaemia, periodic treatment for worm infestation, the promotion of use of iodized salt, organizing talks on relevant nutrition issues and a linkage with the school mid-day meal programme to ensure that this acts as the critical supplement to correct macro nutritional deficiency, rather than being a substitute for food intake at home. School health programme offers a unique opportunity to reach students and through them, their families at home. The nutrition counselling given herein has the potential to last through to the next generation, as these students are the parents of tomorrow.

Providing safe and supportive environment in schools

It is a given pre-requisite that schools need to provide the basic amenities like potable drinking water, separate sanitary toilets for boys and girls and clean classrooms. It is also necessary that schools strive to ensure safety to their students and staff from physical injuries, stress, corporal punishment and abuse. The school environment needs to be supportive of its teachers and students and also to be sensitive and alert to the manifest signs and symptoms of these conditions and provide the opportunity to seek appropriate help in effective and confidential management.

Service provision

Services for minor ailments like headache, fever, cuts can be provided by the trained teachers while all other services can be offered through health care providers.

Programme of School Health

A total school health programme is needed if the school is to function as an effective institution for promoting high-level wellness. A comprehensive school health programme can be divided into three parts:

1. Health services
2. Healthful school environment
3. Health instruction

Each component has a planning, administration and evaluation aspect. Adequate planning for all three components ensures the comprehensiveness of each component. Effective leadership coordinates the components and ensures proper staffing, budgeting, policy fulfillment and evaluation.

1. *School health services*

The basic responsibility for the health of the child lies with the parents, but the school plays an important role sometimes primary, sometimes secondary—in maintaining the health of each child. All teachers should be concerned with student health, as any deviation from normal health is a possible deterrent to the ability to learn effectively. Even minor disturbances such as cold or stomachache can impair a student's ability to concentrate and therefore, the ability to learn. The primary role of the teacher in this part of the health programme is in observation, record keeping, referral and follow up. Teachers can also become involved in screening the students for various health functions, such as vision and hearing. It is important to prepare students for any screening examination they might be taking in the near future. This preparation serves two purposes. First, anxiety of the student regarding the testing will be reduced. Second, the screening exam then becomes a learning experience in health education for the students. The classroom teacher and school nurse should cooperate in all three areas of the comprehensive school health programme. Particularly in the school health services area these two professionals form a vital team in promoting the health of the child.

The specific reasons for providing school health services are: (a) they contribute to the realization of educational aims, (b) they are necessary to minimize the hazards of school attendance, (c) they are important in adapting school programs to individual capacities and needs, and (d) they ensure normal and sound health among the pupils.

There are six phases of school health services which are:

I. *Health appraisal*

It is the process of determining the total health status of a child through such means as health histories, teacher and nurse observations, and medical examination. It is a cooperative process in which the responsibility is shared by physician, nurse, school psychologist, teacher and others. Teachers are in the best position to reveal evidence of a health problemme—their observations need to be followed by a medical examination by the physician. Cumulative health records are used in the school for maintaining information about each pupil as he progresses from his first year at school until he leaves at the end of the high school years.

II. *Health counselling and follow-up*

Health counseling is a procedure for helping pupils and parents to gain insight into the nature and significance of conditions revealed by various appraisal techniques. The specific aims of health counselling are:

1. To give pupils the information about their health status revealed by appraisal procedures, which they can use to good advantage.
2. To interpret to parents the significance of health problems and to encourage them to obtain needed care for their children.
3. To motivate pupils to want and accept needed treatment.
4. To promote each pupil's acceptance of responsibility for his own health in keeping with his stage of maturity.

Actual improvement in the health of children depends more on counselling and follow up than on any other school activity. Teachers, principals, nurses, physicians all have important roles to play in this phase of the school health service. The specific role and responsibility of a school nurse is like this.

The role and responsibility of school nurse:

In a comprehensive school health plan, the school nurse is most visible in the health services area. When schools do employ school nurses, they are either hired directly by the school district or provided by the local health department. The services provided by school nurses are extremely important to the child's welfare. Most frequently they provide direct care to children when they are sick or injured. Important functions are information gathering through assessment of the children, record keeping and routine assessments.

Nurses are excellent resources. They should be included on any health education curriculum planning committee and should be involved in planning the education of special populations, especially in planning the educational programme of the handicapped child. Nurses can assist these children in becoming self-sufficient in the classroom and help alleviate the fears and concerns of the teachers. Finally the nurse should see that emergency procedures for injuries, accidents and sickness are developed, because there are obvious legal concerns when undertaking aid in any of these situations. The nurse can help ensure that proper care will be given by helping to develop guidelines and workshops for teachers and office personnel in emergency procedures. It is recommended that every teacher finds the time to take a basic first course and follows the emergency procedures established by the school district and the nurse. The teacher can be of special assistance in working with the school nurse in areas like:

Observation: The teacher should observe the verbal and non-verbal behaviour of each student for any deviation that might indicate a health problem. Teachers are in an excellent position to appraise the health of the students as they see the child for several hours each day in a variety of situations—in the classroom, in the playground. Teachers familiar with the expected growth and development patterns of students are more likely to be objective in their appraisal than some one more closely identified with a student, such as a parent. When a child poses a possible threat to the health of the other students, appropriate steps to remove the child from the classroom should be taken. When children are allowed to attend school with contagious diseases, epidemics ensue.

Record keeping: The teacher should keep an individual card file for each student. This file can be used as a referral source and can also be useful when discussing specific behaviours with parents or other members of the school health team. The teacher should refrain from making value judgements about a child's behaviour or condition and should avoid attempts at diagnosing the student's condition; thus objectivity should be the goal when making card file notes. The health records can also familiarize the teacher with any specific condition, such as diabetes or epilepsy that might require emergency care in the classroom. All school personnel must remember that information contained in a student's health record is confidential and should not be shared as public knowledge.

Referral: Upon noticing any detrimental change in a student's health or behaviour, the teacher should place the child under his/her care. The classroom teacher should be able to help the school nurse, physician or psychologist understand the everyday behaviour of the child. For instance, whereas the physician might see the child in an isolated situation, a teacher can provide input relative to the history of the student's behaviour and explain whether the current behaviour is usual or represents a drastic change. Teachers should also be familiar with health related agencies in the community that can provide assistance for specific health problems. This knowledge could be valuable to parents in getting help if they cannot afford the services of a private physician.

Follow-up: A dedicated teacher will continue to follow the student's case, even after observation and referral have been completed. If the child is absent from school for any length of time, checking with parents or the school physician concerning the child's health is appropriate. When the student returns to the classroom, the teacher should resume careful observation to aid in the child's recovery.

III. *Emergency care in schools*

The first aid or emergency care programme of a school is a part of the school health service. The school has five distinct responsibilities in case of accidents or in case of sudden illness occurring in school or in school-connected activities:

1. Immediate care and first aid.
2. Notifying the pupil's parents.
3. Getting the child home or to some other place of safety.
4. Guiding parents, where necessary, to further sources of treatment.
5. Complementing the necessary records and reports.

To administer emergency care properly in the school, it is desirable that suitable facilities and appropriate supplies be available at all times. Each school should have a room designated as "the health room" where children can be sent when sick or injured, and where other school health activities can be conducted. It should contain a cabinet with the appropriate first-aid supplies. First aid should be readily available when needed. All school personnel should be trained in first aid.

IV. *Communicable disease control*

Communicable diseases are a big menace to the community. In addition to the health departments and the schools, everybody has to work hard to maintain control of these diseases. School responsibility arises principally from two factors i.e. during the time that children are in school the school is expected to protect their health, and the congregating of children in a classroom increases the possibility of communicating many diseases. The programme, in this direction, includes the education of parents and pupils, the encouragement of immunization during infancy and continuous efforts to have sick children stay at home.

V. *Identification and education of handicapped children*

It is generally observed that among the school population there are children having physical defects. This indicates a need for special school adjustments or adaptations. It is essential that these children be identified through the health appraisal programme of the school health services so that the appropriate educational adjustments can be made for them.

VI. *Health of school personnel*

One of the qualities, which every teacher must have, is good health. A healthy teacher has abundant energy and ability to think clearly and plan carefully. The appraisal, maintenance and improvement of teacher health are an important responsibility of the health service programme of the school. Teachers' health must be preserved and amount of illness among teachers must be reduced. The teacher must be free from handicapping conditions. He must have a periodic check up to discover his health status.

Healthy School Environment

The school and classroom environment should be an outstanding example of health excellence for the student. The teacher can play a critical part in conveying the appropriate message to the students concerning a healthful environment. If teachers demonstrate an interest in the environment, students are more likely to do the same. Teachers require a quality environment in which to work. This is important not only for the teaching-learning process but also for teacher and student morale. Whenever possible, teachers should volunteer as consultants in planning and maintaining the school site and surroundings. Fostering a cooperative relationship with the custodial staff, lunchroom staff and administrators in charge of the various aspects of the environment is beneficial. Lunchroom and canteen are excellent locations for learning opportunity in nutrition and sanitation.

It is important to teach students the significance of safe, sanitary and aesthetically pleasing surroundings in which to live and study; also teaching the proper ways to maintain the school site. It is possible to motivate students to enjoy and maintain the school environment. Few teachers are fortunate enough to be able to work in ideal situations. However, it is desirable to do all that is possible to enhance the teaching environment. The classroom should be physically adequate, pleasant, attractive and comfortable for the students.

The psychological setting is just as important as the physical one and the teacher is responsible for establishing the emotional tone within the classroom. The overall atmosphere should be one of acceptance, one in which the teacher knows the students well and is sensitive to their individual physical and emotional needs. The classroom should be non-threatening. Stress is reduced when there is a relaxed approach to instruction, one in which there is less emphasis on competition that makes the students stand against each other. Students should feel free to express their feelings honestly without fear of ridicule or rebuke.

A teacher can promote students' well-being by being kind but fair in promoting teacher-pupil relationships, setting reasonable goals for each student, praising positive behaviour, challenging students within their capabilities and tolerating occasional frustration. If they are involved in planning, they will become more interested in the subject matter. When students are interested, discipline is less likely to become a problem. Developing a warm, caring relationship with each pupil and by teaching self-discipline, maturity and responsibility for one's actions can minimize discipline problems.

Additional suggestions for creating a pleasing psychological environment include:

- Each student should be called by his/her name.
- Positive reinforcement should be given for appropriate academic and classroom behaviours.
- Teacher should talk with each student everyday.
- The student's behaviour should be corrected in a one-to-one conference.
- It should be made sure that every student gets to perform as a helper in classroom maintenance activities.
- The teacher should be pleasurable, smiling and should use direct eye contact when talking with the students.

Although main emphasis has been given on the classroom environment, there are other considerations that are part of the healthy school environment. Safety in the classrooms, canteen and the gymnasiums and on the school campus is an important aspect of a healthy school environment. The breakfast and lunch programme should be nutritious and appealing to school age children. Thus, all aspects of the comprehensive school health programme are important in order to provide an effective health education programme.

School Health Instruction

The third area of the school health programme is health instruction. Its main purpose is to equip the students with sufficient knowledge, attitudes and practices about health so that they may be able to attain and maintain the highest possible level of health. Health instruction is an important means of bringing about healthful behaviour among students. It emphasizes a scientific attitude towards health, which enables students to conduct themselves according to the recognized scientific knowledge. Many physical defects such as those involving hearing, posture, eyesight, etc. develop in childhood, which can be prevented, to a great extent, by intelligent health behaviour. Similarly scientific attitude toward superstitions and fads is very important for modern healthy living.

Health educators should consider themselves as part of a team whose main mission is to provide optimal conditions to enhance the wellness of each student. Each member of the health team has a particular role to play. Everyone involved with the health of students including the students' themselves—must take responsibility seriously. Each member must work cooperatively with other members in order to reach the ultimate goal of the total health.

It is the responsibility of the school to acquaint every pupil with the need for maintaining excellent health. It is necessary that pupil knows about his own physical condition, what good health is and how to acquire it; how to avoid illness and accidents and how to protect the health of others. It is equally essential that he know about sex, value of good nutritious food, safety, sanitation, and mental and emotional health. In the lower grades, health teaching should be primarily integrated with other subjects. In higher classes, separate classes with the name of 'Health' may be started. Health instruction may be given the same recognition as other subjects in regard to placement in the curriculum. Direct health instruction in physiology and hygiene classes may be taken up. Health instruction may be imparted through subjects like biology, general science, physical education, home economics and social studies.

Basic Principles of Health Instruction

C.L. Anderson, in his book, *School Health Practice* has given the following basic principles of health instruction. These principles are still recognized as fundamental to sound and effective health instruction.

(a) The fundamental principles of anatomy and physiology should be taught in relation to health and hygiene.

(b) The teacher should pay individual attention towards habit formation, rather than giving theoretical knowledge of facts to the children.

(c) The instructions should be given in a positive manner, emphasizing do's than don'ts.

(d) Health is an end to be achieved and not an academic subject.

(e) Health promotion should be one of the objectives of the whole school programme throughout the school life.

(f) Learning experiences must be adapted to physiological, psychological and social development of students.

(g) Instruction must be based on the students' interests, needs, abilities and social background.

(h) Learning results from experiences and opportunities must be provided through participation.

(i) The objectives of any activity must be specified in terms of learner's outcomes.

(j) The learning situation should be created so that the students can adopt it quickly.

(k) Integrated learning is most effective but it will be lasting only when it becomes unified.

(l) Health work in the institution cannot be fully effective unless it is integrated with the life of home and community.

(m) A number of audio-visual aids and illustrative material should be used in explaining the abstract principles of health.

Thus, health instruction should be made as practical as possible. For this purpose, opportunities should be provided and availed of in the institution, neighbourhood and outdoor activities wherein the students get new knowledge and develop good health habits.

Methods of Imparting Health Education

The days when health education was regarded as synonymous with the delivery of public lectures are gone for good. Educators now have at their disposal a whole battery of visual and auditory aids with which to vary and enliven their teaching. It needs to be pointed out that there is nothing unique about the methods of health education. Health education is merely one strand of the total educational weave. It must provide assumptions about the way life is lived, inculcate habits conducive to health, impart information which will provide a rational basis for habits already and yet to be acquired, encourage healthy attitudes and develop appreciations.

All aspects of health education must be carried on at all stages of the educational process although certain aspects are of greater importance and more easily dealt with at particular periods. Some of the important ways and means are given below, through which health education can be effectively imparted in schools.

1. *Healthy school environment*

Environment is one of the most potent educational media. In the matter of human development in various directions it is considered even more important than the heredity. It is the type of school building and the type of schoolteacher, which mould later assumptions about desirable ways of life. Any scheme of health education in schools must first of all ensure a healthy school environment and surroundings. If the school environment is clean and healthy, it is a befitting basic amenity towards health education. It will be unimpressive to talk of health education within dirty and unhealthy school surroundings. There should be suitable arrangement of clean drinking water and place for taking mid-day meals. The provision of suitable urinals and lavoratories also demands attention in the interest of sanitation and health.

2. *Health book*

Each student should be asked to maintain a health book. It will contain the health record of the student. Pictures illustrating important health rules, causes, prevention and remedies of various diseases may be pasted in it. An important health rule should be pasted on the top of every page. This book will provide to the authorities many clues for imparting health education to individuals and groups.

3. *Safety first*

The school has the responsibility for providing an environment that ensures safe living at school. It is necessary that safety be promoted in the classrooms, playgrounds, laboratories, workshops, etc.

4. *Lectures and talks*

The headmaster, teachers, school medical officer, local health authorities and the physical education instructor may deliver special lectures on various requisites of health and hygiene from time to time. After these talks students should be given opportunities to ask questions concerning these topics of health and hygiene to remove their doubts and to bring in their individual health problems. The impact of these lectures and talks should be evaluated from time to time.

5. *Printed material*

The school can accumulate a lot of printed material on health and hygiene, such as books, booklets, charts, posters, pamphlets, leaflets, etc. The health department, hospitals, Red

Cross and other social welfare organizations can be contacted for relevant health literature. The teachers themselves can prepare and display charts and posters on topics like food, exercise, personal cleanliness, healthy habits, prevention, etc.

6. *Health week*

Health week may be celebrated in the school every year, in which special emphasis may be placed on personal hygiene, school cleanliness, community health, etc. The students may engage in the thorough cleanliness of the school campus. Various student committees may be formed regarding different aspects of personal cleanliness. These committees may arrange competitions in their areas and award prizes to students having a better grasp of health education and its activities. Of course, it is desired that the spirit displayed in the health week be maintained throughout the year.

7. *Health projects*

Apart from health weeks, some specific health projects may also be undertaken by the school to promote health education. A campaign may be launched to combat malaria and reduce its incidence. The uneducated adults may be educated about personal hygiene.

8. *Health clubs*

Health clubs like other student clubs and societies can be organized in schools. These clubs can arrange debates, plays, etc. on health matters in cooperation with Red Cross Society and Health Department. The members of these clubs should definitely practice health rules in their daily lives.

9. *Films and film strips*

These are the latest devices for imparting health education. It has the unique ability to portray motion and speed. The Ministry of Information and Broadcasting and also the Public Relations Departments prepare from time to time certain documentary films to acquaint the public with the causes, precautions and remedial measures of important diseases. These films also discourage bad habits like smoking, drinking, addiction, overeating, gambling, etc. Importance of personal and social hygiene can be explained very effectively with the help of these films, which have really done much service in making the people health oriented. These films can also be shown in school from time to time, accompanied by oral commentary by the teacher. Filmstrips depicting various aspects of health can also be prepared in the school at a very low cost.

10. *Radio*

Radio talks are popular and effective medium for giving health education to the pupils and the public in general. Health rules, healthy habits, health standards, health requirements, health hazards, etc. can be presented to listeners through talks, poems, songs, plays, etc. over the radio. The students not only get entertainment from radio programmes but useful health instructions also.

11. *Television*

This device provides a much better device to telecast features on healthful living. It is a most potent instrument in raising the health standards of the community.

12. *Mechanical aids and exhibitions*

Certain mechanical aids can be exploited for giving health education. These can show what happens when a child is inoculated against diphtheria. It would not be difficult to devise a "quiz cabinet" which lights up when the button showing the correct answer to some health query is pressed.

13. *Educational trips*

Learning by experiencing is most effective. Actual field trips provide learning situations for the pupils and they get a first hand experience. Such trips can be organized to visit Red Cross, hospitals, clinics, and exhibitions, yoga centers, public health centers, etc. After the visit there should be further discussions to clarify any doubt or to supplement the material.

14. *Incidental teaching*

At the school stage there are always many opportunities of giving incidental health education to the students. There may be an incident of a communicable disease; the teacher has to educate the students to prevent against it. By frequent checking, personal cleanliness habits may be emphasized among the pupils.

Whatever is the media available, careful consideration must be given to their utilization. The tools should be used properly, for blundering efforts cannot be tolerated at health education. Right methods and right programmes alone can ensure the health of the children. A nation cannot afford to allow the major parts of its children and future citizens to grow up defective, undernourished and ill developed in mind, body and spirit. Keeping a child continuously on the right path through all the periods of development is real achievement and it should result in a well-developed, physically fit adult.

We may conclude by quoting the Secondary Education Commission, "This approach to the maintenance of school children's health may appear impracticable at first sight. But a clearer appreciation of the factors involved and a better coordination of the agencies concerned with the promotion of health will show that the adopting of such measures can produce tangible results within a reasonable time."

Physical Education

5

Physical education is an integral part of the educational system. It aims at building a sound body, a sharp mind and wholesome personality. It is essential for the cultivation of vitality, courage, self-confidence, cooperativeness, leadership, obedience, discipline and positive attitude towards life and the world. Physical education aims to develop the total personality and makes the student, a suitable leader for the future India. In the new education policy more importance is given to physical education at primary and secondary school levels.

Development of physical fitness and health of the student is not the responsibility of the teachers of physical education alone. In fact, every teacher has a role to play in this direction, especially at the elementary stage and must have substantial exposure to physical education. It should be viewed as an integral part of Teacher Education programmes at all levels, especially at primary and elementary levels.

Health education has been included in the national curriculum framework by the NCERT to bring out an all round development in children so that they are physically healthy, socially useful, economically productive and personally satisfied citizen of the country. Hence it is imperative that teachers are properly oriented to plan, implement and evaluate an objective based health education curriculum at the elementary and secondary level. Through health education the teacher training institution endeavours to provide the future teacher the knowledge, attitudes, practices and skills necessary to meet his own health needs, provide a safe, sanitary and healthful environment for his students, help student teachers meet their physical, social and emotional health needs, insist in the prevention and control of communicable and other diseases, assist with planning and implementation of school and community health programmes and impart adequate and basic knowledge on health.

Meaning and Concept of Physical Education

In the words of C.L. Brownwell, "Physical education is concerned with strength and endurance (the principal objectives of physical training). But physical education regards these qualities as a means to an end—the means of obtaining greater satisfaction in a specific activity, and the end which represents the all round educational development associated with participation in the activity. In short, physical education means the physical activities that have characterized the immemorial history of mankind."

According to Elbert Obertenffer, "Physical education is the sum of those experiences which come to the individual through movement."

In the words of J.B. Nash, "Physical education is that field of education which deals with big muscle activities and their related responses."

Charles A. Bucher opined, "Physical education is an integral part of total education process and has as its aim the development of physically, mentally, emotionally and socially fit citizens through the medium of physical activities which have been selected with a view to realizing these outcomes."

Nixon and Cozens defined physical education "as that phase of the whole process of education which is concerned with vigorous muscular activities and related responses and with the modifications in the individual resultant from these responses."

The Secondary Education Commission (1952-53) made it clear that unless physical education is accepted as an integral part of education, and the educational authorities recognize its need in all schools, the youth of the country, which forms its most valuable asset, will never be able to pull their full weight in national welfare. The old concept of physical education as 'mere drill' or a series of regulated exercises has been rejected. It includes all forms of physical activities and games, which promote the development of the body and mind. The commission recommended that physical education should be comprehensive enough to include all aspects of health education; full records of physical activities should be maintained; teachers of physical education should be given the same status as other teachers of similar qualifications; and other teachers of the school along with the physical instructor should actively participate in the physical activities of students.

The Education Commission (1964-66) points out that the concept of physical education has been made broader, as it should contribute not only to physical fitness but also to physical efficiency, mental alertness and the development of certain qualities—perseverance, team spirit, leadership and obedience to rules. It also emphasized the need for re-examining and re-designing the programmes of physical education in the light of certain basic principles of child growth and development.

From the above expressed views it is obvious that physical education is not only concerned with helping the child to grow and develop physically but learning to fit in with his social environment and adjusting to life around, acquiring the capacity to be mentally alert to all environmental responses, expressing emotions without prejudice to others and otherwise reaching his maturity progressively.

Aims and Objectives of Physical Education

The aim of physical education is to provide appropriate opportunities and experiences for individuals to achieve their optimum potential. Physical education is primarily concerned with physical capabilities but the associated aspects of knowledge and understanding are also vital components for all children. Additionally, participating in an appropriate and sensitively designed physical education programme can enhance the development of personal skills within a social setting. Planning, performing and evaluating therefore are important components, which have to be pursued according to each individual's needs and strengths. It is to be acknowledged that the aim of physical education is to encompass enjoyment and satisfaction and thereby encourage a lifelong commitment to an active and healthy lifestyle.

Physical education does not only aim to produce experts in various branches of sports and athletics, nor those who are masses of brawn and muscle. The aim of this part of education concerned with the body is to devote its share in producing an integrated and harmoniously developed personality. The aim is to ensure that the body is given its due share of attention, which it needs so that it can play a positive part in the life of the individual. Physical education is not only a health insurance but a valuable aid to health also. It not only develops physique but also promotes fine adjustment between physical and mental health. It gives the children training for good citizenship. Thus, the main aim of physical education can be pointed out as:

- Conservation of health.
- Development of well built and strong bodies.
- Development of sense of personal hygiene, social hygiene, mental hygiene, moral and sex hygiene.
- Development of regular habits of exercise, cleanliness and play and healthful living.
- Development of personal qualities like self-reliance, endurance, self-control, courage, initiative, etc.
- Development of qualities relating to society, e.g. obedience, cooperation, leadership and fellowship, selfless service, etc.
- Development of regular habits of exercise and play.
- Development of regular health habits.
- Development of character and personality and the whole man.

American Educational Policies Commission gave four main objectives of physical education:

1. *Objective of self-realization*

The realization of self is achieved best through interaction of self with the social group in which the individual moves. Opportunities of this interaction are available in physical education. The pupil understands the basic facts concerning health and disease. He secures for himself and his family competent medical advice and treatment. He strives to improve the health of the community. He wisely plans for hours of wholesome recreation and acquires skills in the leisure pursuits of his choice. He subscribes in full to the general principle that the person who lives most, serves best.

2. *Objective of human relationship*

The person knows the value of preventing the spread of communicable diseases. He knows that his own health care affects others. He learns that safety applies to protecting others as well as himself. He understands that physical education participation should strengthen and not destroy the objectives of friendship, loyalty, fair play, tolerance and others. He gains confidence in his own individual powers of achievement, but utilizes these powers in working effectively with others.

3. *Objective of economic efficiency*

Physical education contributes to economic efficiency especially for those who decide to pursue some aspect of physical and health education as a vocation—physical educators, athletic coaches, professional athletes, health teachers or coordinators, safety directors, medicine, nursing, etc. Many people decide upon a professional career in one of the above areas as a result of their school and college experiences in health and physical education.

4. *Objective of civic responsibility*

Physical education teaches the observance of rules of games and sports and other laws. Law observance is the responsibility of all citizens. Physical education teaches obedience, sense of duty, friendship and sympathy for everyone, inculcates sense of responsibility, promotes tolerance and creates democratic feelings among the pupils.

Three main objectives of physical education particularly suited for India are:

1. *Development of organic fitness*

This is dependent upon a wide selection of activities arising out of the inherent interest of the participants and so conducted that the normal functions of the body are developed and improved.

2. *Development of neuro-muscular skills*

The development of skills in a large variety of physical activities makes it possible for individuals and groups to obtain satisfaction and happiness in a variety of ways during leisure time. Possession of skills in naturalized forms of individual and group play activities enables people to give wholesome expression to innate desires and interests.

3. *Development of character and personality*

Physical activities that give opportunity for self-expression and self-improvement are useful in developing character and personality. The relationships and experience of cooperation and competition on the athletic field call for decisions very similar to those, which have to be made in every day life. Leaders with moral purpose will make it possible for their athletes to act and decide in the light of values and consequence, and will relate the idea of sportsmanship as practiced on the playing field with the desirability of carrying it over into all relationships with their fellow-men (*A National Plan of Physical Education and Recreation,* p. 3).

Principles Underlying Physical Education

Psychological and physiological principles form the bases of physical education and it is but obvious that physical education should include activities pertaining to these principles. Following points should be borne in mind while organizing a programme of physical education.

1. Undue emphasis should not be given to those physical activities, which primarily develop strength of muscles.

2. Activities, which are suitable for the different age groups should be provided. The children should not be judged by adult standards.
3. Too much emphasis should not be laid on inter-school competitions. A large number of students should be encouraged to participate in various physical activities.
4. Classroom physical activities should be encouraged.
5. Physical activities pertaining to the cleanliness of the school should be organized off and on.

Indian Education Commission (1964-66) recommended the introduction of Physical Education as a compulsory school subject and emphasized that a satisfactory programme should be developed on the basis of the following principles:

1. **Interest and capacities:** The physical education programme should be planned for desirable outcomes keeping in mind the interests and capacities of the participants.
2. **Emphasis on traditional forms of play:** The traditional forms of play and physical activities that have developed in our country should receive due emphasis in the programme.
3. **Sense of personal worth and pride:** The activities promoted should develop in each child a sense of personal worth and pride.
4. **Sense of sharing responsibility:** A sense of sharing responsibility in a spirit of democratic cooperation should grow from experience on playground and in the gymnasium.
5. **Supplement other programmes:** The programmes offered should supplement other programmes of education and not duplicate them.
6. **Financial means:** The programmes offered should be within the financial means.

7. **Programmes for all:** The physical education programme should reach and benefit all rather than a selected few.
8. **Special coaching:** Special instructions and coaching should be provided for students with talent and special aptitude.

Importance of Physical Education

Physical education or health and physical education are the areas of knowledge that will ultimately drive our success engine. We are physical and spiritual beings; our mind, body, and spirit are all connected and learning how they work together and how to care for them can save us from unnecessary pain and suffering. Knowing how to take care of our body, mind, and spirit will lead us down the path toward happiness, health, and wealth.

"The physical welfare of the youth of the country should be one of the main concerns of the State and any departure from the normal standards of physical well-being at this period of life may have serious consequences", observed the Secondary Education Commission. Swami Vivekananda has also stressed the importance of well-built bodies when he remarks, "What India needs today is not the Bhagwad Gita but the football field." Our Indian schools must give due importance to this aspect of education. There is a great need of a general philosophy of physical education in India, though it appears to be very strange in a country famous for ancient Yogic system. W.M. Ryburn remarked, "We need in Indian education a general physical education—a conception of education in which physical education takes its rightful place and in which its vital importance is recognized."

Regarding the significance of physical education H.C. Buck has observed that a properly directed physical education should result in health, happiness, efficiency and character. Montague writes, "physical education does neither train up the soul, nor body but the whole man". Physical education plays a vital role in the students' development and growth. According to recent medical studies, physical well-being of a student is directly related to his or her performance whether in class or in the office.

1. *It is a link to good health*

The value of physical fitness can never be overstated. It's only in physical educational classrooms that students learn the value of taking care of themselves through proper grooming, healthy eating and regular exercise.

2. *It is a preventive measure against disease*

Many doctors today agree that obesity is a serious health risk. Without any form of diet management and control with the numerous processed food students intake everyday compounded by a sedentary lifestyle, a student's health can easily be at risk to many diseases like chronic heart disease, hypertension and diabetes. Physical education in school is a preventive measure to teach students the value of regular exercise.

3. *It is a programme for muscle strength and fitness*

Physical education develops the students' motor skills and *hand-eye* coordination. It also develops the upper body muscles through activities like doing push-ups as well as the lower body muscles through stationary jumping jacks, three minutes running and jumping exercises. Programmes usually have core training exercises also like doing abdominal crunches.

4. *It promotes academic learning*

Physical health allows students to function even well in classrooms. A good cardiovascular system developed from regular exercise promotes excellent blood and oxygen circulation. This means more nutrients circulate through out the body, which includes the brain. This circulation produces longer attention span during classes allowing longer concentration and absorption.

5. *It builds self-esteem*

Students who are active in physical activities like basketball, volleyball, martial arts and running just to name a few are more confident with themselves according to most social school studies. It is probably because of the self-discipline and dedication to excel in a sport that brings out the best in students. In school, the physical education programme introduces these sport activities to students allowing them to make choices to which sport areas they want to get involved in.

6. *It develops cooperation, teamwork and sportsmanship skill*

Most physical education programmes are holistic. The programme allows student to interact together to a common goal and that is to win and excel physically. It brings out the competitive sides of students working both body and mind but also promotes sportsmanship.

7. *It promotes a physically active lifestyle*

The purpose of physical education is to instill in students, at an early age, the value of self-preservation and choosing a lifestyle that is good for both the mind and body.

Physical education takes care of the most vital aspect of human life, which is the very basis of human existence and strength. It is the basis of a healthy, happy and harmonious life. It helps in the development of a well balanced, well integrated and vitally alive human personality. It inculcates the habits of self-discipline, self-control, toleration and forbearance, fortitude and spirit of sportsmanship that enable a person to withstand life's setbacks and shocks and brave all risks and hazards with a smiling face and quiet graceful demeanour.

Programme of Physical Education

6

People are physical beings. Health, bodily development, muscular co-ordination and physical dexterity are important in our development as human beings. Education is concerned with developing the physical aspect to capacity in each and every person–through Physical Education and Health Education.

The 1988 Education Act stipulates that through the national curriculum framework all children have an entitlement for physical education during their normal course of study. Within the national curriculum children at various stages of their education will have experience in up to six programmes of study. These being: athletic activities, dance, games, gymnastic activities, outdoor and adventurous activities and swimming. Teachers, after assessing the needs of children should devise an appropriate programme, using all the resources available, to ensure that a broad, balanced, progressive, differentiated, coherent and relevant curriculum is accessible for all children.

The types of activities considered essential under the programme of physical education are:

Developmental activities:

(i) Exercise tables, 'dands', 'baithaks' and yogic exercises.

(ii) Fundamental movements such as walking, running, throwing, jumping, climbing and balancing.

(iii) Mimetic and story plays.

(iv) Stunts, pyramids, weight and conditioning exercises.

Rhythmic activities:

Rhythm fundamentals, rhythm games, folk dances, social dances, singing games, community singing, Indian rhythmic, 'garba', 'phugdi', 'himma', 'tipri', etc.

Games, sports and athletics:

(i) Major games such as 'kabaddi', kho kho, volleyball, basketball, football, hockey, cricket, etc.

(ii) Dual games such as tennis, table tennis, badminton, ring-tennis, etc.

(iii) Recreative games, minor games, relays, social games, group games, etc.

Sports: Cycling, canoeing, shooting, riding, skating, etc.

Athletics: Running, jumping, throwing, walking and relays.

Formal activities: Drill and marching, mass P.T. exercises.

Apparatus: Parallel bars, vaulting, beam, roman rings, ropes, 'malkhamb', etc.

Combatives: Wrestling, boxing, judo, 'lathi' fight, dagger fight, sword fight, simple contests and mass combative based on attack and defence.

Aquatics: Swimming, diving and life saving.

Self-testing activities: All types of tests.

Camping and outdoor activities: Hiking, cross country, camping and mountaineering, picnics and excursions.

Special activities: Demonstrations, ceremonial parades, flag salutations, practical projects, citizenship training, etc.

Physical Education in Secondary Schools

Physical education programmes in secondary schools have evolved over the years, moving from a more sports-oriented curriculum to a balanced approach that stresses the teaching of healthy lifestyle choices. Physical education design diversified programmes that get students moving even if they are not inclined towards athletics. The overall goal of the secondary school physical education programme is to help students find the positive aspects of physical fitness. Students are asked to set fitness goals and to study the role of fitness activities in society. During class time, they are also involved in running or walking and other aerobic activities like jumping rope or running obstacle courses. Students are also instructed in the use of weights and spend time in the weight room. Some schools have access to treadmills and other fitness equipment and use this in the curriculum as well. Activities like yoga and kickboxing are also part of the programme at some schools.

Nearly 10 million children and adolescents in the United States ages 6-19 are considered overweight. Over the last three decades the prevalence of overweight in adolescents has quadrupled from 4 per cent in 1971-74 to 17 per cent in 2003-06. One important way to prevent obesity is to increase physical activity. Schools can play a critical role in increasing physical activity by offering quality, daily physical education and other opportunities to recreate. Physical education not only gives children an opportunity to be active but it teaches them the skills they need to be active throughout their lifetime. Thus, investing in quality physical education in all schools for all grades is a logical and important step toward improving the health of the next generation.

Unfortunately, very few states require daily physical education in grades 10-12. In an era when increasing obesity and rising healthcare costs are threatening our competitive advantage and national security, we are cutting the very programmes that could help reverse this trend. That is why the American Heart Association is working in every state and at the federal level to require that quality physical education be offered in all grades. The Association recommends a minimum standard for elementary students of 150 minutes a week and for middle schools of 225 minutes per week. It also recommended that successfully completing physical education be a requirement for high school graduation. Schools should develop standards for student learning in physical education that reflect national and state standards and should require that physical education be taught by certified/licensed physical education teachers.

Physical education is not merely to be confined to the playground but should pervade the classroom. Physical education in the classroom may take the following forms:

(a) Direct instruction emphasizing the necessity of having a good physique.

(b) Suggestions regarding the maintenance of good health.

(c) Emphasis on right postures.

(d) Provision of good seating and lighting arrangements in the classroom, thereby impressing upon the students the importance of studying under healthy surroundings.

(e) Providing ample opportunities to the children for physical activity.

Physical and mental development is inseparably allied to each other. Classroom should not be devoid of physical activity. Instruction in a play way manner affords ample opportunities to the students to be physically active and a wise teacher would always bring this spirit of play way in classroom work. The students should play an active role in the instruction work. They should not remain merely as passive listeners. A few minutes drill or music after every lesson of the class may introduce bodily activity among the children. J.F. Williams quoted: "Of all the activities of school curriculum, none is as rich with educational outcomes as the plays, games, sports and athletics of physical education."

The Secondary School programme should provide activities that make for organic and structural development, provide opportunity for self-expression, are meaningful, are enjoyed by the participants, and provide situations that encourage social development. The adolescent in the Secondary School desires to imitate the activities of the adults and he should be given sports, games and athletics in their standard form. Skills learnt earlier should be perfected through guidance and practice. It is an age when boys and girls desire excellence and the physical education syllabus must include techniques for good performance. The following items can constitute the scope of Physical Education in a Secondary School:

1. *Free play*

It is mostly based on skill and technique rather than random running, jumping and climbing activities of the primary group.

2. *Organized games*

Organized games include tag games, relay games, basketball, cricket, football, hockey, tennis and volleyball. These games when under wise guidance and leadership, act as one of the best citizenship laboratories we possess.

3. *Self-testing activities*

Self-testing activities are those that allow for a self-assessment to be made in terms of win or lose, pass or fail, success or failure, or time and distance standards. Activities like diving; track and field athletics are self-testing activities.

4. *Dancing and music*

These are also very effective forms of exercises. Dancing especially promotes organic fitness, suppleness and neuro-muscular coordination. It can be a health-promoting activity for people of all ages and fosters desirable social attitudes. It is not competitive rather cooperative. It affords pleasure and is a form of expression of worthy feelings in addition to being highly recreative. Square dancing is common physical education class activity, but more schools have now added social and ballroom dancing to the educational programme. Other activities used in this part of the curriculum are folk dancing, line dancing and even some schools have brought hip-hop into the classroom. Music has a vital place in physical education apart from the usual rhythmic activities. It can be used to give rhythm to pyramid building, vaulting, tumbling, drills, etc. Music at all times must be appropriate to the activity.

5. *Team sports*

The tried and true physical fitness activities are still in wide use as teachers get kids involved in team sports for the fitness benefits of them in addition to helping them learn about different sports. Basketball, volleyball, soccer, softball, field hockey and flag football still have their value in the curriculum, and they are used to teach skills like teamwork and strategy and also to help students learn how to play by the rules and resolve conflicts as they arrive.

6. *Individual sports*

Hand-eye coordination and fun individual exercise options are the goals of individual sports that are part of the physical education coursework. Sports like badminton, golf, archery, tennis, handball and track and field are great for teaching movement and can become sports that non-elite athletes enjoy well into their adult years.

7. *Basic skills*

Basic skills are developed not in one day or in one year. These are developed by continuous efforts and guidance.

8. *Athletics*

Athletics occupy an important place in the Secondary School Physical Education programme. Some sort of instruction in theory is also essential.

9. *Individual corrective exercises*

Such exercises are necessary for the correction of postural defects.

10. *Yoga*

Yoga is a science of the mind and soul. Yoga links the body with mind, mind with *'Atma'* and finally *'atma'* with *'paramatma'*, the universe. It is the treasure of our yogis and rishis. Yoga is suitable for all people, from young age to old age, from family men to sadhus; rather the most of it are for social well-being and mental peace in the normal life of the man. So every teacher has to know of it, has to practice it and make his pupils to follow him, so as to have a balanced, awakened mind for the academic achievement, as well as, to have a total happy life.

Yoga and Physical Education for Fitness and Health of Children

Both yoga and physical education contribute to not merely the physical development of the child but have a positive impact on psychological and mental development as well. Playing group games have a positive influence on individual self-esteem, promotes better interaction among children, imparts values of cooperation, sharing and to deal with both victory and defeat. Similarly yoga practice contributes to the overall development of the child and various studies have shown that it contributes to flexibility and muscular fitness and also corrects postural defects among school children (Gharote, 1976; Gharote, Ganguly and Moorthy, 1976; Moorthy, 1982). In addition it plays an important role in improving cardio-vascular efficiency and helps to control and reduce excessive body fat while contributing to the overall physical and health related fitness (Ganguly, 1981; Bera, 1998; Ganguly, 1989; Mishra, Tripathi and Bera, 2003). Apart from contributing to physical fitness, yoga also contributes to improving learning, memory and dealing with stress and anxieties in children (Kulkarni, 1997; Ganguly, Bera and Gharote, 2002).

Both yoga and physical education have not been given due importance in the school curriculum and neither has their contribution to the health and overall development of the child been adequately acknowledged. The constraints faced by yoga and physical education are related to a number of factors that affect the quality of school education in general and health and physical education in particular. These constraints include lack of appropriate school environment in terms of physical infrastructure, furniture, lighting, ventilation, water supply, etc.; lack of budgetary support, lack of transport services; lack of adequately trained teachers and institutions for their training; lack of proper documentation and systematic evaluation of the area and lack of coordination between the education and health departments (GOI, 1961).

Gymnastics and Athletics

Gymnastics and athletics are two important forms of physical education. The chief aim of athletics is recreation. Gymnastics on the other hand stimulate normal physical development, promote good carriage and secure general efficiency in the individual. The effect of gymnastic exercises is internal and primary. They are based on sound principles. Each exercise has its own value for a specific purpose. Gymnastic exercises are very helpful in teaching correct postures. Gymnastic exercises with apparatus, i.e. Bars, Ladder, Horse, etc., are greatly liked by the boys as these involve a great degree of skill and difficulties. Gymnastic exercises like marching, easy exercises in jumping and skipping, aesthetic dancing and folk dancing appeal to the girls. Athletic activities include running, jumping, disc throwing, hammer throwing and weight throwing, etc.

Free Play

A child derives immense pleasure in free play. He wants to choose games and other kinds of activities according to his interest. He does not like that any time limit should be imposed on him while he is at play. Free play has direct appeal to his natural urges and it satisfies his psychological needs. It is in the nature of the child to play. He is interested in it from the very birth. Stern defines play as "voluntary self-constrained activity". The value of play may be classified as: educational, intellectual, physical, social and emotional development.

Physical Drill

Physical drill should be organized regularly. It should be properly graded; 'simple to complex' and 'easy to difficult' should form the basis of physical drill. The duration of the period should depend upon the age and strength of the pupils. A good system of physical exercises would give beneficial exercise to all parts of the body. The following types of exercises will make the programme interesting and instructive:

(i) Preparing or warming up, running in a circle, marching, etc.

(ii) Corrective exercises

(iii) Educative exercises

(iv) Recreative exercises

(v) Physiological exercises

The playground is said to be the cradle of democracy. Various co-curricular activities and especially the games and sports contribute a lot for the development of all the major qualities needed to be an ideal citizen. Games inculcate the following values in children:

1. *Games teach cooperation*

Teamwork is the pivot around which the games revolve. If the members of the team do not work for the team but for their individual distinctions, the team is sure to go to the walls. Games and sports bring home to the students that loyalty and cooperation are the important contributory factors for the honour of the team. These serve to eliminate selfishness and teach the students to subordinate their own interests for the sake of a broader aim of winning the game.

2. *Preparation for life situations*

The players have to play sometimes against heavy odds. Courage, patience, steadfastness and perseverance are needed to play well and effectively. The players get accustomed to face very critical situations and this stands in good stead when they enter life.

3. *Providing Opportunities for leadership*

Games and sports provide opportunities for leadership of a very high order. The captain of the team has to put right players at the right places and thus bring harmony among the different members of the team.

4. *Development of various senses*

The games and sports involve a variety of movement-physical and mental; most of the senses are called into action. The mind has to be kept alert to meet the changing situation of the ball. Thus body and mind work in harmony.

5. *Physical development*

Games and sports promote good health, which is perhaps more important than wealth.

6. *Emphasis on struggle*

They teach the lesson that struggle is more important than success. Baron de Conbertin states, "The more important thing in sports is not to win but to take part. The important thing in life is not triumph but struggle. The essential thing is not to have conquered but to have fought well. To spread these precepts is to build up a stronger and more scrupulous and more generous humanity."

7. *Satisfaction of various urges of children*

Games satisfy one of the important urges of the children. Play is biological and social necessity for the children. It is the most fundamental thing about a child—play for the child is one of the most serious facts of life; it is a form of work for the young and the basis for all education.

8. *Development of esprit de corps*

Tournaments develop in the minds of the students love for the school. 'We feeling' comes to the forefront. Tournaments if properly conducted help in developing the idea of corporate life in the minds of the students. Tournaments are of great help in raising the standard of sports of different institutions.

9. *Profitable use of leisure time*

Leisure time is utilized in a very profitable way and thus these games fulfil another function of education.

10. *Training in character*

Last but not least, they afford a valuable training in character. For promoting the qualities of character, viz. self-control, steadfastness, perseverance, obedience, morality and health, games and sports are very potent and effective.

Thus, the educative values of these games make it clear that the playground is another school and its function is equally important. We can sum up the importance of games and sports with the quotation of Aldous Huxley, "Like every other instrument that man has invented, sport can be used either for good or evil purpose. Used well, it can teach endurance and courage, a sense of fair play and a respect for rules, coordinated effort and the subordination of personal interest to those of the group. Used badly it can encourage personal vanity and group vanity, greedy desire for victory and hatred for rivals, an intolerant *esprit de corps* and contempt for people who are beyond a certain arbitrarily selected pole. In either case sport inculcates responsible cooperation."

Principles of Organizing Games

- To satisfy individual needs of children, a variety of games should be provided.
- Our motto should be games for all or play for all.
- Regular time should be given to the games by framing games timetable.
- Competitions should be organized frequently but winning of trophies should not become the be all and end all of these contests.
- Students should be associated with the organization of games.
- Supervision of games by competent teachers is very essential to draw the real benefit. Such teachers should get some relief in teaching periods in lieu of that.
- The achievement of the students in this field should receive due appreciation and get a mention in their progress reports.
- The teams should be constituted with the students of the same skill and interest as far as possible.

Drawbacks of Health and Physical Education in India

The present position of physical education in our country is far from satisfactory. Some drawbacks have been pointed out as under:

***Ill-nourished children*:** The children of poor and middle-income families are likely to remain ill fed and undernourished. An average Indian present cannot provide balanced diet to his children. Such children remain physically weak and inactive. The school programme of physical education cannot have much success with them. They cannot take active and vigorous part in games, sports and other physical education activities.

No provision in the timetable: Physical education is not given equal status in the school timetable. If at all a period is allotted to this subject, it is considered as an available period and any other subject teacher can utilize it for his own subject. The subject is neither taught nor evaluated at par with other subjects.

Lack of equipment: Most of the schools have no playgrounds. Funds are not made available for sports material, equipments and facilities.

Indifferent teachers: Teachers do not show an active interest in the organization and supervision of games and sports. They consider this duty as an extra burden and also consider these activities as a hindrance in the way of teaching and learning. They do not develop and maintain a strong interest in them and consider them as wastage of time and energy.

Limited participation: Only a few outstanding players and athletes are encouraged to participate in them with a view to win distinctions in competitions and tournaments. Mass participation of students in sports and games is perhaps nowhere to be seen.

Lack of proper status: Outstanding sportsmen among students do not get due recognition, status or dignity just as the academically bright students enjoy. That is why above average and even average students avoid participation in sports. Most of the sportsmen come from the group of students with low academic caliber.

Shortage of physical directors: There is a shortage of trained physical directors in the schools. The existing facilities for their training are also inadequate. In the absence of experts, the programmes of physical education and games remain handicapped and neglected.

The then position of physical education in India was summed up in the report of the University Education Commission stating, "We may say there are insufficient trained personnel, dearth of playgrounds and equipment, poverty of students, absence of organization, poor types of programmes, small variety of games, conflict with academic work and inconvenience of time."

Present Status of Health and Physical Education in India

A survey of 44 middle schools in Delhi on the status of school health programme showed that health education in schools does not get sufficient time or attention and most teachers are not equipped to deal with this subject. This survey showed that only 12.5 per cent of the teachers had received training in health education. Support facilities like books and audio-visual material were minimal in all the surveyed schools. Apart from health education activities, less than 50 per cent of the schools offered games and physical training and less than that was devoted to health teaching. The school health services were available to around 2 per cent of the schools; the remaining did not have any significant input. As a result regular monitoring of children did not take place at all.

This survey also looked at the physical surroundings of the school in terms of ventilation, cleanliness, drinking water and lavatories. The schools fared poorly on all these inputs and therefore are bound to affect their health in the long run. A morbidity survey among the children in these schools revealed that they are related to poor nutrition and lack of access to safe water and sanitation facilities (Raju, B., 1970).

An evaluation of the school health programme in relation to teacher's knowledge showed that elementary school teachers have misconceptions about health and health education. According to the study, the teachers possessed inadequate knowledge regarding the subject of health education. Though the health authorities were being involved in the school health programme there was little coordination between the education, health and social welfare departments. Health education and management of school health programme were not included in the pre-service or in-service education of teachers and hence the lack of integration of this subject areas with others (Potdar, R.S., 1989).

As far as physical education is concerned the available studies show that this area does not get the importance that it should and this gets translated into a negative attitude on the part of the teachers and headmasters of schools. An evaluation of the physical education curriculum at the lower primary stage in Mysore district showed that 80 per cent of headmasters, 60 per cent of general teachers and 90 per cent of physical education teachers had a positive attitude towards physical education. A significant percentage of general teachers had a negative attitude towards physical education. As far as the curriculum and syllabus is concerned, the aims and objectives of this area was not clearly stated and the existing syllabus for this area did not contain minimum levels of learning and the activities prescribed under yogic exercises were found to be inappropriate. The infrastructure for physical education was found appropriate but 50 per cent of the lower primary schools of Mysore city did not have physical education teachers (Sudarshan and Balakrishnaiah, 2003).

The experience of introducing yoga in school curriculum has been quite a mixed experience. There is a tendency for yoga to be reduced to mere physical exercise that defeats the very essence of this practice. At present there is a shortage of trained yoga teachers that is related to the non-availability of adequate number of institutions that have the capacity and expertise for this purpose. If yoga is to be effectively integrated then the government would need to overcome the shortage of yoga teachers beginning with the senior secondary level and then consider classes from sixth to tenth. In the interim period teachers who are trained in physical education are also getting some training in yoga education. It may be worthwhile to review the syllabus and pedagogy of the teacher's training programme offered by different colleges and deemed universities in this area.

Apart from the concern about availability of trained teachers, there is also the negative attitude of administrators at the central, state and district levels within the education department and authorities within schools with respect to both yoga and physical education. The experience of both these areas has been that where there is a supportive school atmosphere, the transaction of both these subjects has by and large been effective but examples of these are rather few in number.

Measures to Improve Physical Education in Schools

Various Commissions, Committees and Seminars on Education for Physical Education have made valuable suggestions for the improvement of Physical Education programmes in schools. These recommendations are:

1. Physical Education should be made a curricular subject in the school at all levels and should be on par with other subjects. Similarly schools should provide a period for it in the timetable.
2. The programme of physical education and recreation should cater to the needs, interests and capacities of the pupils, and should have a carryover value. It should promote normal growth and development, maintenance of health, acquisition of skills and desirable social attitudes and behaviour.
3. Schools should provide playgrounds of adequate dimensions. Where separate playgrounds cannot be made available for each educational institution, a common pool for a group of institutions should be created.
4. The physical education programmes offered should supplement other programmes of education and not duplicate them.

5. The physical education programme should reach all rather than a selected few.
6. The traditional forms of play and physical activities that have developed in India should receive due emphasis in the programme.
7. Greater facilities should be provided in educational institutions in the form of funds, equipments and trained teachers.
8. For the supervision of physical education activities, qualified persons should be appointed as District Physical Education Officers.
9. Periodical Refresher courses should be organized for in service teachers of physical education and supervisors.
10. All young teachers should actively participate in games and physical education activities and impart to them a charm and significance.
11. Full records of the students' participation in these activities may be maintained and they should get credits for their achievements in these fields.
12. The physical education programmes should be within the financial means.
13. Special instruction and coaching should be provided to students with talent, special aptitude and exceptional skill.
14. Health, power of endurance, physical well-being, energy and stamina of young people should be developed by nutrition and suitable exercises.
15. A sense of sharing responsibility in a spirit of democratic cooperation should grow from experience on the playground and also in the gymnasium.
16. Standard equipment should be manufactured in the country so as to be available at cheap rates to all.
17. Sports and games should be organized in rural areas through *Vyayamshalas, Vyayam Mandals, Akharas,*

etc. and in cooperation with Community Projects. Sports festival should be organized and sports events encouraged on the occasion of fairs. Indigenous sports like *Kabaddi* and indigenous style of wrestling should be encouraged.

Conclusion

True education of the intellect can come only through a proper exercise and training of the bodily organs, e.g. hands, feet, eyes, nose, etc. An intelligent use of the bodily organs in a child provides the best and quickest way of developing his intellect. The Vedic and Epic ages have given special importance to physical culture in providing man sound physique and sufficient strength to survive. Thus, physical education is instrumental in developing strength and stamina for the laborious and strenuous work in life. It works as a great educational force, providing opportunities for the wholesome satisfaction of inherent drives and urges of individuals and groups. It has a direct bearing on healthful school life. It is a great factor in mental and social hygiene of the students. Through an intensive and systematic programme of physical education, the students are acquainted with physiology and human autonomy and the fundamental laws of physical growth and development is brought home to them.

HISTORY OF PHYSICAL EDUCATION IN INDIA DURING PRE-AND POST INDEPENDENCE

PRE-INDEPENDENCE ERA

For the promotion of Physical Education, the following steps were taken by the government and other organizations during the Pre-Independence period.

1882 For the first time it was the Indian Education Organization that recommended physical training be promoted in the interest of youth in each class of school.

1884 The question of making Physical Education as a compulsory subject has considered. What even the Programme of Physical Education existed in Pre-Independence days, it was carried on by the ex-servicemen employed by school/college authorities.

1914 Vidya Borthers founded Sir Hanuman Vyayam Prasarak Mandal, Amaravathi, basically to serve the course of Physical Education in India.

1920 The outstanding development of scientific Physical Education in India in Pre-Independence days goes to the Y.M.C.A. college of Physical Education, Madras founded in 1920 by H.C. Buck. Since its inception this college has been working tirelessly and selflessly to promote and systematize Physical Education in India.

1921 Boys Scout Association of India was formed.

1924 Hanuman Vyayam Prasarak Mandal, Amaravathi, started a five-week summer course for youngmen and women in indigenous activities. A youth completing course was rounded Vyayam Visharad.

1927 Indian Olympic Association (I.O.A.) was formed with the efforts of Dr. A.G. Noehren and Mr. H.C. Buck. Mr. Sorabti Tata was its first President with Dr. D.G. Noehren it secretary. Since Indian Olympic Association has been functioning in India and is affiliated with International Olympic Committee (I.O.A.). This association started to promote and encourage Physical, Manual and Cultural Educations of youth of the nation for the development of character, good health and good citizenship, also to enforce all rules and regulations of International Olympic Committee and to educate the public of the country as to the value of amateurism in sports.

1931 Government College of Physical Education, Hyderabad.

1938 Training Institute of Physical Education, Kandivali (Bombay). The

Contd.

three Institutions were established to promote systematic, scientific Physical Education courses in India.

1947 **POST-INDEPENDENCE ERA**

The Central Government retained the vital affairs of education, by coordinating and formulating the directives to the states keeping in view the national objectives to be achieved. (Thousands of social forces started operating in the life of an Indian citizen. As a result in memorable schools, colleges and many new universities case into existence to give impetus to the course of education, on sure industry development, to helved a free revolution and to raise the thousands of living of millions of country men.)

It is out of these phenomenal charges that Physical Education has been considered part and parcel of school education programme. A considerable number of institutions for training teachers for Physical Education have come up ever since independence. New schemes have been put into operations to boost up the standard of sports and Health standards of people.

1948 National Credit Corps (NCC) and Auxiliary Credit Corps (ACC) at school and college levels were introduced.

1948 Asian Games Committee constituted.

1950 The Central Advisory Board of Physical Education and Recreation was set up (CABPER): In the light of the recommendations of the board the Union Ministry of Education has taken a number of steps in the field such as development training of leaders in Physical Education, institution of scholarship for research in Physical Education, conduct of National Physical Efficiency Drive, conduct of seminar on Physical Education, giving financial assistance to the colleges of Physical Education, giving directions to the state governments for affecting organization of Physical Education in their respective states.

1953 In 1953 Government of India introduced the Rajkumari Coaching Scheme for games and sports with the object of training good athletes and sportsmen. The scheme received wide popularity since famous players like Major. Dhayan Chand, Dr. Ram Singh were working under this scheme.

1954 All India Council of Sports, School Games Federation of India, and National Discipline Scheme (NDS) were established with the aim to regularize the promotions of the sports and working of sports bodies. To make the youth healthy in mind and body and instill in them a sense of patriotism, self-reliance, tolerance and

Contd.

self-sacrifice. To develop human values and to build in them a desire to serve the country and humanity at large.

1956 A National Syllabus of Physical Activities was formed.

1957 With the recommendation of CABPER, Laxmi Bai National college of Physical Education at Gwalior (M.P.) was established. This is the only Physical Education College being sum by the Central Government. This institute conducts research programmes, and provides training and teaching for Physical Education personnel.

1958 Government of India set up on Ad-hoc Enquiry Committee on Games and sports to suggest ways and means to improve the standards of Indian competitions in all games and sports.

1959 In 1959, Government of India appointed a Co-ordination Committee, under the chairmanship of Dr. Hriday Nath Kunzuru, to examining the various schemes for Physical Education, recreation, character building and discipline operating in educational institutions, and to recommend measure for the proper coordination.

The national Physical Efficiency Drive was launched by the Union Ministry of Education in 1959-69. The plan consisted of certain items of physical efficiency tests which prescribed standards for achievement. It was hoped that drive would arouse the interest of young and old men and women to check their performance abilities and thus stimulate their keenness for physical fitness.

1961 As a follow up action to the recommendations of the Ad-hoc Enquiry Committee of 1958 the Netaji Subhash National Institute of Sports was established by the Government of India in 1961 at state Bagh Palace, Patiala stressing to produce coaches of high caliber in various games.

Kaul Kapoor Committee: This committee submitted recommendation on 1961 starting that Physical Education should be considered as a part of general education in schools and colleges. It should be one of the subjects in the universities for graduates.

The Raj Kumari Coaching Scheme ceased to function on 18th October 1961. It has been merged after comes like (MS) in the NIS.

1963 The Kunzur Committee studied the prevailing conditions in other countries, consulted experts including vice-chancellors of

Contd.

	convents, educational administrations, physical educationists, etc. and submitted report. The report is probably first even authoritative assessment of Physical Education in this country. The committee admitted that Physical Education is one of the important basis on which should rest school and colleges for improving the nations physique.
1965	The state education secretaries and direction of public instruction met in New Delhi in February and April 1965, and decided unanimously to introduce the National Fitness Corps (NFC) on a compulsory basis in all universities, college and high and higher secondary schools in the country. With this ACC has managed with NCC and MDS has ended with the function of HFC. NFC Time table allotment has drawn up and inculcated throughout all the educational institutions in the country. The colleges of Physical Education in the country were asked to reformulate their syllabus for various training classes, so that teachers who could handle NFC programme could be produced.
1984	Sports authority of India has been established at Delhi. SAI comes forward to establish sports hostel in each state to encourage the players by generating scholarship and coaching. The University Education Commission (1948-49) felt that the all round development of the individual is facilitated through a various commissions balance programme of education which shall necessarily include Physical Education and Physical Education are complementary to each other and must be integrated in such a way as to form an organic whole. After Independence in India, much emphasis has been given on Physical Education. Recognizing the importance of Physical Education in schools, colleges and universities. The secondary education commission (1952-53) (Mandaliar Commission) said: Unless Physical Education is accepted as an integral part of education and the educational authorities recognize its need in all schools, the youth of the country which form its most valuable assets will never be able to pull their weight in national welfare. The Indian Education Commission (1964-66) (Kothari Commission) emphasized the importance of Physical Education in the following words: It must be emphasized that such education contributes not only to Physical fitness but also to Physical Efficiency, mental alertness and the development of certain qualities like

Contd.

perseverance, team spirit, leadership, and obedience, to rules, moderation in victory and balance in defeat.

A bill was passed in the parliament which was known as National Policy of Education 1986. Emphasized the importance of Physical Education in the following ways:

Sports and Physical Educations are an integral part of the learning process, and will be included in the evaluation of performance. A nation-wide infrastructure for Physical Education, sports and games will be built into the educational edifice. The infrastructure will consists of play fields, equipment, coaches and teachers of Physical Education as part of the school improvement programme. Available open spaces in urban areas will be reserved for playgrounds, if necessary by legislation, effects will be made to established sports Institution and hostels where specialized attention will be given to sports activities and sports related studies, along with normal education. Appropriate encouragement will be given to those talented in games and sports. The stress will be laid on indigenous traditional games. As a system which promotes an integrated duo of body and mind. Yoga will revive special authentic effects will be made to introduce Yoga in all schools, and to this, it will be introduce in teacher training courses. The MPE has recommended for a minimum of 10 periods per week for Physical Education activities in low primary and upper primary stages, and 7 periods per week at the second stage.

1988 The NCERT developed the national curriculum for elementary and secondary educations in 1988 to reflect the postulates of the NPE and the programme of Action, 1986. The main thrust of this exercise was to provide for the national core-curriculum in the school syllabi as postulated in the national policy and to integrate Physical Education with the academic programme of the schools. The core-curriculum states that Health and Physical Education and sports should be integral part of learning process and be included as the evaluation of performance.

1992 The above policy has been reiterated in the National Policy of Education in 1992.

1992 NCERT put forward a revised curriculum for school education in 1992, and the revised edition was introduced in November 2000, under the title National Curriculum Framework for School Education. In this curriculum includes, Health and Physical Education as one of the core subjects in all levels of school

Contd.

educations. This curriculum was to be revised by NCERT, every five years; therefore, a new edition should be made available in the year 2005.

1993 A National Advisory Committee was set up by MHRD, in 1993. The committee report published in 1993 was reprinted in 2004 under the title Learning Without Bonded. This has been discussed in the parliament. The chairman of the committee is Prof. Yashpal.

CONCLUSION

Thus the Physical Education is made to be an ongoing continuous process without a break with participation by the greater number. This is what is required in an country.... A mass fitness movement, a spread of sports culture. With all what is said and done, sports management is primarily a questions of raising over young people by means of appropriate education and judicious measures.

VARIOUS VALUES DEVELOPED THROUGH PHYSICAL EDUCATION

Year	Commission	Inculcation of values
1952	Committee on National College of Physical Education and Recreation	**Physiological values, Psychological values**
1959	Committee for Coordination and Integration of schemes operating in the field of Physical Education, Recreation and youth welfare. Chairman Dr. Hriday Nath Kunzuru.	**Character building Discipline, Recreational values**
1965	Committee on Physical Education Chairman Dr. C.D. Deshmukh	**National Character Building**

Compiled by

Dr. P. Ravi Kumar

Source: www.napess.org

7

Personal Hygiene and Sanitation

Personal hygiene is a term used to denote personal care of the body. The well-being of an individual is really the totality of the all-different and vital organs individually and collectively, plus the necessary precautions and observance in general hygiene. Personal hygiene does not apply merely to washing of the outside skin or putting on clean clothes, etc., though the essential factors in preventing disease, the teeth, the hair, the nose, the eyes, the hands, the feet, all should receive care if we are to be really healthy. One's personal health is one's own personal responsibility.

Personal hygiene is something all of us have learnt at our homes, from our parents and also in early days of school. The good habits learned in the childhood are remembered and followed throughout the life and hence doctors, parents and teachers give a special emphasis on personal hygiene. Even adults are taught the importance of personal hygiene through several awareness programmes, floated by government and private institutions. Some vital tips for personal hygiene for children as well as elders are discussed herewith.

Care of the Skin

Skin is the outer covering of the body, an organ of touch. The skin though it is about a sixteenth of an inch thick, is a complicated organism that lives and breathes and changes constantly. Like every other organs of elimination and absorption, the skin also needs daily attendance. Its greatest care consists in external cleanliness. But it is wrong to suppose that mere baths can improve the health and beauty of the skin and complexion. The hygiene of the skin also depends upon food, air, exercise, sunshine, clothing and cleanliness.

The skin is one of the most important depurating organs of the whole body. A man, who has a perfectly healthy skin, is almost certain to be healthy in other respects. In no way can the health of the skin be preserved, but by regular bathing. The question of proper diet and nourishment bears on beauty culture at every point. The health of the skin, the beauty of the eyes and hair, are all tremendously affected by our eating habits. Our physical personality is governed to a great degree by the food we eat. The best internal skin beautifiers are raw carrots, fresh orange juice, buttermilk, cucumber and honey.

Exercise is one of the secret sources of youthfulness. Physical activity, alternating with relaxation must go hand in hand with nutrition and care of the skin and other outward structures to keep the glow of youth. Exercise quickens the circulation, increases the amount of air breathed and the percentage of oxygen absorbed, stimulates the appetite, activates the digestive power, and lends to more rapid elimination of toxins. Deep breathing and exercises should be made a part of one's daily life.

The skin should be allowed to breathe freely as possible if the human machine is to run regularly. Too much clothing weakens the skin's resistance. The hygiene of clothing also includes freedom from pressure, moderate warmth and cleanliness. One set of clothing should never be worn day and night. The under clothing should be washed, aired very thoroughly and dried in open sunshine. Dark coloured clothes are not very desirable as they obstruct the penetration of sunrays. Light colored clothes should be used as far as possible. The mental and emotional side of life cannot be separated from health and beauty culture as it may affect the nervous system and through it, the skin. The body is profoundly affected by the emotion that enters the mental state.

Care of the Hair

The hair is strongly governed by one's physical condition. It has been called the thermometer of the system. As the hair is ruled by the body so bodily health must be maintained if beautiful hair is desired. The hair serves four great purposes: preservation of body heat, a protective agency, and an organ of touch and promotion of beauty. Being a poor conductor of heat, the hair protects against exposure to the sun's rays, and helps to keep in the body heat when exposed to cold. Hair disorders result from poor physical condition, improper diet, deficient exercise and elimination, and poor hair hygiene.

If the scalp is kept well nourished and free from binding and if the blood is provided with adequate elements, it usually is possible to maintain a normal head of hair. Preventive measures are very important. If one wishes to prevent loss of hair, care should really begin in childhood. Hair like every other part of the body requires three things for health and beauty: cleanliness, exercise and nourishment. Healthy hair grows only on a clean well-nourished scalp.

No single measure is of great value to the hair than daily brushing. It keeps the hair from falling, reduces or prevents dandruff, activates the oil glands, increases its luster and in every way improves its health and beauty besides maintaining the scalp in good condition. Brushing is the best tonic for the hair. It exercises and stimulates the erector pile muscles, which are so important to the life of the hair shaft; it exercises the hair follicles themselves, and it cleanses the hair-shaft until it glistens. Fresh air and sunlight serve as an excellent tonic to the hair and scalp. The best time for the sunbath is immediately after washing the hair, though the hair should receive the sunlight at other times also. Cleanliness, brushing and moderate exposure to sunshine will do as much as can be done to keep the hair lustrous and to retain its colour but excessive washing and frequent shampooing will remove the natural oil, the luster and elasticity and the life of the hair.

Care of the Ear

The ear is divided into three parts: the external, the internal and the middle ear. The part that we see on the outside of the head simply forms a funnel like arrangement to pass the sound on into the middle and internal ear. Sound is the result of the vibrations of air. The mechanisms for hearing is constructed as to receive these vibrations, concentrate and transmit them to the deeper portions of the ear, where they are communicated to the end organs of the special nerve of hearing. They are then carried to the brain where they are recognized as sound.

To all appearances the hygiene of the ear is unnecessary, mainly because nature has sufficiently provided for the renewal of the earwax, which dries up, and falls off itself. Efforts to keep the ear free from wax increase the difficulty by irritating the membrane and causing it to make more wax. The outer ear needs some special attention by keeping it clean with soap and water because of its irregular surfaces, but the ear canal should be left alone. Nature has made provision for its protection by supplying a growth of hair to protect against draught and a little wax to prevent invasion by insects. However, the unhygienic condition of the ear has a remote bearing upon the general health of an individual and is equally responsible for certain diseases. Hence rules respecting the care of the ears should be observed.

PROPER CARE FOR THE EAR

Ear Cleaning

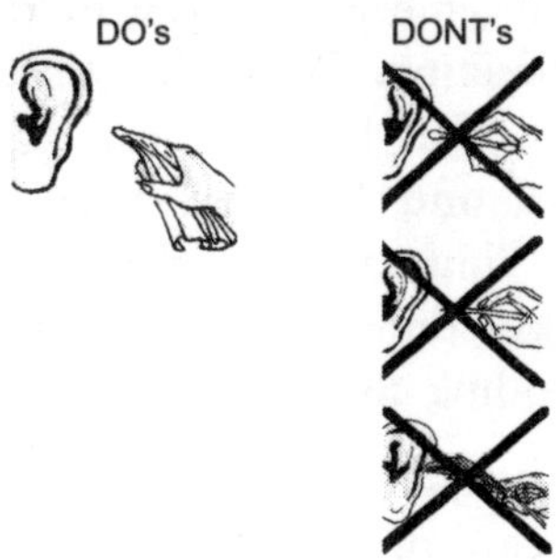

The ear should never be cleaned with toothpicks or hairpins; one is apt to rupture the eardrum or cause deeper infection. Cold water should never be allowed to enter the ears; neither cold wind should be blown into them. Shouting into the ear may cause deafness. Slapping or boxing the ears may often cause loss of hearing, and sometimes diseases of the ear, which prove fatal. Violent blowing of the nose should be avoided; this may cause the germs in the nose or throat to be forced through the Eustachian tube (a small tube that connects the throat to the middle ear) into the middle ear and cause deafness. Above all, general health should be maintained; cold and cough should be avoided which are responsible for ear trouble.

Care of the Nose and Throat

The nose and throat are external organs that are very useful in protecting the body from the invasion of a large array of bacteria that would otherwise find an easy entrance into the system. The nose and throat are a reservoir of bacteria from which infectious germs get dispersed over the body, both internally and externally, and in various ways are communicated to other persons.

A person, who is suffering from an acute cold, influenza or a chronic nasal discharge, should use soft napkins or bits of cheesecloth to receive the discharge and these should be destroyed after being used once. In this way an active source of infection may be eliminated. The mouth and nose should be carefully protected during the act of coughing or sneezing, by a handkerchief or in an emergency even by the hand, to prevent the spreading of infection. With the increase of population, housing and traffic, it has become very difficult to avoid dust inhalation, crowding and foul air. Even many diseases like tonsillitis, mumps, sinusitis, diphtheria, infantile paralysis, influenza, etc. could be prevented by taking proper care of nose and throat and attending to general hygiene.

Nasal and throat hygiene therefore, should form a part of the daily toilet and care of the body. This would not only help in preventing disease but is equally important for the health of the body. Water sniffing is the most simple and harmless operation for hygiene of the nose. In order to clean the throat, which is a source of infection, tonsillitis, sore throat, diptheria, etc., rinsing the throat with plain water or gargling with saline water or diluted limejuice are good hygiene and preventive measures.

Care of the Teeth

The teeth serve three very important functions: preparing food for digestion, aiding in speech, and aiding in one's facial attractiveness. The work of the teeth is to grind food into fine particles, mix it with saliva, and to begin digestion. The teeth also aid in speaking; for when they are lost certain syllables cannot be pronounced clearly.

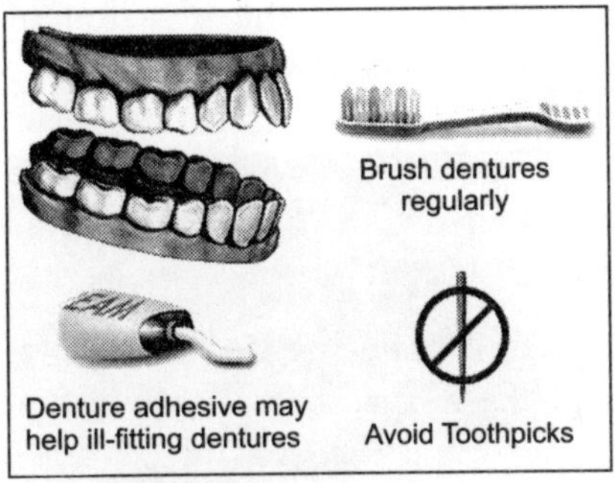

Modern foods and "civilized" dietary habits are responsible for the ruination of healthy teeth. The replacing of fresh fruits and vegetables by too much of fast foods is responsible for decay and diseased condition of the teeth in modern times. A healthy tooth is a natural thing and the greatest care it needs is not only its external cleanliness, but also proper nutrition and care of the body. Teeth should be cleansed as often as they are used, but at the very least they must be cleansed in the morning, and at night before going to bed with a moderately stiff tooth-brush, with or without powder or paste or with salt or lemon juice.

A most important matter in relation to the health of the teeth is cleanliness. When the tongue is coated, cleanliness is impossible, for the mouth is constantly swarming with billions of bacteria. The tongue must be kept clean by means of regulated diet and increased intestinal activity. Not only teeth decay and disease of the gums result from neglect of mouth hygiene, but rheumatism, neuritis, asthma, indigestion, diseases of the eyes, heart diseases and probably many other serious maladies, may owe their origin to this apparently insignificant cause. Thus, diseased teeth should receive prompt attention.

Thus, some apparently trivial local ailment or infection of the teeth, mouth and the tongue may have the most far-reaching consequences in shortening life and should never be permitted to persist untreated. The hygiene of these three organs consists of simple daily care that calls for no special sacrifice of time or money.

Care of the Eyes

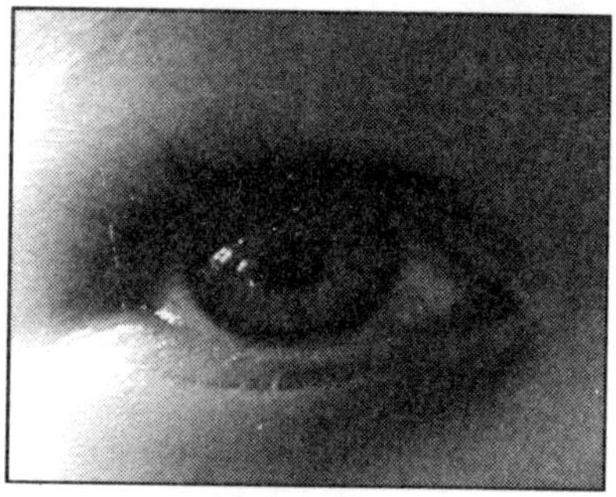

Of all the five senses with which humanity is endowed, sight is undoubtedly the most highly prized. Sight is an inestimable blessing. The eye is not a detached organ; it is an intimate part of the entire organism. Any habit that reacts harmfully upon the body as a whole will react harmfully upon the eyes. Not only are the eyes important in themselves but if they are strained or injured or if there is a visual defect the general nervous system is affected and headache, nausea and dizziness become marked. Just as visual defects affect the general health of the body constitutional diseases, like diabetes, high blood pressure, kidney disease affect the eyes. The care of the eyes, therefore, must in a certain sense be constitutional, that is, pertaining to the general care of the body and not merely local.

A perfect digestion, healthy and energetic circulation of the blood, a delicate nervous poise, and proper nutrition are all prerequisites to beautiful eyes. Emotions and expressions are mirrored in the eyes. Eyes are the windows of the soul; certainly they are the index of one's health. Just as there are ways of keeping the skin fresh and clear and young, so there are ways of keeping the eyes sparkling and charming.

Of all the ailments due to the highly artificial conditions in which men are living on account of civilization, eye-trouble may be placed in the forefront. Reading and writing, painting, embroidery and other fine artistic work, living in crowded cities full of dust and heat, obstruction to the range of vision, and continuous physical and mental strain caused by the exacting conditions of life have created a state of affairs which affects the eye-sight so much that, it would be no exaggeration to say that above 90 per cent of people nowadays suffer from defective eyesight. Resorting to glasses, the most popular and most commonly used accessory at the present day is no solution at all.

In order to prevent the eyes from injury and disease it is not overuse but misuse of the eyes is the chief cause of eye strain. It is important to keep the following points in mind:

1. Never try to read or do work requiring close application of the eyesight in poor light.
2. When reading, writing or using the eyes care should be taken that the light is neither too bright nor too dim and that it falls over the shoulder, at a correct angle.
3. Reading in a moving vehicle is not desirable on account of the shaking which continually changes the distance between the book and the eye and thus taxes the eyes.
4. The study room, office and especially the schoolroom where children study should be well lit.

5. Avoid using towels, soap, wash-pans or handkerchief that are being used by other people. One can easily contract eye diseases.
6. Neglected colds and sinuses affect the eyes at times very badly. Rubbing the eyes with unclean fingers is also harmful.
7. Practice palming and blinking for relaxation of the eye muscle. An excellent way, in fact one of the best ways, to bring about relaxation from strain of the eyes, is to cover the eyes with the palms of the hands so that the eyelids are untouched yet light is excluded, while thinking of something, as for instance imagining a dark curtain in front, that will help the mind to rest.

Care of the Feet

There is probably no part of the body, which is so much neglected and abused as the feet, especially when we consider that the feet bear the burden of the entire body. Proper footwear is a matter of no small importance, as many diseases arise from the wearing of shoes or boots of improper shape. Tight and ill fitting shoes or boots prevent the proper circulation of the blood in the feet and produce corns, swellings and sometimes still worse diseases of the feet. The toes are forced out of shape, and even the bony structure of the feet is often changed. All this affects the spine and the nerves. It spoils the shape of the muscles and makes an ungraceful walk.

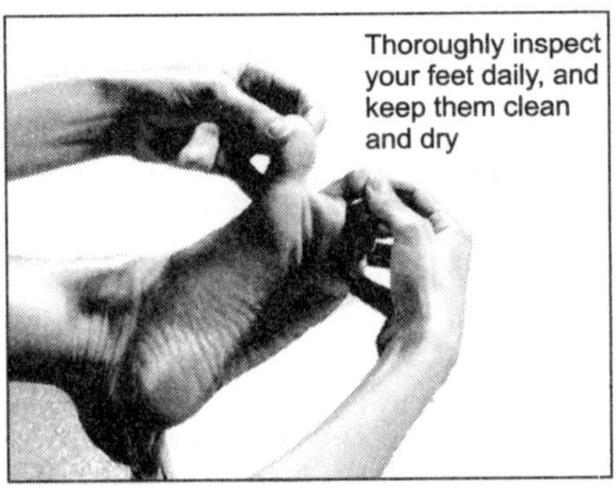

To keep the feet clean and healthy they should be bathed frequently, because shoes and stockings prevent the evaporation of the perspiration, which the skin constantly exudes. After bathing the feet should be carefully wiped. No moisture should be left between the toes. The stockings should be changed regularly and the feet should be exposed to the air and sun regularly. High heels are disastrous to arches; worn constantly, they strain the muscles and tendons of the calf so that when one puts on low heel shoes for sports or walking, a very painful strain develops. Finally, it is always advisable to wash the feet in hot or cold water before retiring.

Some Good Personal Habits

Personal hygiene

Personal cleanliness and hygiene is one of the determinant factors to a healthy life. A daily bath is the basic good habit that has to be inculcated in children from an early age. Maintaining personal hygiene is important to remain healthy.

Eating healthy

Following a healthy and balanced diet is one of the good personal habits that one should have. Frequent consumption of junk foods and constant deviation in meal timings affects the health negatively. A balanced diet is important.

Sleeping well

Sleeping well does not mean to sleep for long hours. The statement rather implies that habit of going to bed early and rising early keeps one fit and fine. An eight-hour sleep is sufficient for a human being. Taking excess of it and sleeping late in the morning is bound to bring laze and ill health.

Exercising

Daily exercise is one of the most important personal habits. It is one habit that applies to every phase of life and it reaps plentifully. One needs to understand the importance of daily exercise and should follow it with dedication.

Meditation

Along with making physical activity an integral part of daily life, mental exercise is equally important. A daily habit of meditation is very helpful for one's mental health. It helps to achieve mind control and peace of mind. It is beneficial in the fostering of a positive spirit. Making meditation a daily habit can actually lead to enhancement of mental strength and feeling of happiness.

Reading

This habit should be developed since childhood. Children need to be made to take interest in reading during their initial years of learning to read. Once a child develops the habit of reading, it will stay with him for lifetime. Reading good books opens doors to new horizons and exposes a child to new experiences. Reading is one of the most effective ways through which a child learns the values of life. Moral stories are the most effective media of cultivating moral values in a child. Reading thus proves a very good personal habit that all of us should have.

Being humane

This personal habit is the one that makes one a human being. Humanity is one value that needs to be fostered since one's early years. Man is a social animal and hence needs to take everyone along. We should develop a helpful nature, help the less fortunate ones to fight their difficulties.

These were some of those personal good habits that one should have. The basic understanding of bad habits helps to differentiate between the good and the bad. Everything that is positive should be followed. Every principle that makes one a better human being should be adopted.

Community Health and Sanitation

blue A foundational public health measure

Community health, a field of public health, is a discipline that concerns itself with the study and betterment of the health characteristics of biological communities. While the term community can be broadly defined, community health tends to focus on geographic areas rather than people with shared characteristics. Success of community health blue rely on the transfer of information from health professionals to the general public using one-to-one or one to many communication. Hygiene and sanitation merge into one another, but hygiene is chiefly personal, whereas sanitation is linked with the environments of the body and its relation to physical well-being. Hygiene usually relates to the consideration of individual health. It pertains to personal care of the body as to cleanliness, clothing, and moral self-control and so on, whereas sanitation generally refers to matters of corporate life regarding health.

As sanitation is applied to the correction of environmental faults, which tend to produce disease or otherwise impair health, and since the environment is commonly shared with others, sanitary science deals mainly with community problems, such as the management of sewers, the safeguarding of milk and water supply. It is the science, which aims at the prevention and reduction of infectious diseases and this necessitates improved sanitation in matters of drainage, sewerage, housing accommodation, the abatement of any social nuisance, and the inspection of food and water supply. Sanitation is therefore, not an independent science nor does it stand-alone. It embraces acknowledge of medicine, bacteriology, engineering, meteorology, architecture and geology.

In order that the individual or the nation may progress, health is indispensable, and since it is the multiplication of individuals that makes the community and the state, the participation of government in matters relating to health has become a necessity. It is a matter of great predicament that the health consciousness of the great mass of people is poorly developed that it is even necessary to consider legislation in matters pertaining to our physical well-being.

Sanitation of Buildings

To preserve the health of the occupiers of the buildings, it is imperative that all polluted water and solid organic refuse be removed from the premises at frequent intervals. Where the buildings are in a town it is usual for the local authority to remove the solid dry refuse by carting, but where public water supply is available liquid wastes are flushed away through a system of pipes to carry human excreta. All drains that carry solids should be provided with accessible clean-out caps, which can be readily unscrewed for the admission of cleaning rods to remove obstructions, which may choke the drains.

Air, Light and Ventilation

Oxygen is the life-supporting element in air. Fresh air is inimical to certain forms of disease carrying organism while foul air may easily contain and is conducive to their growth. The throwing of rubbish outside or on the streets renders the air impure. In fact, no kind of decaying matter should be allowed to lie exposed to the air. We should be as much against the breathing of impure air as we are against the drinking of polluted water and the eating of unclean food.

Poor ventilation in homes, combined with insanitary conditions, is a prolific cause of poor health and susceptibility to epidemics. Bad housekeeping in general, plus the impurities arising from dust, burning of fuel and faulty planning, makes many dwellings not only unfit but also dangerous for human habitation. It is increasingly recognized that insufficient lightening has a harmful effect upon the eyes, the comfort and production of workers, the efficiency of school children, and the general health of everyone obliged to use the eyes to any appreciable extent whether in reading, studying, drafting or otherwise by natural or artificial light.

Water Supply

In towns and cities the water supply is under municipal control. So far as hygiene is concerned water may be said to be pure when it contains nothing injurious to health, hence every supply of water from whatever source it is obtained, should be investigated by local authorities and steps taken to make it safe. Wells located in closely built up communities are polluted and dangerous. The drains passing near the wells are the main sources of pollution of water causing infectious diseases like typhoid, dysentery, and cholera besides infections from various parasitic worms. The drains and the municipal water supply pipes for domestic purposes should be checked frequently as due to leakage in the pipes there is a mixing of freshwater with the drain water. This has been responsible for virus and virulent infectious diseases, which usually take a very heavy toll in cities.

The area of water supply should be well guarded and watched as the bodies of dead animals and even human corpses are no infrequently found in lakes or in such locations; the dangerous products of decomposition are carried from them to the dwellings where water is used for drinking, cooking, washing or bathing purposes. Mere adding of chlorine does not make the water safe for drinking or health, as it should be noted that chlorine by itself is a poisonous gas.

Food

Proper care of food, the manner and environment in which produced is of extreme importance in the preservation of public health. Healthy stock should provide the food whether from animal or vegetable kingdom. Meat or milk of diseased animals could be dangerous to consumers. Every effort should be made by local authorities to prevent disease of animal stock of all kinds.

Vegetables should not be contaminated by any substance harmful to health. If any foods are intended for use in an uncooked state they should not be fertilized by human or animal wastes, nor watered by house drains. It is dangerous to purchase foods that are kept in insanitary conditions or exposed to flies, dust and to contamination. The inspection of food in all its forms and stages is an important duty of the Health Department in cities; strict measures should be taken to eliminate adulteration, contamination, poor quality of eatables and food which are found unfit for human consumption. These measures are very necessary to prevent infectious diseases, ill health and for the preservation of good health.

Infectious Disease

Infectious diseases are due to the entrance into the body of certain poisons, which multiply in the system, and can be given off from the person affected and passed on to other individuals in whom they may reproduce the disease. These diseases are known as "infectious diseases". If the person is susceptible to the disease, a period elapses after the organism is received, known as the incubation period, during which no symptoms develop but during which the organisms multiply and produce poison.

It is a fact that most diseases can be prevented because sickness is due either to ignorance or carelessness in observing the laws of health. It is, therefore, one's own doing and nobody else can be blamed. It is the duty and privilege of every intelligent person to acquire sufficient knowledge of health, hygiene and sanitation to live a healthy life.

Conclusion

Good hygiene is an important barrier to many infectious diseases and it promotes better health and well-being. To achieve the greatest health benefits, improvements in hygiene should be made concurrently with improvements in the water supply and sanitation, and be integrated with other interventions, such as improving nutrition and increasing incomes. The installation of a safe, plentiful and easily accessible water supply combined with adequate sanitation in a rural community will have a positive health impact only if combined with hygiene education.

Hygiene education is crucial to increase the community's knowledge and awareness of the link between water, sanitation, hygiene and health. Hygiene education enables a behavioural change to ensure a lasting health and economic benefit from the improved water and sanitation facilities. Further hygiene education enhances appropriate utilization, reduces recurrent cost of maintenance and improves the sustainability of the water and sanitation facilities.

8

Correct Posture and Physical Exercise

Bodily posture means the balancing of body in a proper manner while sitting, standing, reading or writing or during any other body action. In a proper posture, the whole body weight falls on the two legs without any effort and the entire body appears a vertical line. In this state, all the limbs perform their functions and do not tire easily. Proper bodily posture indicates a healthy and strong body, while improper faulty postures represent a sick and weak body. The proper posture also reveals a sound mind. Self-confidence, happiness and determination are the results of correct posture and on the contrary anxiety, unhappiness and pessimism are the outcome of wrong posture. The child should possess from the early days the knowledge of correct posture of standing, sitting and reading. In the absence of this knowledge, he adopts faulty postures as the results of which the backbone bends, the chest becomes like a pigeon-chest, the shoulders turn dropping, feet become flat, and vision turns defective and many other deformities appear in the body.

Achieving proper posture is the focal point of the science of body mechanics. Body mechanics is defined by *The American Heritage Medical Dictionary* as "the application of kinesiology to the use of proper body movement in daily activities, to the prevention and correction of problems associated with posture and to the enhancement of coordination and endurance". *Nursing Fundamental* defines body mechanics as "the utilization of correct muscles to complete a task safely and efficiently, without undue strain on any muscle or joint". The principles of body mechanics directly relate to the goal of achieving proper posture. Posture cannot be stressed enough for all physical activity, be it activities of daily living or activities that are athletic in nature. Posture is the position from which movement begins and ends; the better the posture, the better the movements. Poor spinal alignment is often caused by muscular imbalances where there is some tightness and/or weakness somewhere in the body.

Not only does good posture improve movement, but it also improves visceral functions such as respiratory system. In "Advanced Program Design" Paul Chek cites Joel E. Goldthwaite's book *Body Mechanics in Health and Disease* where Goldthwaite states that poor posture may reduce respiratory volume by as much as one third. The spinal cord and brain make up our central nervous system. The brain is the center of sensory awareness, movement, emotions, rational thought, behaviour, memory, speech, language, planning, foresight, and interpretation. The spinal cord is an extension of the brain; it is the receiver of sensory input below the head, as well as the source of motor commands for muscles below the head. It attaches to the medulla of our brain stem in order to send messages from and to the brain. The brain stem also contains the thalamus and it is here where our conscious state (awareness) is regulated and maintained.

We experience the world through our senses and that information is sent to the brain via neurological messaging where the brain determines an appropriate response. That response or reaction will then be sent to the appropriate part of the body or to the body as a whole, if necessary. The fight or flight mechanism occurs here. Having optimal messaging back and forth is obviously the ideal condition for all sorts of situations. It is good posture that allows for that kind of inner bodily communication to take place freely. The brain only understands movements and not particular muscles. With neural messaging being at, or close to optimal, the brain will activate all of the appropriate muscles necessary for a certain response to a condition. Whether we think about the movement or not, is irrelevant in some cases.

Even in this beauty and health conscious age, majority of humans tend to overlook the importance of a correct posture. A good posture benefits one in a number of ways. First of all, it makes the individual look in-shape, and thus healthy and attractive. Secondly, it lays the foundation for a balanced exercise. Thirdly, it allows taking deeper breaths. Fourthly, it boosts the digestive system. Fifthly, it assists the efficient functioning of the body organs. Thus, a good or correct body posture improves the overall health; one tends to feel more energetic and confident.

Kinds of Postures

There are two basic kinds of posture:

1. Static posture: It is the position from which movement begins and ends. It is during a state of ideal posture that the muscles will function most efficiently and effectively (P. Chek, Scientific Core Conditioning, p. 31).

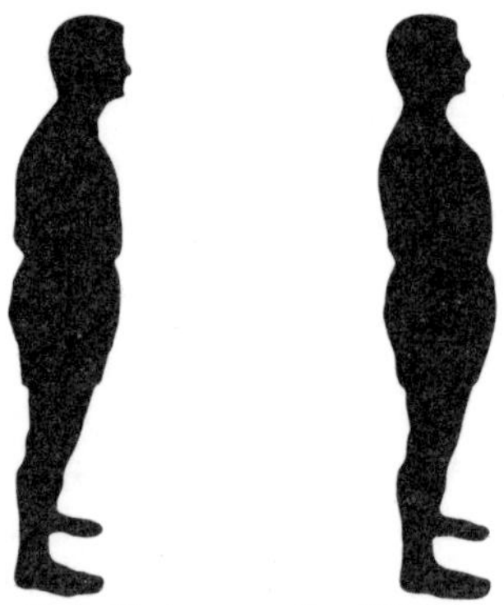

Poor Static Posture Good Static Posture

When observed from the side you should be able to draw a line from the earlobe down through the vertebrae of the neck (cervical vertebrae) and center of the shoulder, down through the mid-trunk, approximately through the centre of the hip (greater trochantor), slightly anterior to the knee joint and slightly anterior to the ankle.

2. Dynamic posture: It is the ability to maintain an optimal instantaneous axis of rotation in any combination of movement planes at any time in space. This means that stress is distributed equally throughout all portions of a joint as we move. Dr. Moshe Feldenkrais (1904-1984) showed that the poorer the posture, the more energy it takes to move our body. Therefore, the better our posture, the better our body will move, function and last. The musculo-skeletal system fights the relentless force of gravity on a daily basis. Individuals who don't fight gravity well frequently have poor posture, which manifests itself in the form of Forward Head Posture, increased Thoracic Kyphosis (rounded shoulders) and altered spinal curvatures.

The following illustrates good and poor dynamic posture during three commonly performed movements—the squat, the lunge and the bend.

1. The squat: Whenever someone gets onto or off a chair, bed, bench or toilet they perform the squat. When the squat is performed with good posture as shown, the load is distributed evenly across the body, and the thighs, hamstrings, glutens, lower back and upper back all shares the load.

Starting Squat position Good Posture

Lower Squat Position Good Posture

When the squat is performed with poor posture as shown, the load is distributed unevenly across the body. In the case of the faulty posture the lower back is taking too much of the load and the risk of injury is increased.

Starting Squat Position Poor Posture

Lower Squat Position Poor Posture

2. The lunge: We can examine this movement pattern in the pictures below. Whilst people may not lunge as long or as deep as illustrated in the picture, they will still use it on a daily basis; they just may not notice themselves doing it.

Poor Lunge Posture

Good Lunge Posture

The picture on the right above shows the lunge performed with good posture. Once again the load is shared evenly across both legs and the upper body. However, in the picture on the left, with poor posture the load is once again unevenly distributed. On the left leg, the knee has gone beyond the toes and is exposed to increased stress and loading, whilst the upper body is pitching forward and increasing the load on the low back.

3. The bend: Once again, on a daily basis many people bend down to pick objects up off the floor, regardless of whether they are heavy or light. The picture on the left below shows how someone with good posture would hopefully choose to pick up an object. The back is kept in neutral alignment and the load spread across the legs, back and upper body. The picture on the right shows how someone with poor posture would have to pick up an object, and how the loading on the low back is increased with poor posture.

Good bend Posture

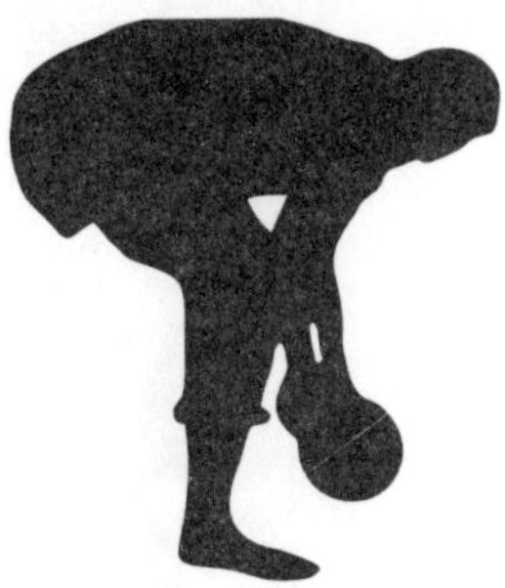

Poor Bend Posture

Correct Postures

Good and correct postures can be described as under:

Sitting posture: In correct sitting posture, various organs of the body and the body as a whole are balanced; the legs may be crossed; the hips are properly and comfortably placed at the seat; the head, shoulder and the hips are in a straight vertical line; and the vertebral column is perfectly vertical.

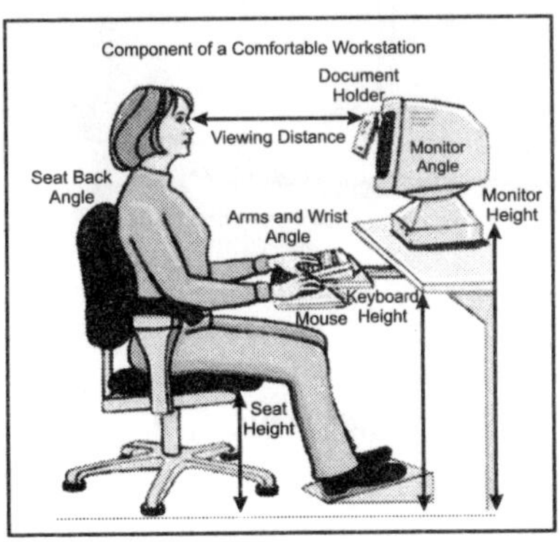

Standing posture: In correct standing posture, the body weight should equally fall on both the legs; the whole body should be vertical and erect; the heels should rest evenly on the flat floor; the two arms should rest on the thighs in a straight line; the head and the body should not bend forward; the body should not bend on one of its sides; and the body as a whole should be balanced.

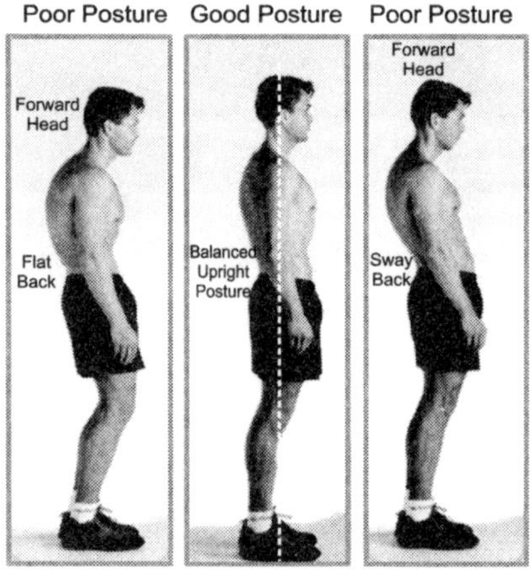

Reading posture: While reading, the book should not be placed very close to the eyes, it should be at least 12 inches away; and the hand holding the book should form an angle of 45 degree with the eyes.

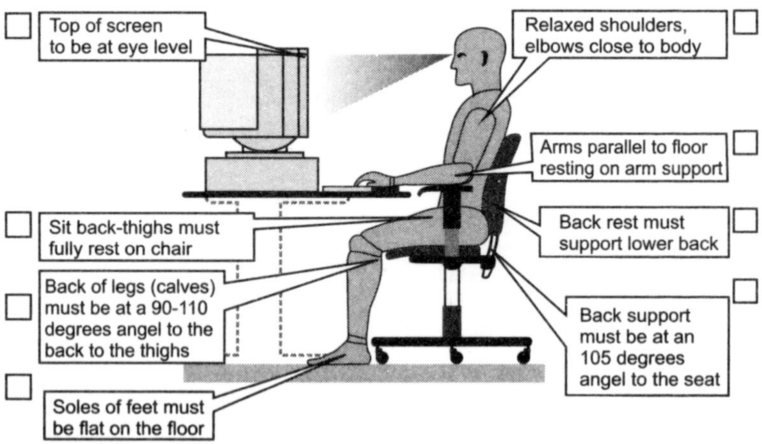

Writing posture: While writing, the position of the table or desk should be very close to the body; the body should be in an upright position and not bent over the note book; the legs should rest on the ground; the note book should be at a distance of 12 inches from the eyes; the paper should be placed parallel to the edge of the desk, and the pen should be held in between the thumb and two fingers.

Walking posture: While walking, the body as a whole should be erect and upright; the eyes should look straight at an angle of 90 degrees; the arms should swing alternately along with steps preferably upto an angle of 90 degrees with the body; the heels should touch the ground first and then the middle portion and the toes; and one should take steps of normal dimension.

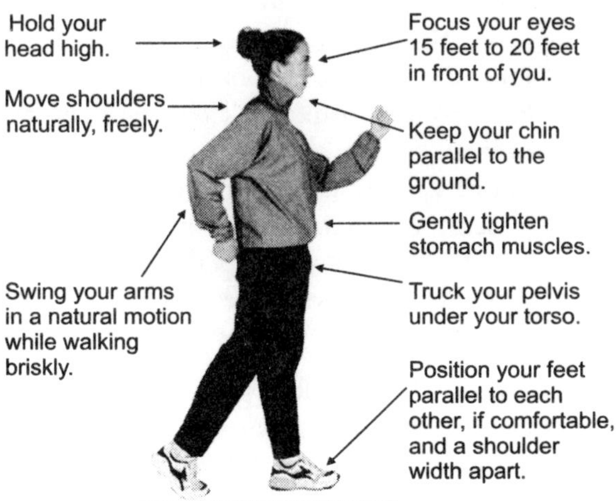

Adverse Effect of Poor Posture

Most of us underestimate the importance of good posture. Poor posture can have a surprisingly adverse affect on many aspects of our lives. Whether an office worker, housewife, builder or Olympic athlete, everyone can benefit from better posture.

For example, the average office worker who spends most of his/her day at a computer may develop forward head posture where the head and neck protrude forwards, just like it does with mannequins. They may also experience pain in the low back, hip, shoulder, knee and ankle or many other discomforts including poor breathing and low energy as a result of the way they habitually sit at work.

Individuals with poor posture experience greater stress on their joints and the muscles surrounding them, are more susceptible to injury, may suffer from any number of ailments including low back pain, chronic neck tension/pain, headaches, rotator cuff problems, pain in the mid to upper spine, and knee or hamstring strain. Conversely a person with a good posture has better alignment, which translates into less injury, better balance, agility and overall physical performance and recovers quicker from exercise or physical exertion, and feels more energetic.

Dr. Mosher says, "As a result of poor postures, constipation, diarrhea, flatulence, disturbance of the circulation, nervous irritability and most marked of all fatigue out of proportion to the effort expended lessen the efficiency of the individual and often make life a burden." Some of the bad effects of wrong postures are given below:

- Interference in the normal working of digestion, respiration and blood circulation.
- Defective physical development, such as crooked bodies, drooping bodies, round shoulders, poor build, devoid of charm, etc.
- Bad effect on eyesight due to excessive strain.
- Poor physical efficiency and laziness.
- Poor handwriting because of wrong handling of the pen and paper.
- Undesirable traits, like shabbiness, poor impression, timidness, lack of courage, etc.

If the school-going children are examined in relation to body postures, at least 50 per cent of them will be found adopting faulty postures in some way or other. The defect arising from poor posture is:

Spinal Curvature

This defect is generally found in a large number of children. Excessive strain during childhood on the vertebral column makes it curve and the following defects arise:

1. Appearance of Kyphosis
2. Lordosis
3. Scoliosis

The following deformities appear with the Kyphosis:

(a) Bending of head and the body in the forward direction

(b) Round back

(c) Flat chest

(d) Round shoulders

(e) Round hallow back

(f) Bulging out of the belly

The above-mentioned defects are caused by non-nutritive and unbalanced diet, lack of fresh air and inadequate physical exercises. Besides, faulty desk sitting posture, myopia, excessive strain on shoulders and rickets also deform the waist region.

Causes of Bad Postures

People with poor posture are often thought to have little or no confidence or self-esteem. After all, how we carry our body has a lot to do with how people perceive us. Not only does good posture come across as strong and confident, but also it helps to strengthen the muscles around the spine and neck. The following are some of the root causes of poor posture and how to correct the problem.

Poor nutrition

Nutrition has a lot to do with how well one feels and looks. The old adage, "you are what you eat" is popular for a reason—our spine and bones need nutrients to grow strong and straight. Lack of Vitamin D, calcium and protein will have a negative impact on the bones and muscular system. Malnutrition will also weaken the skeletal structure and may lead to osteoporosis in later years.

Disease

Likewise, the presence of disease has a debilitating effect on our bones and muscles. Any condition that weakens our immune system, drains nutrients from our body or creates poor cell growth will be harmful in the long run. *Scoliosis*—named for the Greek word "crooked"—is a medical condition, not a disease that plays havoc with the spine by creating a painful, lateral curve. Two per cent of women and 0.5 per cent of men are affected, most cases are found in adolescence. The Adam's Forward Bend Test is a cursory test for scoliosis, in which the patient leans forward at a 90-degree bend and the trunk, is checked for imbalance. Treatment is observation, orthopedic braces, or surgery.

Injuries

Breaking bones, poor healing, and uneven legs can be contributing factors toward poor posture. Even after a bone breaks and re-heals, the adjacent muscles may shrink, and the injured person tends to alter his step or the way he walks to protect that area. All of this creates an imbalance, which causes a deviation in the way one moves, sits and stands.

Stress and tension

Two of the body's dreaded culprits to health: stress and tension, certainly affect the way we carry ourselves. Unhappy people hunch over, tired folks curve into themselves and stress shows like the weight of the world on our shoulders. Repeated behaviours such as this create muscle weakness, poor breathing habits, and the inability to knowingly stand erect.

Repeated behaviours

Additional bad "posture" habits include working at a computer for long hours, playing video games or driving for long periods of time. All of these factors contribute to our inability to keep our spines straight. Certain jobs also lead to spine fatigue, such as therapy positions, which requires bending over for extended periods of time.

Poor fitting shoes

Women who spend a lot of time walking around in three-inch high heels are likely wreaking havoc with their posture. Shoes that wear unevenly due to overpronation—pronation is a symptom of the foot rolling in and flattening the arch—can certainly create poor posture.

Some other causes are, weakness of the muscles and bones, which may be due to poor diet and lack of exercise, lack of information regarding correct posture, defective shape and size of desks and benches compelling the students to stretch or cramp their bodies, wrong writing and reading positions, defective vision or hearing and illegible blackboard writing by the teacher, defective postures of teachers and other adults, unduly tight and unsuitable dress, chronic illness and excessive fatigue, and lack of light, air, rest and sleep.

The teacher in order to remove these causes and defects thereof should impress upon the students the importance of adopting correct postures while standing, reading and writing.

Importance of Proper Posture

1. Using proper body mechanics, or achieving proper posture, is particularly important for people recovering from a spine-related injury. Proper posture can alleviate two of the most common physical complaints—neck and back pain. Incorporating proper body mechanics into routine activities can reduce the amount of stress exerted on the spine. Awareness of proper posture and correct movement can lead to a tremendous reduction in chronic pain.

2. The spine is composed of 33 vertebrae. Disks lie between the vertebrae and act as shock absorbers in addition to allowing the spine to move. The modern work environment is ill designed for maintaining proper posture and body mechanics, but proper spine alignment can be corrected and encouraged through the performance of simple exercises throughout the day.

3. The Colorado Spine Institute recommends two simple exercises: the chin tuck and the shoulder squeeze. The chin tuck is a series of neck retractions, performed by imagining that the person is a turtle pulling his neck into the shell and then extending it straight up as though someone is pulling a string attached to the back of the neck straight up to the sky. The movement has to be followed by leaning the neck completely back in a state of relaxation. The chin tuck aids in realigning the upper spine and neck. This exercise can be performed numerous times throughout the workday.

Another beneficial exercise is the shoulder squeeze. It is performed by bringing the elbows behind while squeezing the shoulder blades together. This position should be held back for five seconds. This can be done numerous times to relax the back muscles and to correct a slumped body posture that often occurs after hours spent focusing on a computer screen. Dr. Harry N. Herkowitz, an orthopedic surgeon, has determined that using simple exercises, such as the chin tuck and shoulder squeeze, significantly improves an individual's posture and body mechanics.

4. Proper posture is of utmost importance when lifting objects because spinal strain occurs most commonly as the result of not lifting correctly. When lifting objects, it has to be made sure that the back is straight and a stable base of support is maintained. One should always bend from the hips and knees rather than from the waist.

Ways to Improve the Posture

The first step to better the posture is to learn what a correct posture is. The natural body posture of a human has three curves, forming 'S'. These three curves are the neck curve, mid back curve and low back curve. A proper alignment means that when we stand, our back in an 'S' shape while we sit on a chair or bench, our back should be straight, chest up and out and tummy should be completely pulled in. If it is the case, we are in a good shape otherwise we need to work to get in. Standing, sitting, walking, working in an uncomfortable or incorrect stance for long periods of time results in bad posture. There are a number of ways that can help poor posture. Some of the important ones are briefly described as under.

1. *Yoga*

Yoga can help a lot in correction as well as maintenance of our body posture. We need to perform them properly and on a regular basis.

Some of the yoga poses recommendable for posture correction are mentioned below:

1. *Adho Mukta Svanasana* (Downward-facing pose)
2. *Tadasana* (Mountain pose)
3. *Vṛksasana* (Tree pose)
4. *Trikonasana* (Triangle pose)
5. *Balasana* (Child's pose)

2. *Exercises*

Exercising is a great way to have good posture. Actually, there are certain exercises to improve posture. To get accustomed to the posture correction exercises, we should start doing a set of each exercise once a day for a couple of weeks. When we get comfortable, the count can be increased to three times a day.

3. *Ergonomic posture chair*

Bad posture is often the result of sitting in an uncomfortable chair for long hours for an extended period of time. Many health care professionals recommend using an ergonomic chair while sitting for a long time.

4. *Posture braces*

Medical professionals for posture correction commonly prescribe posture correction braces. These braces are soft, non-elastic straps, which are designed in a way to provide a safe and non-binding fit. The posture braces are often equipped with easily adjustable hook-and-loop closures. Their function is to increase or decrease the amount of support and pressure, as per requirement. The posture braces support the back muscles.

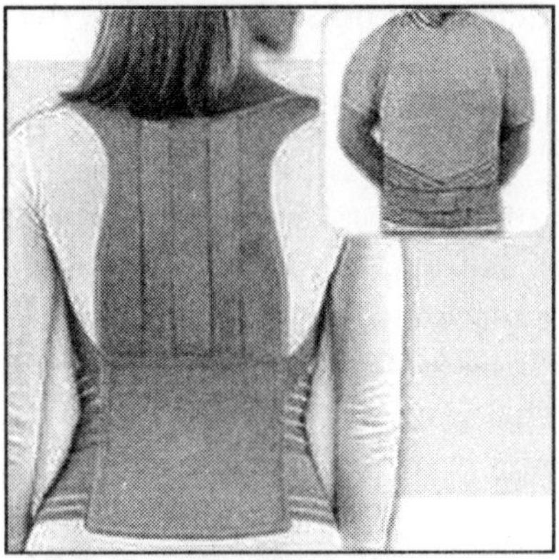

5. *Comfortable shoes and clothing*

We should avoid wearing high heels as they put pressure on the lower back. Also, high-heeled boots, wide belts and tight clothing harm us over a period of time, as they tend to shift our center of gravity. Therefore, we should always wear comfortable fitting clothes and flat-heeled shoes. This is because they provide us relaxation and good support.

In order to correct the defective postures of the students, we must first ensure balanced diet for them. They may be asked to take regular exercise to strengthen their muscles and bones. Fresh air, rest and sleep should also be ensured. Overwork should be avoided and excessive fatigue should not be allowed to happen. Good postural habits should be inculcated in them by paying proper attention to them while they are sitting, standing, walking, reading or writing. Their vision and hearing should be examined and students with defective eyesight and hearing should be seated in the front row. Along with mass drill, march past and yogasans, suitable corrective exercises should be recommended for the needy. There should be suitable uniform or dress for all. Books used should be of bold type and classrooms should be spacious and well ventilated. Stools should be provided for smaller children so that they may learn to sit without reclining against the back of the chair. The suitability of the furniture should be ensured. In the case of serious postural defects or body deformities, the aid of competent medical authority may be sought.

Physical Exercises

The beauty of life rests a lot in your physical well-being along with other aspects. If you stay fit, fine and healthy, you will surely enjoy the life to its best.

Physical exercise is the performance of some activity in order to develop or maintain physical fitness and overall health. It is often directed toward developing athletic ability or skill. Frequent and regular physical exercise is an important component in the prevention of some of the diseases of affluence such as cancer, heart disease, cardiovascular disease, Type 2 diabetes, obesity and back pain. Exercises are generally grouped into three types depending on the overall effect they have on the human body: *flexibility exercises* such as stretching improve the range of motion of muscles and joints, *aerobic exercises* such as walking and running focus on increasing cardiovascular endurance, and *anaerobic exercises* such as weight training or sprinting increase short-term muscle strength.

Physical exercise is considered important for maintaining physical fitness including healthy weight building and maintaining healthy bones, muscles, and joints; promoting physiological well-being; reducing surgical risks; and strengthening the immune system. Proper nutrition is just as, if not more, important to health as exercise. When exercising it becomes even more important to have good diet to ensure the body has the correct ratio of macronutrients whilst providing ample micronutrients; this is to aid the body with the recovery process following strenuous exercise. When the body falls short of proper nutrition, it gets into starvation mode developed through evolution and depends onto fat content for survival. Research suggests that the production of thyroid hormones can be negatively affected by repeated bouts of dieting and calorie restriction. Proper rest and recovery is also as important to health as exercise, otherwise the body exists in a permanently injured state and will not improve or adapt adequately to the exercise.

The above two factors can be compromised by psychological compulsions (eating disorders such as exercise bulimia, anorexia, and other bulimias), misinformation, a lack of organization, or a lack of motivation. These all lead to a decreased state of health. Delayed Onset Muscle Soreness can occur after any exercise, particularly if the body is in an unconditioned state relative to that exercise.

Benefits of Physical Activity

Regular physical activity is one of the most important things one can do for his/her health. It can help:

- Control weight.
- Reduce the risk of cardiovascular disease.
- Reduce the risk for type 2 diabetes and metabolic syndrome.
- Reduce the risk of some cancers.
- Strengthen bones and muscles.
- Improve mental health and mood.
- Improve the ability to do daily activities and prevent falls.
- Increase the chances of living longer.

Controls weight

Both diet and physical activity play a critical role in controlling the weight. We gain weight when the calories we burn, including those burned during physical activity, are less than the calories we eat or drink. When it comes to weight management, people vary greatly in how much physical activity they need. We may need to be more active than others to achieve or maintain a healthy weight.

Reduces risk of cardiovascular disease

Heart disease and stroke are two of the leading causes of death in the United States. But following the guidelines and getting at least 150 minutes a week (2 hours and 30 minutes) of moderate-intensity aerobic activity can put one at a lower risk for these diseases. We can reduce the risk even further with more physical activity. Regular physical activity can also lower the blood pressure and improve our cholesterol levels.

Reduces the risk of type 2 diabetes and metabolic syndrome

Regular physical activity can reduce the risk of developing type 2 diabetes and metabolic syndrome. Metabolic syndrome is a condition in which the person has some combination of too much fat around the waist, high blood pressure, low HDL cholesterol or high blood sugar. Research shows that lower rates of these conditions are seen with 120 to 150 minutes (2 hours to 2 hours and 30 minutes) a week of at least moderate-intensity aerobic activity. And the more physical activity one does, the lower the risk will be.

Reduces the risk of some cancers

Being physically active lowers the risk for two types of cancer: colon and breast. Research shows that:

- Physically active people have a lower risk of colon cancer than do people who are not active.
- Physically active women have a lower risk of breast cancer than do women who are not active.

Strengthens bones and muscles

As we age, it is important to protect the bones, joints and muscles. Not only do they support our body and help us move, but keeping bones, joints and muscles healthy can help ensure that we are able to do our daily activities and be physically active. Research shows that doing aerobic, muscle-strengthening and bone-strengthening physical activity of at least a moderately-intense level can slow the loss of bone density that comes with age.

Improves mental health and mood

Regular physical activity can help keep our thinking, learning, and judgement skills sharp as we age. It can also reduce the risk of depression and may help in sleeping better. Research has shown that doing aerobic or a mix of aerobic and muscle-strengthening activities 3 to 5 times a week for 30 to 60 minutes can give us these mental health benefits. Some scientific evidence has also shown that even lower levels of physical activity can be beneficial.

Improves the ability to do daily activities and prevent falls

A functional limitation is a loss of the ability to do everyday activities such as climbing stairs, grocery shopping, or playing with grandchildren. Regular exercise will definitely improve the ability to do daily activities and avoid and prevent falls.

Increases the chances of living longer

Science shows that physical activity can reduce the risk of dying early from the leading causes of death, like heart disease and some cancers. This is remarkable in two ways:

- Only a few lifestyle choices have as large an impact on the health as physical activity. People who are physically active for about 7 hours a week have a 40 per cent lower risk of dying early than those who are active for less than 30 minutes a week.

- One need not do high amounts of activity or vigorous-intensity activity to reduce risk of premature death. One can put oneself at lower risk of dying early by doing at least 150 minutes a week of moderate-intensity aerobic activity.

Everyone can gain the health benefits of physical activity—age, ethnicity, shape or size do not matter.

Other Benefits of Physical Activity

- Physical activity builds healthy bones, muscles and joints, and reduces the risk of colon cancer. Millions of Americans suffer from illnesses that can be prevented or improved through regular physical activity.
- Physical activity also helps psychologically. It reduces feelings of depression and anxiety, improves mood and promotes a sense of well-being.
- The 1996 Surgeon General's Report on Physical Activity also suggests that active people have a lower risk for stroke.

Importance of Regular Exercise

Every person should try to remain fit and healthy throughout his or her life. Fitness has a lot to do with physical exercise. And the practice of doing physical exercise cannot be taught in a day or two. The orientation to physical exercise and fitness must begin right at early ages. Exercising makes one more energetic.

Children develop spontaneity in activities and they are always in their best spirit when they exercise regularly. Physical exercise keeps away obesity in children, builds muscular strength and mighty bones, helps in overall growth, development and strength, helps them perform better in school and studies and defends diseases like type 2 diabetes and controls cholesterol.

The practical part of physical exercise has to be maintained in a proper and regular schedule. Children do have a specific time for playing and doing exercises. Therefore, the kids have to be guided in a routine way to play and practice exercises. Parents must encourage their children to play along with studies. Computer games and television watching should be cut short. Researches have found that more young children are becoming inactive and inert due to TV watching. The children must be encouraged for different outdoor games. They must be admitted to swimming classes, general gymnasium or aerobics, if available. Otherwise they should be helped with some regular exercise including skipping, running or other activities. This will help the child even remain mentally fit because the little ones will find friends and will take more interest in these activities. Children always follow role models, particularly their parents.

Thus, the parents should find time to play with their children. They can also fix up a particular schedule of exercising along with the child. This will boost their spirit and build a natural instinct to remain fit from the young age itself. It is a matter of encouragement, culture and cultivation. If parents can really encourage their children with a proper education of physical exercise from the very beginning, no one can stop them to remain fit.

9

Balanced Diet and Nutrition

Nutritive and balanced diet provides the body with the required energy for doing everyday work. Body depends on food for its growth, maintenance and health. Food acts as its fuel and provides energy. It makes good the consumed energy, keeps the body temperature and invigorates the mind and nervous system. Besides, the responsibility of keeping the body temperature is that of the food; it is the food that helps the body to grow. As the old tissues are broken, consumed or spent in work through the process of catabolism, food replaces the same through the process of anabolism. Combination of these two processes goes on continuously in the human body and the combined process is known as metabolism. Both the quantity and quality of the food are important for the body. The quantity of food needed daily by a child or adult varies according to the nature of occupation, general health and the rate of metabolism. Both over-eating and under-eating are harmful. Therefore, there is a need for knowing the exact amount of nutrition needed by a person or his balanced diet. Lack of proper nutrition or balanced diet is called malnutrition. In India, malnutrition is a common problem with most of the children and adults.

Balanced Diet

A diet is considered "balanced" when all food groups are represented in healthy proportions or percentages. This means following the recommended daily allowances for micronutrients and for macronutrients—fats, carbohydrates, and proteins. Thus a balanced diet is that which fulfils all the nutritive needs of a normal and healthy individual. It should contain all the constituents like proteins, fats, starch, vitamins, etc. in needed quantity. The quantity will vary in accordance with the requirements of age, sex, body build, nature of occupation and climatic conditions.

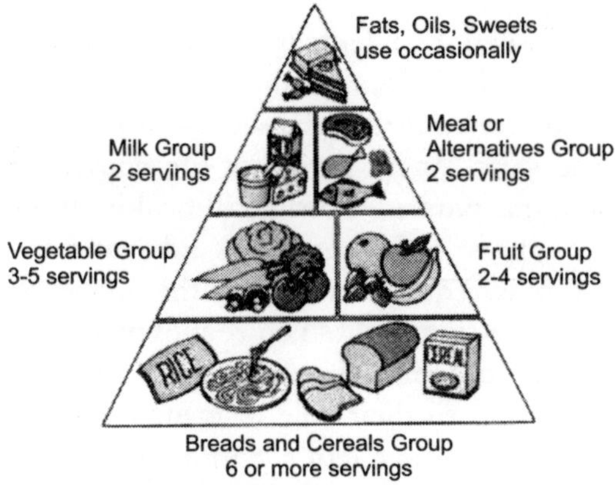

A well balanced diet consisting of vitamins, nutrients and minerals will help one to remain fit and healthy. A healthy balanced diet is required for children as well as adults. Diet plays a significant role to maintain health of an individual. The objectives of a balanced and healthy diet as recommended by the World Health Organization are:

1. To achieve a healthy weight and energy balance.
2. Elimination of trans fatty acids and saturated fats.
3. Consumption of unsaturated fatty acids.
4. Intake of simple sugar should be limited.
5. Include a high amount of vegetables, fruits, nuts, legumes and whole grains.
6. Intake iodized salt and limit consumption of sodium.
7. Essential amino acids and proteins should form a major part of diet.
8. Avoid consumption of food substances containing artificial preservatives and carcinogens.
9. Foods contaminated with human pathogen should be strictly avoided.

10. Limit intake of caffeine and alcohol.
11. Inclusion of vitamins, minerals and fibers in diet.
12. Consumption of plenty of water.

Most of the school students in India get nothing except *Dal* and *Roti* as food. They remain short of required minerals and vitamins. Apart from *dal-roti*, the diet must include milk, fruits, vegetables and salts. At no period of life does unbalanced diet play such a large part in causing ill-health or in promoting defects of growth as in the periods of adolescence. A balanced diet for children is required to supply the nutrients and energy needed for the growing child. The requirement of all nutrients is increased, but the pattern of increase varies for different nutrients in relation to their role in growth of specific tissues. A child of one year of age can eat most of the dishes that are prepared for the rest of the family, but they require less spicy food. Kids need five to six meals a day because of their smaller appetites. Healthy and balanced diet for kids such as whole wheat bread, cereals, fruits and vegetables should make up the major part of the diet of the children. Foods such as meat, fish, Soya products, milk, pulses and cereals provide the proteins necessary for this age group.

Balanced Diet for Children

It is important for parents to plan a balanced diet for their children. The nutritional requirements in each and every child vary, depending upon the age, height, weight and sex. Balanced diets help in weight loss and strengthen the immunity system of a child.

Balanced Diet Chart for Children

The chart contains the food intake required by the child on a daily basis:

Food Type	Per Serve	Per Day Serving from this group
Whole Grain Foods (Bread, Pasta, Cereal)	Bread-2 slices, Pasta-1 cup, Cereal-1 cup	5-9 serves per day
Vegetables (Broccoli, Cauli-flower, Salad, Spinach	Half a cup each	4-5 serves per day
Fruits (Oranges, Apple, Banana)	1 piece, Juices (1 glass)	2-3 serves per day
Dairy Products (Milk, Cheese, Yogurt)	Milk (250 ml), Cheese (40 grams), Yogurt (200 grams)	2-4 serves per day
Lean Proteins (Meat, Fish, Egg)	1 piece	1-2 serves per day

Child's overall development depends upon a healthy balanced diet. A stipulated amount of oils like coconut oil and olive oil include healthy fats. Essential fatty acids aid in proper functioning of the brain and help in maintaining mental health. Oily fish are rich in essential fatty acids. Folates refer to Vitamin B which helps produce red blood cells. Green leafy vegetables (spinach and turnip) and citrus fruits are good sources of folate. Vitamin A is required for the proper growth and development of cells and is good for the eyes. Carrots, pumpkin and broccoli are rich sources of Vitamin A. Vitamin C, an antioxidant, helps in iron absorption. Fruits (apple, oranges, dark berries) are rich in Vitamin C. Deficiency of Vitamin D causes rickets in children. Eggs and oily fish contain Vitamin D. Fibers should be incorporated in the diet to prevent constipation. Fibers help in proper digestion and body metabolism. Water intake should be 6-8 glasses per day to keep body dehydration at bay.

A healthy balanced diet for children is necessary to boost their energy levels. The child should be encouraged to eat different varieties of foods. Ultimately, a proper balanced diet can keep the child fit and healthy.

Basic Guidelines for Nutrient Requirement in Balanced Diet for Children of Different Age Groups

Calories requirement

The calorie requirements are increased due to the high cellular activity in children above 5 years of age. Children under 5 year of age should not be given skimmed milk to restrict on fat and cholesterol, as they need the extra calories, but grilled and baked foods are always preferable to fried and fatty ones. Whole grains or enriched cereals increase the calories. Concentrated sweets and foods that are very high in fat should be avoided.

Protein requirement

Protein has a very important role in the diet of the preschool child because there is considerable increase in muscular development during these years. The requirements for essential amino acids are higher for children than adults. So protein should be selected from complete protein foods such as milk, egg and meat.

Vitamin and mineral requirement

Vitamins and minerals must be supplemented adequately. Calcium and iron requirements are relatively greater during early childhood. Deficiency of calcium can affect the bones of growing children. Foods rich in calcium such as milk and milk products, ragi, green leafy vegetable and fish should be included in the diet of children.

Balanced Nutrition

Nutrition may be defined simply as the science providing the body with the nourishment, which it needs for growth, maintenance and repair. The primary aim of nutrition education should be to establish good habits and attitudes, which will result in intelligent selection and consumption of nutritious food throughout life. Children cannot be depended upon to select by instinct a diet that meets nutritive values. Some sort of formal instruction is necessary.

In order to begin creating a healthy diet, it is important to understand the basics of good nutrition. There are six classes of nutrients: carbohydrates, proteins, fats, vitamins, minerals and water. All of these nutrients are necessary as sources of energy and to create chemical reactions within the body to make it function.

Proteins

The substance formed by the combination of carbon, hydrogen, oxygen, nitrogen, sulphur and phosphorous and that builds tissues for growth and repair is called protein. The body also uses protein to stabilize blood sugar levels by stimulating glucagons. Protein is found in the shape of albumin in the egg, as myosin in meat, as gluten in wheat and as legumin in various pulses and leafy vegetables. Ordinarily, the protein found in the vegetarian edibles as inferior to that found in non-vegetarian edibles or in other words protein derived from vegetation is inferior to that received from animals. The cells of animals are very much similar to those found in man; therefore, the protein derived from them is more useful. This is the reason why protein received from animals is comparatively superior.

The protein helps the formation of new tissues replacing those, which are destroyed during exertion. It produces protoplasm. Because of this, protein is also called tissue producer. Protein is absolutely necessary for life; the growth of the body is retarded in its absence and many diseases set in. When excessive protein is formed in the body it accumulates in the form of fat and produces heat and energy in the absence of carbohydrate. Protein produces in the body power to resist diseases. It helps in the production of digestive juices and also helps the ductless glands to produce juices.

Proteins can be found in meat, poultry, foul, fish, eggs, milk and milk products, beans, nuts, yeast, grains, soya and wheat germ. Protein should account for about 20 to 30 per cent of a healthy diet.

Carbohydrates

Carbohydrates are our main source of producing heat and energy and are found in starch, sugar and fiber. Chemicals like carbon, hydrogen and oxygen are also found in it. This is essential for the formation of fat. Muscles need it when a man puts in hard physical labour. The digestive system changes it to glucose, which mixes in blood and reaches muscles and proves a very useful diet for them. The glucose in excess of body requirement collects in the liver in the shape of glycogen and when required again turns into glucose and supplies heat and energy to the muscles.

Starch is found in potatoes, rice, wheat, corn, millet, etc. Sugar is found in sugar canes, beet and different fruits. Lactose is found in milk. Starch is also found in some non-vegetarian diets, but the vegetarian diet is its main source. It is important to eat the right kinds of carbohydrates. Natural sugars such as those found in fruits and vegetables are good. Refined sugars are very unhealthy. Carbohydrates and fiber can be found in whole-meal bread and pasta, vegetables and fruit. Foods containing starch and fiber should make up about 40 to 50 per cent of the diet.

Fat

Fat keeps the body functions working properly and should account for about 30 per cent of the diet. Many of us cut fats from our diets, in attempting to lose weight. We need to remember that a certain amount of fat is necessary in our diets. Saturated fats should be used sparingly as they increase blood cholesterol to dangerous levels. Polyunsaturated fats are mainly derived from plants and have greater health benefits. Saturated fats are of animal origin and found in meat, milk, butter, cheese, olive oil and nuts. Polyunsaturated and monounsaturated fats are found in fish and seaweed, flaxseed oil, green leafy vegetables, liver, olive oil and soya oil. Fats should make up 30 per cent of the diet.

Carbon, hydrogen and oxygen are found in fats like carbohydrates but the proportion of these chemicals differ in them. Mixture of fatty acids and glycerin also exists in fats. Fat produces heat in the body and energy for muscles; it produces more heat and energy as compared to starch. Excessive fat in relation to body requirement is deposited below the skin in the body. Consequently, the body becomes healthy and the bones, joints and other body parts get protection against external injuries. Fat produces smoothness in the skin, which minimizes the loss of body albumin. The fat below the skin protects the body from outside heat and cold. The bones, joints and other body parts become safe from external injuries. The fat produced by non-vegetarian food has Vitamins A and D as well. Ordinarily fat is found in butter, cheese, ghee, mustard and coconut oil.

Vitamins

Vitamins are natural substances found in plants and animals. The human body makes use of these vitamins for proper function of its various organs and for staying healthy. Vitamins in everyday diet, keeps one healthy, because the body's metabolism also depends on the vitamin intake. The human body cannot manufacture vitamins, so the appropriate supply of vitamins have to be taken in through the food we consume, or by vitamin supplements, to prevent from falling ill and maintain a healthy body. Prevention is always better than cure.

Classification of vitamins

Vitamins are classified into two types: Water-soluble vitamins and fat-soluble vitamins.

Fat-soluble vitamins like Vitamins A, D, E and K, as the name suggests, are soluble in fat and are absorbed and stored in the body for being used later. But these vitamins should not be consumed in excess. Fruits and vegetables are rich in vitamins.

If we consume them daily, the body will get the sufficient source of multivitamins.

Vitamin A fights infection, prevents dry skin and poor bone growth. It provides the body organs with the necessary diet. It increases appetite and helps digestive system to function properly. It increases vitality and builds resistance capacity against diseases. This vitamin also enhances vision by helping the retina function properly, permitting us to distinguish between light and shade and see various colours distinctly. Vitamin A is not destroyed by long exposure to sunlight or cooking.

The deficiency of Vitamin A causes night-blindness, bronchitis, cold, cough and intestinal diseases. Its continued deficiency produces stones in the kidneys. **Source:** Found in fish liver oils, green vegetables, carrots, ripe tomatoes, and milk, butter, and margarine and egg yolks. Overdoses of Vitamin A may result in yellowish and dry skin and irritated eyes.

Vitamin D is essential for bone growth and calcium absorption. It can be found either through consuming food rich in this vitamin or through sunlight. It is needed to prevent and cure rickets. Vitamin D is also called anti-rickets vitamin because calcium and phosphorus, needed most for the development of bones and teeth require this vitamin. In the absence of Vitamin D, phosphorous and calcium go out of the body without performing their function and without being digested. Its deficiency in children is most harmful because the proper development of bones and teeth takes place in this early age. Diseases like small pox, whooping cough, tuberculosis is likely to attack a person suffering from deficiency of this vitamin. The intake of this vitamin should be increased in children in order to cure bone and teeth diseases. **Source:** Found in tuna fish, eggs, butter and cheese.

Vitamin E promotes blood clotting and is an activator in certain enzyme reactions. It affects the reproductory power of the body and is called anti-sterility vitamin. This vitamin also protects Vitamins A and C from being used up too quickly.

Source: Found in milk, vegetables, liver, rice and sprouts of wheat and yolk.

Vitamin K maintains the involuntary nervous system, vascular system and involuntary muscles. It is essential for the synthesis of prothrombin, a substance needed for normal blood coagulation. The presence of this vitamin is essential in a woman during pre-natal and post-natal periods. **Source:** Found in abundance in spinach, cabbages, tomatoes, potatoes, wheat germ, vegetable oil and whole-grain breads and cereals.

Water-soluble vitamins include the B vitamins and Vitamin C or ascorbic acid. The B vitamins, a combination of hydrogen, oxygen, carbon and sulphur, are essential to daily human nutrition. It has ten different varieties and collectively it is known as the B complex vitamins. They help body systems combat stress and maintain energy reserves. The B-complex group is comprised of Vitamin B_1 (thiamine), Vitamin B_2 (riboflavin), Vitamin B_3 (niacin), Vitamin B_5 (Pantothenic acid), Vitamin B_6 (Pyridoxine), Vitamin B_{12} (Cobalamin), Folic acid and biotin. In these varieties, Vitamin B_1 and Vitamin B_2 are particularly useful for the human body. These are crystal like and soluble. They continue to exist in heat but are destroyed in high temperature. These can exist in acids but are destroyed in alkalies. These varieties of vitamins are found in sufficient quantity in seeds, plants, and the yolk of eggs, wheat, rice, fruits, vegetables, fresh peas and milk. Since these vitamins get eliminated in urine easily, the body has to be continuously supplied with them.

Brief description of these vitamins along with their food sources is discussed as under:

1. **Thiamin (B_1)**—It is necessary for carbohydrate metabolism. It aids in the release of energy from food. Its deficiency thins the intestine membrane; consequently it does not function smoothly. It causes indigestion, constipation and many other stomach ailments. The disease of Beriberi is caused by its deficiency in which

the development of the body is checked and it becomes weak. Source: It is found in whole-grain nuts and seeds. It is also found in yeast, pulse, rice, leafy vegetables like turnips, radish, dry fruits, onions, etc. It is destroyed when cooked in open utensils for a long time.

2. **Riboflavin** (B_2)—It is necessary for growth. It helps body cells use oxygen, promotes tissue repair and helps the nervous system function properly. Its deficiency makes one prematurely old and causes the skin and membrane to become unhealthy and eyes and eyelids feel pain. **Source:** Found in yeast, milk, meat, eggs and leafy vegetables.

3. **Niacin**—It promotes a glowing complexion, prevents disease and improves the mood. It is essential for growth. **Source:** Found in milk, eggs, cheeses and fish.

4. **Panthotenic acid**—It is essential for energy metabolism and helps increase vitality and influences glandular functions. **Source:** Found in meat, fish, poultry, whole grain cereals and dried beans.

5. **Folic acid** aids in the proper growth and reproduction of blood cells and contributes to healthy skin. **Source:** Found in leafy green vegetables, chicken, liver and kidneys.

6. **Biotin** is necessary for the proper utilization of fats, carbohydrates and protein. It also helps to produce antibodies. **Source:** Found in liver, peanuts and cheese.

7. **Vitamin** B_6—important for metabolism of proteins. **Source:** Found in spinach, broccoli and bananas.

8. **Vitamin** B_{12}—maintains the nervous system and promotes healthy skin. **Source:** Found in meat, milk, eggs, cheese and fish.

9. **Vitamin C**—It is also called anti-ascorbic vitamin because it protects an individual against the disease of scurvy. This disease reduces the strength of blood vessels.

Consequently these burst and start bleeding. Blood generally flows from teeth gums. This vitamin also heals wounds, boosts the immune system, protects us from toxins, prevents colds and is essential for normal metabolism. Vitamin C is destroyed when food containing it is cooked in open utensils. It is better to cook food in a short time than prolonging the process of cooking. **Source:** Found in green vegetables and citrus fruits.

Vitamins sometimes serve as catalysts for important body functions. They are required only in small amounts and are vital to nourishment. They are unlike minerals, however, in that they do not become part of the body, as calcium does in the teeth and bones.

Harmful effects of vitamins

Too much dose of vitamins can also cause harmful effects. For example, excess of Vitamin A can aggregate liver problems. Vitamin B_6 can cause nerve damage if in excess. Too much consumption of Vitamin C can cause diarrhea. High dose of calcium can lead to kidney stones and also cause constipation. But that does not mean vitamin is harmful. One should eat a balanced diet consisting of essential vitamins, in the required quantity. People with medical problems should consult a doctor before taking vitamins as it can worsen the conditions. People with diabetes should use Vitamin B_6, niacin, chromium and Vitamin C only under the supervision of a physician, as these vitamins can affect the sugar level. People with asthma should not use tryptophan.

Minerals

The body needs organic compounds, such as carbohydrates, fats and proteins for proper nutrition, but it also needs inorganic materials, such as minerals. These inorganic elements are present in the body in small amounts, but they play a vital role in nutrition. Mineral salts have their value for health of the body. Calcium, iron, iodine, phosphate, sodium chloride, magnesium, sulphur and copper are important amongst the mineral salts. These fill up the 20th part of the body and contribute towards the general development of the body and activate the digestive juices. The nerves, muscles and blood receive strength from them. These help in keeping the acids and alkaline in proper proportion.

1. *Calcium*

Calcium is found in good quantity in edibles—like milk, cheese, yolk, orange, fish and the green vegetables. Prevents blood clotting and is necessary for bone growth, healthy teeth and iron absorption. It is needed most in the formation of teeth and bones. Tooth decay is the result of calcium deficiency. The growth of children is retarded and bone diseases appear when there is calcium deficiency in them. It controls the action of heart, blood and nerves. The muscles lose their activeness during calcium deficiency in the body. Asthma and skin diseases appear and the nerves become excited in the absence of adequate quantity of calcium in the body. Vitamin D is necessary for calcium.

2. *Iron*

Edibles like meat, eggs, carrots and green and leafy vegetables produce iron in body. Those two are, therefore, useful during anemia. Iron is the main part of hemoglobin. This gives strength to blood corpuscles in carrying oxygen to the body parts. Lack of iron in the body causes anemia.

3. *Iodine*

It regulates energy use in the body. It is found in healthy food and some vegetables, seafood and seaweed. It is also found in fish liver oil. It is useful for thyroid glands. Its deficiency retards the growth of body causing a serious disease called goiter. The brain also is not fully developed in its absence. Iodine is the most necessary constituent of medicines prescribed for goiter.

4. *Phosphate*

It is found in meat, eggs, dry fruits, liver, milk yogurt, yeast, wheat germ and cheese. It is essential for growth of teeth bones and nervous system. It is also useful for blood. Its deficiency retards the development of the body and teeth and bones become weak.

5. *Sodium Chloride or Common Salt*

This special type of salt is found in meat and milk. It can be mixed in food separately. It is particularly useful for health and maintains adequate water in cells. It is present throughout the body tissues and is the main source of hydrochloric acid found in digestive juices.

6. *Magnesium*

It is involved in normal brain, spinal cord and nerve functioning, and aids in the formation of bones. Bones and teeth are formed by magnesium. It helps the carbohydrate to become useful for the body. Its deficiency like the calcium deficiency causes contraction of the muscles, of hands and legs. It functions as a digestive juice and expels the foul matter of the body through urinary passage. It is found in milk, grains, vegetables, fruits and cereals.

7. *Sulphur*

Sulphur is also an important object that is needed for keeping the body healthy. This is an essential part of the body cells. It helps in the formation of brain, nails and hair. Sulphur deficiency is the cause of falling hair and nail decay. The hair remains glossy as long as sulphur remains in good proportion in the body. It also helps in the digestion of food. It reaches the body in adequate quantity through eggs, beans, radish, spinach, pulse, cabbage, etc.

8. *Fibrous Edibles*

Fibrous edibles are also necessary for the body. The muscles of intestines get some useful matter from the fibrous edibles, which help in passing out stool because this matter helps in contraction and relaxation of muscles. These edibles keep the digestive system in order. Constipation is caused in the absence of fibrous edibles in the food. This matter is found in green vegetables, fruits, figs, meat and beetroots in sufficient quantities.

Other mineral elements, known as trace elements and required in lesser amounts are iron, zinc, magnesium, copper, iodine, fluorine, chromium and cobalt. Minerals function in the body in several ways. Minerals act as regulators and are necessary for certain body functions. For example, minerals contribute to the water and electrolyte balance of the body and are important in the functioning of the transmission of nerve impulses.

Elevated amounts of some minerals may cause health problems. For example, elevated levels of sodium are associated with high blood pressure and cardiovascular disease. Sodium can be restricted through the diet by eliminating table salt, using sodium free salt substitutes, drinking low salt milk, and using vegetable salts as spices. A lack of essential minerals can cause malnutrition. For example, iron deficiency causes anemia. Children deprived of iron show lack of motivation and less ability to work and play (Sizer and Whitney, 1988). This deficiency occurs most frequently in infants, adolescent males and females during childbearing years.

Water

Our bodies are made up of about two-thirds water. It also acts as a solvent for minerals and other physiologically important compounds. Further, water helps regulate the body temperature. Water comes from fluids and solids in the diet and is also produced by the metabolism of energy nutrients within the tissues. The effects of water deprivation are dramatic; blood volume is reduced so it does not circulate to the tissues effectively. The brain is the most effected that includes dizziness, disorientation and fatigued. The amount of activity and the climate are important factors influencing the amount of water a person needs. Because children usually participate in physical activities, they perspire more and therefore need more water than many adults. Six to eight ounce glasses of water should be ingested a day. Much of this is gained from solid foods.

Balanced Diet Plan

Simply avoiding consumption of carbohydrates and fats doesn't imply that one is on a balanced diet. It is important to know that carbohydrates and fats energize the body to perform activities. It allows one to remain active. The balanced diet for children accentuates their growth with increasing age. It helps to strengthen their immune system and makes their body strong. Health nutritionists and dietitians suggest consumption of small meals in a gap of 3-4 hours, instead of devouring huge meals. A proper combination of fruits, vegetables, grains and dairy product will undoubtedly ensure a balanced diet. A healthy balanced diet plan is presented below:

Group 1: Vegetables and pulses

Vegetables are rich in vitamins and minerals. Pulses are a source of protein and monounsaturated fatty acids, essential for body. One can consume boiled or cooked vegetables one or two bowls daily. For lunch one can have the vegetables like lettuce, cauliflower, spinach, tomato, cabbage, beans, lentils, lady's finger, carrot, etc.

Group 2: Fruits

Fruits are also a source of multivitamins and minerals. Citrus fruits are rich in Vitamin C. One can consume a fruit dish everyday for breakfast. They are also natural source of carbohydrates and fibers. Some of the healthiest fruits are apple, orange, grapes, lime, strawberries, banana, etc.

Group 3: Dairy

Dairy products are not only rich in proteins but also in unsaturated fatty acids. A glass of skimmed milk is ideal for breakfast or before going to bed. Children can consume cream enriched milk. They are rich in calcium, required for health of bones and teeth. Some of the most nutritious dairy foods are: milk, eggs, cholesterol free butter, cottage cheese, etc.

Group 4: Grains and cereals

Healthy balanced diet for women and men is extremely important and a balanced diet must contain adequate proportions of protein. Therefore, grains are consumed which are extremely rich in proteins. Cereals form an ideal source of carbohydrates. Pulses are rich in fatty acids. Whole grains contain nutritious substances like iron, magnesium and phosphorous that act as cofactors for the enzymatic activities inside the body. The examples are: wheat bread, brown rice, oatmeal, pasta, soya bean, cereal, corns, etc.

Group 5: Others

There are some other sources of proteins that play a vital role for body's metabolism. For example, a piece of chicken or fish is considered healthy for lunch. Nuts are extremely loaded with omega-3-essential fatty acids, a vital component for body. Walnuts, almonds, peanuts, chicken, meat, etc. provide a good source.

Malnutrition

Malnutrition has been an Indian phenomenon for years. By some estimates, over half of India's children are underweight or malnourished today. This is the highest number in the world. In fact, together with our South Asian neighbours, we account for half the world's malnourished children. Malnutrition is the condition that occurs when a person's body is not getting enough nutrients. The condition may result from an inadequate or unbalanced diet, digestive difficulties, absorption problems, or other medical conditions. Malnutrition can occur because of the lack of a single vitamin in the diet, or it can be because a person is not getting enough food. Starvation is a form of malnutrition. Malnutrition also occurs when adequate nutrients are consumed in the diet, but one or more nutrients are not digested or absorbed properly. Malnutrition may be mild enough to show no symptoms. However, in some cases it may be so severe that the damage done is irreversible, even though the individual survives.

Worldwide, malnutrition continues to be a significant problem, especially among children who cannot fend adequately for themselves. Poverty, natural disasters, political problems, and war all contribute to conditions—even epidemics—of malnutrition and starvation, and not just in developing countries.

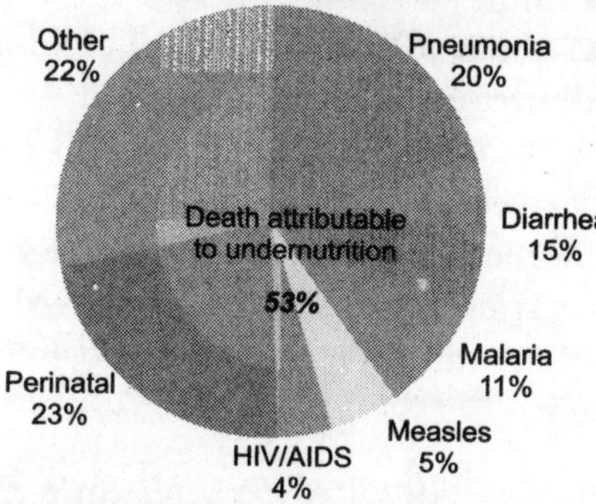

There are two types of nutritional problems—one is under-nutrition and another is over-nutrition. Under-nutrition means too little food, too little care and too little health. More emphasis should be given not only to food but also to care and health, the reason being that even if children in the age group of 0-2 years are able to get food, they may have mothers who do not have enough time to pay attention to their children. Similarly, if there is no health-guaranteeing environment, and children suffer from diarrhoeal diseases, no amount of food will help prevent malnutrition.

Over-nutrition, on the other hand, means either too many calories or the wrong types of calories such as saturated fats or highly processed sugar that lead to obesity, vascular diseases, etc. Many developing countries have under-nutrition and those in Europe and North America have over-nutrition problems. There is this in-between category with countries like India that still have an enormous amount of under-nutrition and significant over-nutrition problems. In India, for instance, around 50 per cent of its children under the age of five are undernourished or malnourished. But in urban areas, the over-nutrition problem is shooting up, thanks to the change in lifestyle and food habits. The point is that many countries in Asia face the problem of having to deal with the over-nutrition and under-nutrition simultaneously. As a result, their health systems are under huge stress.

Causes of Malnutrition

Malnutrition limits development and the capacity to learn. It also costs lives: about 50 per cent of all childhood deaths are attributed to malnutrition. In India, around 46 per cent of all children below the age of three are too small for their age, 47 per cent are underweight and at least 16 per cent are wasted. Many of these children are severely malnourished. The prevalence of malnutrition varies across states, with Madhya Pradesh recording the highest rate (55 per cent) and Kerala among the lowest (27 per cent).

Malnutrition in children is not affected by food intake alone; it is also influenced by access to health services, quality of care for the child and pregnant mother as well as good hygiene practices. Girls are more at risk of malnutrition than boys because of their lower social status. one in three of the world's malnourished children lives in India. Malnutrition in early childhood has serious, long-term consequences because it impedes motor, sensory, cognitive, social and emotional development. Malnourished children are less likely to perform well in school and more likely to grow into malnourished adults, at greater risk of disease and early death. Around one-third of all adult women are underweight. Inadequate care of women and girls, especially during pregnancy, results in low-birth weight babies. Nearly 30 per cent of all newborns have a low birth weight, making them vulnerable to further malnutrition and disease.

Vitamin and mineral deficiencies also affect children's survival and development. Anaemia affects 74 per cent of children under the age of three, more than 90 per cent of adolescent girls and 50 per cent of women. Iodine deficiency, which reduces learning capacity by up to 13 per cent, is widespread because fewer than half of all households use iodized salt. Vitamin A deficiency, which causes blindness and increases morbidity and mortality among pre-schoolers, also remains a public-health problem.

Micronutrient and/or protein deficiency is shown in a very large group of malnourished people. They either do not receive adequate amounts of vitamins and minerals (micronutrients), or the correct proportion of protein in their diets. This can also have very debilitating effects on people and societies. The health symptoms may not be immediately visible to either the individuals themselves or to health workers or they can take years to manifest themselves. The result is lost productivity, and a great increase in health care costs, which negatively affects other government attempts to improve the quality of life.

For example, many older people in all countries have serious protein and micronutrient deficiencies. As people age, their traditional foods may be difficult to chew, swallow or digest, or it may seem bland, and eating then loses its appeal. They may also simply forget to eat. And many aboriginal groups worldwide now suffer from a host of diseases previously unknown to them such as diabetes and certain cancers. This is largely due to a shift from more traditional diets, which included fresh meat, vegetables, fruits, legumes and nuts, to some of the highly processed foods of the "modern" society, which are often very nutrient-deficient.

Over-consumption, taking in many more calories than required, is often accompanied by a deficiency in vitamins and minerals. Many food companies sometimes exploit the human inclination towards fatty and sugary foods by offering consumers cheap and often nutritionally empty products. Compounded with their reduced physical activity and greater meat consumption, these people, the overweight and obese, are a fast-growing segment of the world's population. Ironically they often live, as the middle and upper class, in those countries where hunger is prevalent, such as in India and China. The health care costs, missed productivity and environmental costs associated with this group are huge.

There are a number of causes of malnutrition:

1. Food of poor quality and quantity is the main cause. Malnutrition is caused when a person does not get proper food according to his age and nature of work.

2. Due to poverty, the parents cannot afford proper nourishment for the children. The children get the diet, which is neither balanced nor nutritive.
3. Unhealthy physical surroundings and insanitary conditions in school and outside is another cause. The children do not get fresh air, sunlight and likeable surroundings.
4. Meals taken irregularly and untimely may also cause indigestion and dyspepsia. School children have generally to take meals at odd hours.
5. Some children are otherwise unhealthy. They do not benefit even from the most nutritive food. This may be due to lack of appetite, indigestion, constipation or any other cause.
6. If the child remains over burdened, worried and upset due to any reason, and does not get adequate rest or sleep, malnutrition will be caused in spite of good nutrition.

7. The adulteration of the eatables is another reason why even the costly food articles obtained from the market do not provide expected nutrition.

Symptoms of Malnutrition

The main symptoms of malnutrition are of two types—physical and mental. The physical conditions are laziness, dry hair, loose skin, depressed eyes and pale face, below normal weight, drowsiness, extreme weakness, fatigue and exhaustion, attack of diseases like rickets and beriberi, bad postures, unable to stand the strain of drill or sports in the sun and may faint, charmless and sorrowless face. The mental conditions are lack of concentration, irritability, unenthusiastic, gloomy nature, forgetful memory, slow comprehension and maladjustment. A seeming contradiction occurring in undernourished children is that although they might be lacking physical endurance, they are often hyperactive. A simple solution to the problem is to eat more of the proper nutrients. A balanced diet that includes a variety of foods, sufficient complex carbohydrates, and a minimal level of fat, sodium and cholesterol can be extremely beneficial to an undernourished child.

Role of a School Teacher

Food is one of the delights of every civilization. Eating a fine meal is an aesthetic experience, not just fulfillment of nutritional requirements, but even the simplest dish can provide great pleasure. Teachers can use this positive approach in presenting nutritional concepts. Too often nutrition is taught as a grim and dry subject, divorced from the human perspective. The development of positive lifetime eating habits among children is a critical issue. A parent or a teacher should not resort to using a punishment reward system when trying to get to eat; neither should each mealtime become a war zone.

Teachers should provide accurate information concerning nutrition and teach children how to make wise decision in order to help prevent undernourishment among students. They need to emphasize the importance of eating a good breakfast and lunch, as well as encourage sociability among students when they are eating. Teachers can help the students enjoy the taste, smell, colour and texture of food and thereby increase in it. In addition, teachers have an excellent chance to be exemplary role models by eating the right foods in the right way while at school.

Nutrients do not work as drugs might to cure an illness. Nutrients delivered from foods work with one another under the body's directions. The nourished, healthy body best keeps itself well. The well-built body—the body that best resists disease, lives the longest and enjoys the highest quality of life in the later years—is a body that receives all the nutrients necessary for optimum living. This kind of thinking is an example of the attitude of preventive nutrition, which supports a person's well being.

Mid-Day Meal Scheme

10

Introduction

With a view to enhancing enrolment, retention and attendance and simultaneously improving nutritional levels among children, the National Programme of Nutritional Support to Primary Education (NP-NSPE) was launched as a Centrally Sponsored Scheme on 15th August 1995, initially in 2408 blocks in the country. The programme also seeks to promote hygienic and sanitary practices, break caste prejudices through the sharing of meals, and foster gender equality among schoolchildren.

मध्याह्न भोजन योजना
Mid-Day Meal Scheme

By the year 1997-98 the NP-NSPE was introduced in all blocks of the country. It was further extended in 2002 to cover not only children in classes I-V of government, government aided and local body schools, but also children studying in EGS and AIE centers. Central Assistance under the scheme consisted of free supply of food grains @ 100 grams per child per school day, and subsidy for transportation of food grains up to a maximum of ₹ 50 per quintal.

In September 2004 the scheme was revised to provide cooked mid-day meal with 300 calories and 8-12 grams of protein to all children studying in classes I-V in Government and aided schools and EGS/AIE centers. In addition to free supply of food grains, the revised scheme provided Central Assistance for (a) Cooking cost @ ₹ 1 per child per school day, (b) Transport subsidy was raised from the earlier maximum of ₹ 50 per quintal to ₹ 100 per quintal for special category states, and ₹ 75 per quintal for other states, (c) Management, monitoring and evaluation costs @ 2 per cent of the cost of food grains, transport subsidy and cooking assistance, and (d) Provision of mid-day meal during summer vacation in drought affected areas.

In July 2006 the scheme was further revised to provide assistance for cooking cost at the rate of (a) ₹ 1.80 per child/school day for States in the North Eastern Region, provided the NER states contribute ₹ 0.20 per child/school day, and (b) ₹ 1.50 per child/school day for other States and UTs, provided that these States and UTs contribute ₹ 0.50 per child/school day.

Objectives

The objectives of the mid-day meal scheme are:

- Protecting children from classroom hunger.
- Increasing school enrolment and attendance.
- Improved socialization among children belonging to all castes.
- Addressing malnutrition, and social empowerment through provision of employment to women.
- Improving the nutritional status of children in classes I-V in Government, Local Body and Government aided schools, and EGS and AIE centers.
- Encouraging poor children, belonging to disadvantaged sections, to attend school more regularly and help them concentrate on classroom activities.

- Providing nutritional support to children of primary stage in drought affected areas during summer vacation.

The scheme has a long history especially in Tamil Nadu and Gujarat, and has been expanded to all parts of India after a landmark direction by the Supreme Court of India on November 28, 2001. The success of this scheme is illustrated by the tremendous increase in the school participation and completion rates in the state of Tamilnadu. Allocation for this programme has been enhanced from ₹ 3010 crore to ₹ 4813 crore (₹ 48 billion, $1.2 billion) in 2006-07. Akshaya Patra Foundation is running this programme and is the world's largest school meal programme being implemented across seven states in India and covering about ten lakh students in over 4,800 schools. The allocation was of ₹ 8000 crore for the Mid-Day meal schemes in the Interim Budget 2009.

Akshaya Patra Foundation a non-profit Bangalore-based secular trust evolved the free meal programme in schools in the year 2000. It is one of the most successful public-private partnerships, which has successfully proved that the government in association with the private sector can achieve much if they get together. The mid-day meal provided by Akshaya Patra is funded equally by Government mid-day meal grants and by the generosity of the private sector. What started as a pilot project in five schools in Bangalore, feeding 1,500 children, has now grown into a mammoth endeavour covering over 9,83,000 children in over 4,500 government, government aided schools and anganwadis (day care centers) in 17 locations spread across seven states in India, day after day. This is amongst the largest school meal NGO run programme in the world. The foundation expects to reach a magical figure of five million children by 2020.

Six days a week, without a stop, the foundation provides unlimited, nutritious, hygienically cooked noon meals in government schools and government-run day-care centers (anganwadis). Ushering in a technology-intensive operating model that ensures high-quality, hygienic food on the one hand

and increases internal efficiencies on the other, the programme has brought about policy changes at the state government levels and created a new image for mid-day meals in India. A study in the year 2006 by AC Nielsen Org Marg, has vouchsafed for the efficacy of the programme in increasing attendance in schools, improving nutritional status of these children, enhancing their learning abilities and reducing drop out rates. The foundation's work has been praised by all quarters and a recent feather in its cap has been the study conducted by Harvard Business School.

Programme Intervention and Coverage

To achieve the above objectives a cooked mid-day meal with nutritional content as shown in column 3 of the table below will be provided to all children studying in classes I-V:

Nutritional Content	Norm as per NP-NSPE, 2004	Revised Norm as per NP-NSPE, 2006
Calories	300	450
Protein	8-12	12
Micronutrients adequate	Not Prescribed	Quantity of micronutrients like iron, folic acid, Vitamin-A, etc.

Monitoring Mechanism

The Department of School Education and Literacy, Ministry of Human Resource Development has prescribed a comprehensive and elaborate mechanism for monitoring and supervision of the Mid-Day Meal Scheme. The monitoring mechanism includes the following:

Arrangements for local level monitoring

Representatives of Gram Panchayats/Gram Sabhas, members of VECs, PTAs, SDMCs as well as Mothers' Committees are required to monitor the (i) regularity and wholesomeness of the mid-day meal served to children, (ii) cleanliness in cooking and serving of the mid-day meal, (iii) timeliness in procurement of good quality ingredients, fuel, etc., (iv) implementation of varied menu, and (v) social and gender equity. This is required to be done on a daily basis.

Display of information under Right to Information Act

In order to ensure that there is transparency and accountability, all schools and centers where the programme is being implemented are required to display information *suo-moto*. This includes information on:

- Quality of food grains received, date of receipt.
- Quantity of food grains utilized.
- Other ingredients purchased and utilized.
- Number of children given mid day meal.
- Daily Menu.
- Roster of Community Members involved in the programme.

Inspections by state government officers

Officers of the State Government/UTs belonging to the Departments of Revenue, Rural Development, Education and other related sectors, such as Women and Child Development, Food, Health are also required to inspect schools and centers where the programme is being implemented. It has been recommended that 25 per cent of primary schools/EGS & AIE centers are visited every quarter.

Responsibility of Food Corporation of India (FCI)

The FCI is responsible for the continuous availability of adequate food grains in its Depots (and in Principal Distribution

Centers in the case of North East Region). It allows lifting of food grains for any month/quarter upto one month in advance so that supply chain of food grains remains uninterrupted. For the NP-NSPE, 2006, the FCI is mandated to issue food grains of best available quality, which will in any case be at least of Fair Average Quality (FAQ). The FCI appoints a Nodal Officer for each State to take care of various problems in supply of food grains under the MDM Programme.

Periodic returns

The State Government/UT is also required to submit periodic returns to the Department of School Education and Literacy, Government of India to provide information on: (i) coverage of children and institutions, (ii) Progress in utilisation of Central assistance, including cooking costs, transportation, and construction of kitchen sheds and procurement of kitchen devices.

- Monitoring by Institutions of Social Science Research

Forty one Institutions of Social Science Research, identified for monitoring the Sarva Shiksha Abhiyan, are also entrusted with the task of monitoring the Mid-Day Scheme.

- Grievance Redressal

States and Union Territories are required to develop a dedicated mechanism for public grievance redressal, which should be widely publicized and made easily accessible.

Extension to Upper Primary Stage

The Finance Minister has announced in the Union Budget 2007-08 that the Mid-Day Meal Scheme will be extended to cover children in Upper Primary Classes in 3427 Educationally Backward Blocks (EBBs) in 2007-08. A Budget provision of ₹ 7324 crores has been made for this purpose, representing 37% increase over the budget for 2006-07. The programme would cover all areas across the country from 2008-09. According to state government statistics, at present over 171 crore primary students and 41 lakh secondary students are getting mid-day meals in schools.

The MDM programme has helped in promoting school participation, preventing class room hunger, instilling educational values and fostering social and gender equality. The scheme, in its first year of implementation, has led to some positive outcomes: elimination of class room hunger; increase in enrollment, more significantly of girls; surge in daily attendance, particularly of girls and children from poorer sections; improvement in retention, learning ability and achievement; curbing of teacher absenteeism and narrowing of social distance.

In a new path-breaking initiative, it has been decided to empower mothers of children covered under the scheme to supervise the preparation and serving of the meal. Mothers are being encouraged to come forward and take turn to supervise the feeding of the children, thus ensuring regularity and quality of the meal. This initiative is aimed at giving mothers a voice and a role and greater ownership of the programme. States have been requested to launch a concerted campaign for mass mobilization of mothers. In 16 districts, Mahila Samakhya has been given responsibility of serving mid-day meal to the children.

Anomalies in Midday Meal Scheme for schools in India

The Controller and Auditor General of India's annual report have revealed several irregularities in the implementation of the midday meal scheme in a north Indian state. This has left many children deprived of the benefits of the programme and has severely affected the goal of universalization of primary education. According to a recently released annual report by the Controller and Auditor General of India, around 76 per cent of schools in Uttar Pradesh use low-quality food grain for midday meals. The report also highlights several irregularities in the scheme's implementation. "Inspection of food grain used revealed that broken grains in excess of permissible limits, foreign matter and damaged grains were used in 243 schools of the 320 inspected," says the annual report by the Controller and Auditor General of India that contains audit observations of the midday meal scheme for 2006-2007.

"Improvement in the nutritional status of the children was not ensured by providing micro-nutrient supplements and de-worming medicines. No periodical health check-up of the children was conducted either," it adds. Stating that the Uttar Pradesh Government did not conduct a baseline survey during 2004-05 to determine the enrolment of children, as directed by the Centre, the report says: "The data relating to attendance and retention of children was not also collected." Further, the report indicates misuse of funds and financial irregularities. It reports that food grain worth ₹ 121.98 crore remained with the transporting agencies (2002-2007) and fair price shops (2005-2007), indicating poor transportation of grain.

Limited Reach

Apart from these irregularities, the report also focuses on the reach of the scheme. Around 1.63 crore children in drought-affected areas did not receive the benefit of the scheme during the summer vacation of 2005 and 2007, violating the directives of the Supreme Court. Of the 96,457 schools in the state, 36,489 did not have kitchen sheds. Of the 320 schools inspected, around 61 did not have adequate kitchen devices and potable water. Earlier, in May 2009, the Uttar Pradesh Government found that many schools were not implementing the scheme and initiated action against the principals and teachers of around 105 government-run schools in Hamirpur district. About 150,000 schools are covered by the midday meal scheme in Uttar Pradesh. Under the scheme, lunch is provided to students till Class 8. Over 18.6 million students are enrolled under the scheme. According to the rules, every child must be given a meal each day for at least 200 days a year.

Immunization

11

Immunization is the process by which an individual's immune system becomes fortified against an agent known as ***Immunogen***. It is a process whereby a person is made immune or resistant to an infectious disease, typically by the administration of a vaccine. Immunization prepares our bodies to fight against diseases in case we come into contact with them in the future. Vaccines stimulate the body's own immune system to protect the person against subsequent infection or disease. Immunization is a proven tool for controlling and eliminating life-threatening infectious diseases and is estimated to avert over 2 million deaths each year. It is one of the most cost-effective health investments, with proven strategies that make it accessible to even the most hard-to-reach and vulnerable populations. It has clearly defined target groups; it can be delivered effectively through outreach activities and vaccination does not require any major lifestyle change.

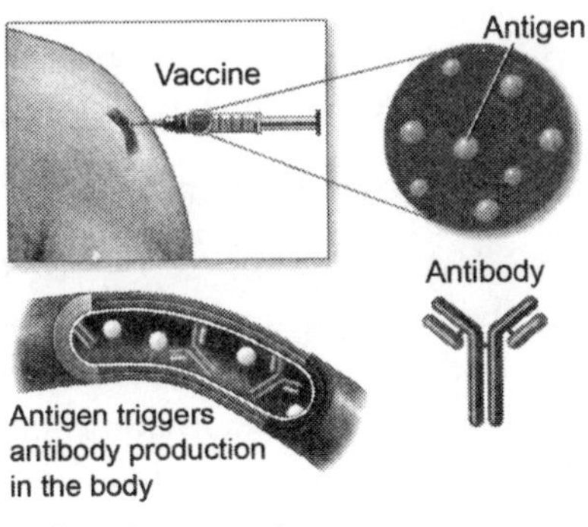

Active and Passive Immunity

Active immunity refers to the process of exposing the body to an antigen to generate an adaptive immune response: the response takes days/weeks to develop but may be long-lasting—even lifelong. Active immunity is usually classified as natural or acquired. Wild infection for example with hepatitis A virus (HAV) and subsequent recovery gives rise to a natural active immune response usually leading to lifelong protection. In a similar manner, administration of two doses of Hepatitis A vaccine generates an acquired active immune response leading to long-lasting (possibly lifelong) protection. Hepatitis A vaccine has only been licensed since the late 1980s so that follow-up studies of duration of protection are limited to <25 years—hence, the preceding caveat about duration of protection.

Passive immunity refers to the process of providing IgG antibodies to protect against infection; it gives immediate, but short-lived protection—several weeks to 3 or 4 months at most. Passive immunity is usually classified as natural or acquired. The transfer of maternal tetanus antibody (mainly IgG) across the placenta provides natural passive immunity for the newborn baby for several weeks/months until such antibody is degraded and lost. In contrast, acquired passive immunity refers to the process of obtaining serum from immune individuals, pooling this, concentrating the immunoglobulin fraction and then injecting it to protect a susceptible person.

Types of Acquired Immunity

There are thus four types of specific resistance or acquired immunity that are generally recognized. These are:

1. *Naturally acquired active immunity*

This immunity develops after antigens (e.g., microbial pathogens) enter the body by natural processes such as infection and, in response the body's immune system forms antibodies. In some cases, the immunity may be lifelong as with smallpox, measles, chickenpox, yellow fever, etc. In other cases, however, the immunity may be lost after only a few years (e.g., diphtheria, tetanus) or even for lesser period.

2. *Naturally acquired passive immunity*

When antibodies produced in the body of an individual (called donor) are naturally transferred into the body of other individual (called recipient), the latter develops immunity, called naturally acquired passive immunity, in its immune system. This immunity is natural because the transfer of antibodies from donor to recipient occurs under natural conditions, and it is passive because the recipient does not synthesize antibodies but picks them up from the donor. The best example of this type of immunity is the natural transfer of antibodies from the mother to the foetus across the placenta.

Certain antibodies are also transferred from mother to infant through colostrums and milk during nursing. These antibodies, called maternal antibodies, remain with the child for about three to six months or, sometimes, twelve to fifteen months, and after the specified time the immune state disappears. The maternal antibodies generally provide resistance against whooping cough, diphtheria, German measles, disease of respiratory and gastrointestinal tract, etc.

3. *Artificially acquired active immunity*

When a carefully chosen antigen (e.g., vaccine, chemically altered toxins called toxids) is intentionally introduced into a body to be immunized, the latter develops immunity that is called artificially acquired active immunity. This immunity is artificial because the antigens are intentionally or purposely introduced, and it is active because the recipient's immune system synthesizes antibodies. Vaccines provide usually long-term immunity. Vaccines are now available against many infectious diseases such as cholera, tuberculosis, plague, pneumonia, rocky mountain spotted fever, smallpox, polio, tetanus, influenza, measles, rabies, yellow fever, etc. Toxids are currently available for protection against diphtheria and tetanus, the two diseases whose major effects are due to toxins.

4. *Artificially acquired passive immunity*

Artificially acquired passive immunity is that which develops as a result of the international introduction of antibody-rich serum (blood plasma devoid of clotting factors) taken from diseased individual to another susceptible individual. It was an important therapeutic device for disease treatment before the vaccines were developed and is still used for viral diseases such as hepatitis B, chicken pox, arthropod-borne encephalitis, and for bacterial disease such as botulism, diphtheria, tetanus, staphylococcal-poisoning where toxins are involved in disease causation. Since these diseases are very dangerous and fatal, already-made antibodies present in serum are introduced into the blood of the susceptible individual for quick response and no risk is taken for introduction of antigens. Artificially acquired passive immunity is immediate but short-lived (only for two to three weeks).

How does Immunization Work

Immunization operates on the premise that once we have had a disease, we are unlikely to contract it again. Through injections, oral drops or scratches on the skin, the body is exposed to weakened or dead disease-producing microorganisms or to the toxins they produce. This will cause the individual to develop the same antibodies and antitoxins that would have been developed if the person had actually contracted the disease, in order to fight the disease. Once the body has been exposed to an infection, the immune system will "recognize" if the disease were to recur, and produce antibodies or antitoxins to destroy the infection. The body has to be exposed to infection once for the immune system to recognize it. This is done through immunization. The most important elements of the immune system that are improved by immunization are the B-cells (and the antibodies they produce) and T-cells. Memory B-cells and memory T-cells are responsible for a swift response to a second encounter with a foreign molecule.

Child Immunization

Babies are born with some natural immunity, which they get from their mother and through breast-feeding. This gradually wears off, as the baby's own immune system starts to develop. Having the child immunized gives extra protection against illnesses, which can kill. Vaccinations should start when the baby is 1½ months old. Even if the baby is brought late for vaccinations, she/he should still receive all the vaccinations. While it is the best to follow the ideal immunization schedule, on no account should the baby be denied vaccinations, even if she/he is brought late for them. But every attempt must be made to complete full immunization, before the age of one year.

Ideal Immunization Schedule for the Infants

(Recommended by the Ministry of Health, Government of India)

At 1½ months	B.C.G. (injection)
	D.P.T. - 1 (injection) and
	O.P.V. - 1 (dose)
At 2½ months	D.P.T. - 2 (injection) and
	O.P.V. - 2 (dose)
At 3½ months	D.P.T. - 3 (injection) and
	O.P.V. - 3 (dose)
At 9 months	Measles (injection)
16 to 24 months	D.P.T. Booster (injection) and
	O.P.V. Booster (dose)

If the infant has been delivered in a hospital/clinic. She should be given the B.C.G. injection at birth.

Vaccine Preventable Diseases

1. *DPT vaccine*

This is given when the child is 1½, 2½ and 3½ months old with a booster at the age of 1½ years. It protects against three diseases, viz. Diptheria, Polio and Tetanus.

2. *Diphtheria*

It is an acute infectious disease of childhood caused by bacteria. It usually manifests with sore throat and quickly progresses to fever, headache and loss of appetite. It can damage the heart, the nervous system and in severe cases it can kill. Though the incidence of diphtheria has greatly reduced but it has not yet completely wiped out.

3. *Pertussis*

Also associated with whooping cough is a highly contagious disease of the respiratory tract. It starts with features of a common cold but quickly progresses to a severe exhausting cough. The cough comes in prolonged bouts during which the child appears unable to breathe and looks anxious. It lasts for upto 6-8 weeks and leaves the child extremely weak and malnourished because of vomitting associated with cough and the disinclination to eat because of the fear of precipitating bank of cough.

4. *Tetanus*

The germs of tetanus are found in soil. They can enter the body through a cut, a bruise or a prick of thorn. The toxin of tetanus acts on the nervous system, which then affects the muscle causing severe stiffness of spasms. It is a very painful and distressing illness which if not treated promptly can lead to death. It can start innocuously as stiffness in the neck or spasm of the jaw and then rapidly progresses to lead to breathing difficulties and severe painful spasms of the limbs or the back, etc.

5. *Polio vaccine*

Polio is a disease caused by a virus that attacks the nervous system and can cause permanent muscle paralysis or weakness. When the virus affects the muscles of the chest, it can kill because of the paralysis of the muscles used in respiration. It is given at the age of 1½, 2½ and 3½ months, usually along with the DPP vaccine. Booster doses are given at the age of 18 months. Additionally for the last few years the Government of India has been running the Pulse Polio Program in which all children under the age of 5 years are given polio drops twice a year in addition to their vaccination schedule.

6. *BCG vaccine*

The vaccine can be administered right after the birth and if not taken then it can be taken as early as possible with other vaccines. This vaccine affords protection against Tuberculosis, a disease, which primarily affects the lungs, though it can involve virtually any system of the body. It usually manifests coughs of long duration, loss of weight and night sweats.

7. *Measles vaccine*

It is a given at the age of 9 months. It is a disease of the respiratory tract, which begins with fever, cough, running nose and watery eye. The rash of measles is very characteristic of the disease, starting on the neck and quickly spreading to the trunk and limbs. Measles is very infectious; the complications occur in a fair percentage of children who feel it. These include chest infectious, fits, brain damage, etc.

Side Effects of Vaccinations

Very rarely, one hears of cases where immunization has resulted in the development of fatal complications. Most children have a mild reaction to immunization, but a few have become seriously ill. With some vaccines there is a negligible risk of serious or permanent damage or even death. One should take certain precautions before vaccinating the child. It him/her to be made sure that the child is in good health before taking her for the vaccine and report any side effects to the doctor immediately. It has to be remembered that the advantages of immunization far outweigh its drawbacks. It is because of immunization that a disease like small pox has been eradicated.

Only very few infants and children develop side effects after a vaccination. After the D.P.T. injection, the infant may have pain at the site of the injection and may even develop fever. In that case the baby may be given 1/2 a table or 1/2 a teaspoon of paracetamol. After the measles injection, measles like rashes may appear. These are normal. Very rarely, children can have allergic reactions straight after immunization. Also if the baby develops high fever or loses consciousness, a doctor should be consulted immediately. People giving immunizations are trained to deal with allergic reactions and if the child is treated quickly, he or she will recover fully.

Routine Immunization in India

Delivering effective and safe vaccines through an efficient delivery system is one of the most cost effective public health interventions. Immunization programmes aim to reduce mortality and morbidity due to vaccine preventable diseases (VPDs). Following the successful global eradication of smallpox in 1975 through effective vaccination programmes and strengthened surveillance, the Expanded Programme on Immunization (EPI) was launched in India in 1978 to control other VPDs. Initially, six diseases were selected: diphtheria, pertussis, tetanus, poliomyelitis, typhoid and childhood tuberculosis. The aim was to cover 80 per cent of all infants. Subsequently, the programme was universalised and renamed as Universal Immunization Programme (UIP) in 1985. Measles vaccine was included in the programme and typhoid vaccine was discontinued. The UIP was introduced in a phased manner from 1985 to cover all districts in the country by 1990, targeting all infants with the primary immunization schedule and all pregnant women with Tetanus Toxoid immunization.

The UIP envisages achieving and sustaining universal immunization coverage in infants with three doses of DPT and OPV and one dose each of measles vaccine and BCG, and, in pregnant women, with two primary doses or one booster dose of TT. The UIP also requires a reliable cold chain system for storing and transporting vaccines, and attaining self-sufficiency in the production of all required vaccines.

In 1992, the UIP became a part of the Child Survival and Safe Motherhood Programme (CSSM), and in 1997, it became an important component of the Reproductive and Child Health Programme (RCH). The cold-chain system was strengthened and training programmes were launched extensively throughout the country. Intensified polio eradication activities were started in 1995-96 under the Polio Eradication programme, beginning with National Immunization Days (NIDs) and active surveillance for acute flaccid paralysis (AFP). The Polio Eradication Programme was set up with the assistance of the National Polio Surveillance Project.

Routine Immunization Monitoring Systems (RIMS)

India's Immunization Programme is one of the largest in the world in terms of quantities of vaccines used, numbers of beneficiaries, and the numbers of immunization sessions organized, the geographical spread and diversity of areas covered. Under the immunization programme, six vaccines are used to protect children and pregnant mothers against Tuberculosis, Diphtheria, Pertussis, Polio, Measles and Tetanus. It is also proposed to include Hepatitis B vaccine in UIP in phased manner.

For a complex and extensive programme like immunization an efficient management information system is necessary to get timely reports at State and National level. It is also equally important to provide feedback to the States and Districts for undertaking management interventions. At present the programme has to depend upon routine reports received as part of the reporting under the Reproductive and Child Health (RCH) programme. This system provides feedback on coverage data only. Important information regarding the vaccines and cold chain logistics which are high cost areas does not get captured in the present system and a lot of effort and time is required in getting the critical data on these issues for planning and forecasting requirements and monitoring the status of vaccine supply and availability. To address these issues now and to collect data from District/PHC level a computer based monitoring system (RIMS software) is underdevelopment for implementation throughout the country. A prototype of this software to assess practical applicability in the field has been developed.

Routine immunization monitoring system (RIMS) is a computerized implementation, to enter data, generate reports and perform queries. The system is presently developed in Microsoft Access as a standalone CD version. It is user friendly and no special training is required to operate the system. Online system is underdevelopment in a different platform using other database and programming tools. The data are collected at district level from PHCs/Reporting Units in the standard pre-designed UIP format and entered on five broad categories namely (a) Immunization and Vitamin A, (b) Vaccine Supply, (c) VPD Surveillance, (d) Status of Cold-Chain Equipment and (e) AEFI (Adverse Event following immunization). The system is capable of performing data analyses and generating useful reports for the use of UPI managers at all levels, i.e. district, state and national. RIMS will be very useful tool to monitor UIP programme as reports from all the 600 districts will be collected in a short period and then analyzed automatically by the software.

In the field of immunization, WHO's roles and responsibilities include:

- supporting and facilitating research and development;
- improving the quality and safety of vaccines;
- developing policy recommendations and strategies for optimizing the use of and maximizing access to vaccines;
- facilitating reduction of financial and technical barriers to the introduction of vaccines and technologies;
- supporting countries in acquiring the skills and developing the infrastructure needed to expand

immunization services delivery and achieve disease control and eradication;

- providing technical assistance where needed;
- developing and maintaining collaboration between partners; and
- monitoring global progress towards the achievements of immunization goals.

Medical Inspection and Health Records

12

The question of school medical service was considered by the Central Advisory Board of Education at their 7th meeting held in January 1942 on the basis of a report made by the Joint Committee appointed by the Central Advisory Board of Health and the Central Advisory Board of Education. The Committee made detailed recommendation on the question of Medical Inspection, Treatment and Follow up, Nutrition, Personal and Environmental Hygiene in Schools, Physical Education and Administrative set-up. The recommendations of the Joint Committee were further considered and approved by the Central Advisory Board of Education in their report on post-war Educational Development in India.

Periodical and systematic medical examination in schools once or twice a year is very important for the health and physical well-being of the students. It helps to keep the students physically and mentally fit so that they can carry out their studies properly. This objective of medical inspection can be fulfilled only when it is carried on in an effective way. It should be thorough and comprehensive and should not be treated as a mere routine. It should not merely concern itself with the height, weight and chest measurements but should also concern itself with ears, teeth, eyes, nose, heart and lungs, etc. In fact no part of the body should be left unexamined as far as possible. The first inspection should be at the time of admission of the child in the school. If it is found out that the child is suffering from some chronic disease, he may be refused admission. Child should be examined every year. The last inspection will be just prior to leaving the school, which reveals the strength and weakness of the child and helps him to choose some vocation suited to his physical development also.

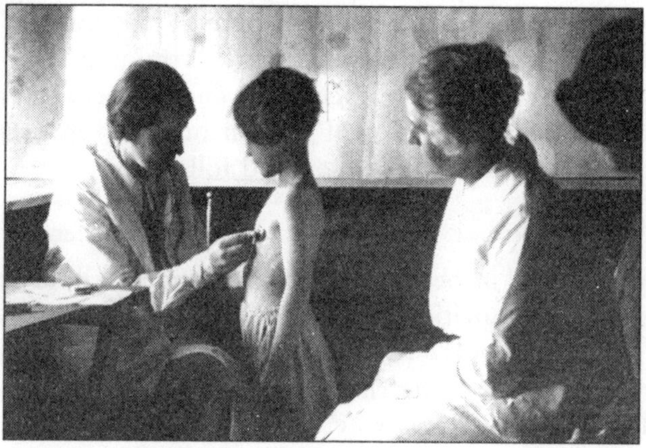

Students with serious defects should be examined more frequently. Remedial measures should be taken to remove defects. Three copies of the report should be prepared. One should be sent to the parents, another should be kept by the teacher-in-charge and the medical officer should keep the third one. Effective collaboration between the home and the school is required to discharge responsibilities towards health check up and follow-up.

Some Recommendations

We may follow some of the recommendations given by the Joint Committee appointed by the Central Advisory Board of Health and the Central Advisory Board of Education to make medical inspection in schools more effective.

1. *Improving financial conditions*

The conditions of government-aided secondary schools are very miserable in India. School management faces lack of finances. So, more finance should be made available for health schemes in schools and colleges. The general economic position of our country is not good therefore, immediate efforts must be concentrated on the maximum utilization of the existing resources.

2. *Team work and training*

Much of the work of improving medical inspection can be taken up by teachers and students both in the form of social work and a part of their normal practical training. Along with this, refresher courses for teachers to enable them to take up some of the routine work will help in building up eventually machinery for medical inspection and follow-up.

3. *Nutrition*

After medical inspection, it is often found that poor students suffer from mal-nutrition. So states should start small projects under which schools, parents and state governments may cooperate to provide nutrition to undernourished groups in secondary schools. In this way, we will get better results in the field of medical inspection improvement.

4. *Health education and physical education*

The health education of adults will have a wholesome effect on children and hence all adult education centers should include health education as an integral part of their syllabus so that the knowledge may filter down to the children. In other words, along with school's efforts, health and physical education given to adults help the family members of students to take medical inspection seriously and this awareness will be learnt by students themselves.

5. *Pilot projects*

With regard to the improvement of school medical service, the Board suggested for pilot projects. In these projects, medical students, teachers, social workers, existing clinics, youth clubs and youth hostels should be included to complete the project related to making medical inspection effective.

6. *Compulsory specialized subject*

The committee suggested that schools should provide education to students with a specialized subject in secondary schools. In this way students will understand the importance of medical inspection and will cooperate their teachers in its effective procedure.

Other Efforts

Along with these efforts suggested by the committee other steps should also be taken to make medical inspection effective in schools. These efforts are:

1. *Opportunity to medical inspector*

In a study done on Asian school in September 2009 it was found that when medical inspectors of schools get proper opportunities by education authority to voice their opinion, standard of medical inspection in school improves. Similarly, Dr. Abdurrahman (2009) says that for better medical inspection in schools remedies suggested by medical inspectors should be adopted. Therefore, in the light of these studies, it can be said that as medical inspectors are experts and professionals, so for making medical inspection effective their suggestions should be welcomed.

2. *Healthy and effective policy*

For making medical inspection effective, a healthy and effective policy is specially needed. Seeing the poor conditions of school medical inspection D.K. Sriniwas and Adkoli (2009) suggested that serious efforts should be made to develop a National Health Profession Education Policy. Through policies efforts are made in systematic and organized way.

3. *Efforts by parents and teachers*

Parents and teachers too should try on their own level. For example they should bring the defects in the child to the notice of the doctor in the period intervening between two periods of medical inspection. Parents and teachers should be aware and conscious for their children and students respectively. They should be present at the time of inspection and should know the physical and mental condition of children and should try to improve it.

4. *Doctor's visit*

Frequent visit of a doctor to the school will be helpful in making medical inspection effective. It will develop positive attitude in parents that scientific procedure is being adopted for their children's medical inspection and the treatment suggested by the doctors will give effective results.

5. *High standard qualifications of inspecting staff*

Only a qualified staff should carry out the medical inspection. The head of the staff should be a registered practitioner of modern scientific medicine and all the staff should have the experience of special training, otherwise medical inspection done by untrained persons might create a big problem. For example, eyesight loss, any sort of infection, etc. Therefore, needed qualification of the inspecting staff will help in making medical inspection effective.

6. *Inspection place*

For making medical inspection effective, presence of all the teachers and students is needed. So, inspection should be done in the school premises during school hours. In this way, all the students will get the opportunity to be present in the medical inspection.

The school physician should regularly examine the health of the student. On his advice, special diet should be given to the students and they should be admitted in schools, according to his advice. It is the duty of the school doctor to find out children suffering from infectious diseases and make arrangements for their isolation so that other students may not catch the infection. He should supervise the work of the school nurse and maintain a record of child's health. He should also inspect the arrangements of light, air, sanitation and physical exercise in the school.

Provision of a nurse is also necessary besides a physician, because with her cooperation, it becomes easier to gain knowledge of children's health. The school nurse should daily keep an eye over the cleanliness of children. She should inform the students of the date and time of medical examination so that they may appear at the appointed hour. It is also her duty to maintain a card recording the facts about the student's health. It is necessary to have the previous history of the student in preparing his card. She should visit every house and acquaint herself with the family and home environment of the student.

The medical examination work in the school will remain incomplete in the absence of teacher's cooperation with the doctor. It is, therefore, necessary that their cooperation is available to the doctor. Besides, the teacher should have a reasonable knowledge of infectious diseases, their diagnoses and treatment. Proper treatment should be started of the diseases diagnosed during medical examination. If careful and proper treatment is not undertaken, all the labour of the school doctor will be lost. A school dispensary for proper treatment is necessary for treating cases of ear, nose, throat, teeth, eyes, and vertebral column diseases.

Follow-up

Medical inspection is of no use unless proper follow-up work is undertaken. Mere diagnosis will not serve the purpose of health education. Rather no time should be lost while undertaking follow-up. In many cases it will not involve heavy expenditure or extra burden. A slight care or a timely and simple treatment will bring about good results. The cooperation of the parents should also be sought. If they are unable to take remedial steps due to poverty, the school should take upon itself the entire responsibility. The state or public hospitals should be involved in poor cases and acute cases. In any case such remedial measures as the school medical officer may suggest should be adopted, and the school authorities should see that they are carried out.

School Staff and Health of the Students

Apart from medical inspection by the doctor, the teacher as a follow-up of instructions regarding personal hygiene should make daily inspection of the general cleanliness of the students. It does not cost much and can be carried out quickly.

Personal cleanliness

The daily morning inspection of the cleanliness of the students by the teacher is very helpful in enforcing personal cleanliness. A rapid survey of the class should be made. Competition may be introduced among the students, cleanliness chart may be prepared and marks allotted to them.

Development of habits regarding air

Stress should be laid on the need of fresh air at all times and especially while sleeping. The students should be asked not to cover their mouth at night and should be taught to breathe through their nose.

Training in first-aid habits

The students should be instructed to give immediate attention to cuts and bruises.

Vaccination and inoculation

At times of epidemics, precautionary measures should be suggested to them and they should be vaccinated and inoculated.

Development of habits of hygienic feeding

The student should be taught to take right type of food in a suitable quantity. They should be warned of the dangers of over-eating. The students should be made to understand the importance of drinking plenty of water.

Selection of suitable physical exercises

A variety of physical activity programmes should exist in a school so that the students may choose activities to their liking.

Formation of good classroom habits

A wise teacher would always pay due attention to the postures of the students. The students may be instructed in other classroom matters where the students can form good habits.

Development of better human relations in matters concerning health

Every child should be asked to make it a point to do his best for the betterment of the health of his friends, relatives, neighbours and the whole community.

Medical inspection and follow-up work

Medical examination should be thorough and the follow-up work taken seriously.

Thus, we see that there are a number of ways for the improvement of medical inspection. If the school administration along with teachers, students and parents follow these ways, medical inspection can be made effective.

School Health Records

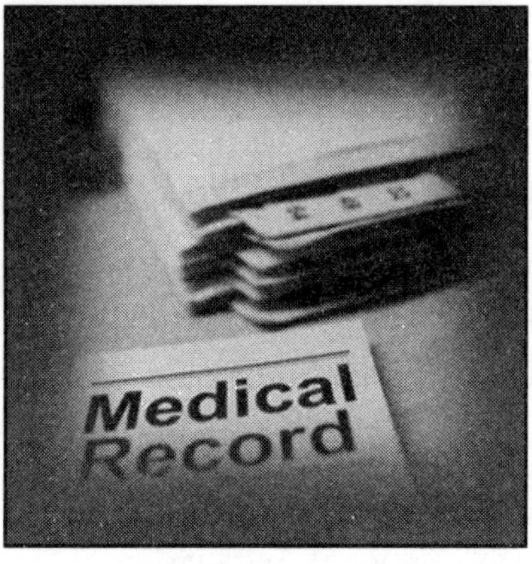

One of the most challenging responsibilities of school medical inspector is managing the many types of student health records, both paper and electronic. They include documents such as immunization records, screening records, progress notes, physician orders, physical examination records, medication and treatment logs, individualized health care plans, emergency health care plans, consent forms, medicaid and other insurance billing forms.

School health records provide the mechanism for a school doctor and nurse to communicate information to students, families, the school multidisciplinary team, emergency personnel, other health care providers, and school nurse substitutes. Data from school health records can be used to show evidence of student health problems that should be addressed. Data can also be used for evaluation of school health programmes, quality assurance, and evaluation of programme outcomes. School health records are transferred to new school sites when a student progresses to other buildings within a district or moves to another district or school.

It is important for school districts to have policies and procedures regarding the types, maintenance, protection, access, retention, destruction, and confidentiality of student health records. State laws and regulations may dictate these policies and procedures (Harrigan, 2002). As society and the health care system are moving from paper to electronic technology, so too is the school health office. Technology currently in use to receive and transmit student health information includes: Answering machines, Cellular and cordless telephones, E-mail via computer, Fax machine (fax), Voice mail, etc.

The following areas are considered when examining a school health records system:

- The foundation and rationale for any school health records system should be based on who needs the information, what information they need for the benefit of the student, and who has the expertise to interpret the records (National Association of State School Nurse Consultants, 2000; Schwab and Gelfman, 2001).

- School health records are maintained for purposes of communication, legal evidence, research, education, quality assurance monitoring, statistics, accrediting/licensing, and reimbursement (Schwab, Panettieri, and Bergren, 1998).
- Management of student health records includes their generation, maintenance, protection, disclosure, and destruction. Privacy, confidentiality, and consent are related to record management (NASN, 2002).
- Paper records are generally kept in locked files. Some school staff will need immediate access to some health information, such as that in emergency care plans, and written instructions for care providers (Schwab and Gelfman, 2001).
- Fax machines are widely used for transmitting health information. In schools, fax machines streamline accessing such records as immunizations, parental permissions, doctor's orders, clinic records, and pharmacy communications regarding medications (Bergren, 2001).
- E-mail has become a standard method of communicating in the school setting among staff in and outside of the school district. E-mail is self-documenting and can be retained in a paper or electronic health record at the time of the exchange, eliminating the need for additional notation. The original message is preserved into a file by downloading (Bergren, 2001).

Health information in either paper or electronic form must be confidential, secure, accessible only by authorized staff, and protected from loss or destruction. Information transmitted via the newer technologies is different from paper records in that it can be fairly easily misdirected, intercepted, and read by recipients for whom it is not intended. Because of this, new methods of security must be undertaken.

Student Records: Three Categories

Student records fall into three basic categories: permanent, temporary, and directory information.

Permanent records shall contain the following information:

- Basic identifying information, including both the student's and parent's names and addresses, and student birth date, birthplace, and gender.
- Academic transcript, including grades, class rank, graduation date or grade level achieved, and scores on college entrance examinations.
- Attendance record.
- Health record and accident reports.
- Record of release of permanent record information.
- Honours and awards received.
- Information concerning participation in school-sponsored activities or athletics, or offices held in school-sponsored organizations.

Temporary records must contain a record of release of temporary record information and may include the following:

- Family background information.
- Intelligence test scores, both group and individual.
- Aptitude test scores.
- Elementary and secondary achievement level test results.
- Reports of psychological evaluations, including information on intelligence, personality, and academic information obtained through test administration, observation, or interviews.
- Participation in extracurricular activities, including any offices held in school sponsored clubs or organizations.
- Honours and awards received.
- Teacher anecdotal records.

- Disciplinary information, including information regarding serious disciplinary infractions that resulted in expulsion, suspension, or the imposition of punishment or sanction.
- Other verified information of clear relevance to the education of the student.

Directory information is that information that may be released to the general public in publications such as athletic programmes or news articles, and in school publications, such as year books. This information is limited to the following:

- Identifying information to include name, address, gender, grade level, birth date and birthplace, and parents' names and addresses.
- Academic awards and honours.
- Information in relation to school-sponsored activities, organizations, and athletics.
- Major field of study.
- Period of attendance in the school.

Parents have the right to request that any or all directory information not be released for their child. Prior to the release of directory information, school districts must notify affected parents in writing and the notification must include date of notification, parents' names, student's name, directory information to be released, and scheduled date of release.

Contagious and Infectious Diseases

13

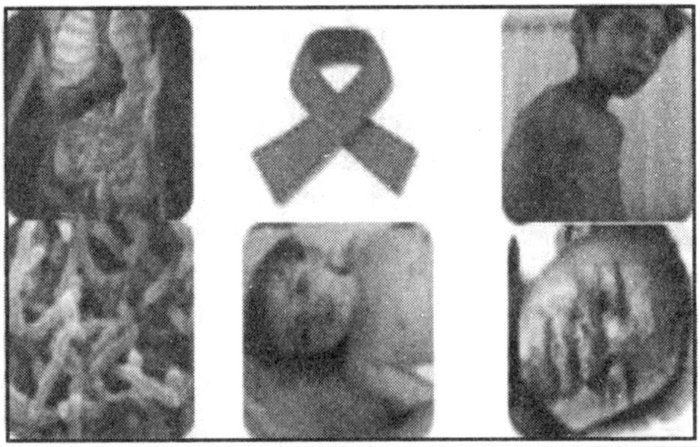

Diseases are an inevitable part of our lives. At some point or the other, each of us experiences some disease or the other, making us realize that in spite of so much of scientific research and technological advancement, mankind is yet nowhere close to emerging victorious over morbidity and mortality. Every time that he invents a new medicine, vaccine, or procedure to cure the existing diseases, newer ones keep cropping up. We are left blaming our genes, altered immunity, microorganisms, and the environment. The intelligent few have therefore realized that prevention certainly makes more sense than a cure. In fact, the indiscriminate use of medicines has given rise to a new range of diseases called estrogenic diseases. Under these circumstances, the value of imparting information responsibly should not be underplayed.

Communicable diseases are those that are infectious and hence, easily transmitted. Tuberculosis, cholera, malaria are examples of such diseases. The mode of transmission for such diseases differs. For example, malaria is a blood-borne disease and is spread by mosquitoes. Now mosquitoes breed in warm damp areas—areas usually associated with filth. In effect, dirty unkempt surroundings do play a role in harbouring the germs and the carriers of malaria. Hygiene is of paramount importance in dealing with such diseases. Also, a well-balanced diet that incorporates the right amount of every type of essential nutrient is also needed. Proper eating habits also must be inculcated.

Then there are communicable diseases such as gonohorrea, syphilis, etc., that are sexually transmitted. The treatment for sexually transmitted diseases is rather tedious and a number of precautions need to be taken. The best precaution is of course to abstain from sex. And the best preventive measure is to stick to just one partner.

Non-communicable diseases are those that are not infectious and one does not run the risk of being infected if one sits next to the carrier of the disease or share the same towel or plate. Examples of such diseases are cancer, hypertension, diabetes, and cardiovascular diseases. Usually, non-communicable diseases are hereditary. A person might suffer from diseases due to genetic factors or lifestyle factors. For example, diseases such as Hemophilia A and Duchenne muscular dystrophy are known to be genetically linked. They are caused due to X-linked recessive disorders that occur because of mutations effected on the X chromosome. On the other hand, a disease such as depression is a result of the modern hectic and haywire lifestyle. Too much work pressure, lack of time for any kind of social involvement are some of the causes for depression. Some other known non-communicable diseases are obesity, acne, and chronic renal failure.

Causes of Infection

Infection is caused when bacteria attack human body. The bacteria are very tiny germs, which cannot be seen with naked eyes. Such bacteria are generally present in the air, raw, stale, rotten things, water, etc. Other causative agents of infectious diseases are viruses, metazoa, protozoa and fungi. Contagious diseases are such that directly and knowingly spread from one person to the other. Their germs are so strong and so numerous that they are sure to reach from the patient to any other person. On the other hand infectious diseases are those, which spread from one person to the other, but without the direct knowledge of the patient. Infection may be caused either through the mouth due to contaminated food or liquid or unwashed and unclean hands. It can also take place through the skin when there are wounds or cuts on it. It is caused either by direct or indirect contact. In direct contact one touches or is touched by a patient. This includes hand to body and hand to mouth contact, inhaling of the air containing germs of infection, sexual intercourse, remaining face to face for long, shaking hands, etc. Indirect contact takes place through contaminated food or contaminated materials like utensils, clothes, beds, books, doors etc.

The following media of infection (causes or agencies) through which infectious and contagious diseases spread need special mention and explanation.

1. *Air*: Air is a very important carrier of all types of germs. When a patient breathes, coughs or sneezes, he sprays out infected droplets and germs in the air. Such infected droplets and germs enter into the system of a healthy person when he inhales the same infected air. That is why such an infection is called droplet infection. Sometimes while breathing we inhale certain dust particles that are infected. The infectious diseases that spread through air are cold, cough, influenza, measles, smallpox, chicken pox, tuberculosis, etc.

2. *Eatables*: The germs also spread through food and drinks. When a healthy person takes the food that has come in contact with a patient suffering from infectious disease the germs enter his body. The germs of tuberculosis are sometimes present in the milk of diseased milch cattle. Diseases that are caused by infected food and drinks are cholera, dysentery, diphtheria, typhoid, enteric fever, scarlet fever, tuberculosis, etc.

3. *Insects*: Insects like flies, mosquitoes, bugs and lice serve as carriers of germs. When these insects suck the blood of a patient, the germs stick to their trunks or stings and when the same insect bites a healthy person the germs are transferred to him. Infectious diseases that are caused by these small creatures are cholera, diarrhoea, malaria, plague, typhoid, yellow fever, filarial, sleeping sickness, etc.

4. *Skin*: Skin is also responsible for certain infectious diseases and cause diseases like tentams and anthrax, which are infectious in nature.

5. *Hands*: Dirty hands are sometimes responsible for carrying the germs of infectious diseases. These diseases are very common with children. They should be specifically trained to keep their hands clean. The infectious diseases of this type are polio, dysentery, mellitus, etc.

6. *Genital organs*: Dangerous diseases like syphilis and gonorrhea get communicated from one person to another through intercourse.

7. *Contact*: Generally persons who look after certain patients run the risk of catching the infectious diseases. This contact may be both direct and indirect. In direct contact the healthy person comes in contact with the patient. A healthy person may catch infection by indirect contact also, that is, when he comes into contact with the clothes, handkerchief, books, stationery, utensil, furniture, etc. of a person suffering from infectious disease. Diseases like ringworm, smallpox, eczema, scarlet fever, impetigo, etc. spread through contact.

Chief Characteristics of Infectious Diseases

- Each infectious disease has a fixed time limit during which the man remains ill.
- It spreads from one person to another.
- A person suffers only once from one type of infectious disease, because once he is attacked, he becomes immune

to it. Influenza and diphtheria are exceptions to this general rule.

- Each infectious disease is caused by a different kind of germs. For example, plague is caused by plague bacillus, measles by measles virus and so on. These germs multiply in number as soon as they enter the body and produce poison. The poison produced by one particular type of germ differs from that produced by another.
- The first stage of an infectious disease is called incubation period. During this period neither the symptoms appear nor can it be said that a particular person is affected by a particular disease. The ill effect of the disease is not visible till their number multiplies and they gain in strength. The incubation period of each infectious disease differs, but it is fixed in each case. After the incubation period comes the onset period during which the symptoms of disease appear.

Symptoms of Infectious Diseases

- *Temperature:* A person suffering from infectious disease may have temperature and his temperature may not remain steady.
- *Shivering:* If there is an internal infection in the body it may cause shivering in the person.
- *Pain:* There may be pain in the head, throat or some other part of the body.
- *Granules:* Some granules may appear on different parts of the body, which are poisonous in nature.
- *Raised patches:* In certain infectious diseases, raised patches appear on the forehead below the hair, which spread out, to the whole body. These patches are more or less red in colour. They indicate the functional inactivity of the skin.

Prevention of Infectious Diseases

In the case of infectious disease, prevention is far better than cure. As far as spreading of infectious diseases in school is concerned, the school authorities should adopt the following measures to check the spread of these diseases:

- *Notification:* As soon as any student is detected suffering from infectious disease, the teacher should immediately notify or refer the case to the school doctor as well as parents of the student.
- *Separation:* Similarly the student who is found suffering from an infectious disease should be at once separated from other students. It would prevent the spread of the disease.
- *Vaccination:* The authorities should arrange in time the vaccination in the case of smallpox and inoculation in the case of cholera, typhoid, diphtheria, etc. The vaccination and inoculation should take place from time to time even without the onset of a disease to keep the student population immune from that or similar diseases.
- *Chlorinating drinking water:* The drinking water to be supplied in the school should be chlorinated properly.
- *Environmental sanitation:* Environmental sanitation is an essential preventive measure. Urinals, toilets, washbasins, floors, canteen, lunchrooms, classrooms, corridors, etc. of the school campus need disinfectants. Various disinfectants like phenyle, lysol, carbolic acid, iodine, sulphur dioxide and potassium permanganate are very effective in destroying germs.
- *Disinfecting the belongings:* The things used by the students suffering from infectious diseases need also be thoroughly disinfected.
- *Testing foodstuffs and drinks:* The authorities should check the foodstuffs and drinks, which are sold to the

students. The rotten, infected and adulterated articles should not be allowed to be sold.

- *Disposal of sewage, waste and garbage:* Arrangements should be made for quick removal, cleaning and disposal of sewage, waste and garbage. In case of inadequate disposal, these dirty materials will provide breeding places for insects, rodents and germs.
- *Reporting local health authorities:* When the situation takes a serious turn local authorities and hospitals should be immediately informed.
- *Education:* Students and public should be educated about the diseases—how they are caused, how they are communicated, how they spread, how they are prevented and what steps they should take to control their spread.

Some Infectious Diseases

1. *Measles*

Measles is a highly contagious vaccine-preventable disease caused by the measles virus, a member of the genus *Morbillivirus* in the family paramyxoviridae. It affects mostly children. It is transmitted via droplets from the nose, mouth or throat of infected persons, less commonly by airborne spread or by articles freshly soiled with secretions of nose and throat. Measles is one of the most readily transmitted communicable diseases and probably the best known and most deadly of all childhood rash/fever illnesses. There is no specific treatment for measles and most people recover within 2-3 weeks. However, particularly in malnourished children and people with reduced immunity, measles can cause serious complications. Measles can be prevented by immunization.

Signs and symptoms

The first sign of measles is usually a high fever, which begins about 10 to 12 days after exposure to the virus, and lasts four to seven days. A running nose, a cough, red and watery

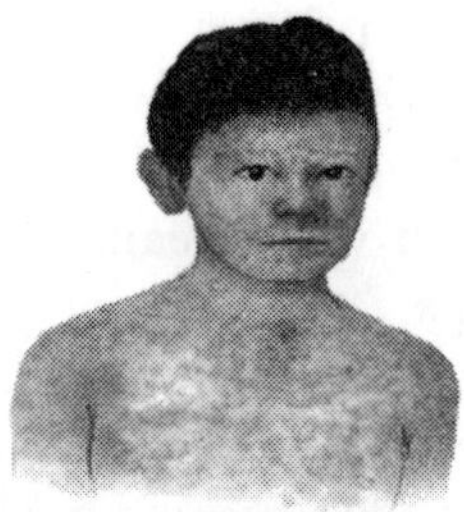

eyes, and small white spots inside the cheeks can develop in the initial stage. After several days, a rash erupts, usually on the face and upper neck. Over about three days, the rash spreads, eventually reaching the hands and feet. The rash lasts for five to six days, and then fades. On average, the rash occurs 14 days after exposure to the virus (within a range of seven to 18 days).

Severe measles is more likely among poorly nourished young children, especially those with insufficient vitamin A, or whose immune systems have been weakened by HIV/AIDS or other diseases. Most measles-related deaths are caused by complications associated with the disease. Complications are more common in children under the age of five, or adults over the age of 20. The most serious complications include blindness, encephalitis (an infection that causes brain swelling), severe diarrhoea and related dehydration, ear infections, or severe respiratory infections such as pneumonia. As high as 10 per cent of measles cases result in death among populations with high levels of malnutrition and a lack of adequate health care. People who recover from measles are immune for the rest of their lives.

Population at risk

Unvaccinated young children are at highest risk of measles and its complications, including death. Any non-immune person (who has not been vaccinated or previously recovered from the disease) can become infected. Measles is still common in many developing countries—particularly in parts of Africa and Asia. More than 20 million people are affected by measles each year. The overwhelming majority (more than 95 per cent) of measles deaths occur in countries with low per capita incomes and weak health infrastructures. Measles outbreaks can be particularly deadly in countries experiencing or recovering from a natural disaster or conflict. Damage to health infrastructure and health services interrupts routine immunization, and overcrowding in residential camps greatly increases the risk of infection.

In 2008, there were 1,64,000 measles deaths globally—nearly 450 deaths every day or 18 deaths every hour. More than 95 per cent of measles deaths occur in low-income countries with weak health infrastructures. Measles vaccination resulted in a 78 per cent drop in measles deaths between 2000 and 2008 worldwide. In 2008, about 83 per cent of the world's children received one dose of measles vaccine by their first birthday through routine health services—up from 72 per cent in 2000.

Measles global annual reported cases and MCV coverge, 1980-2009

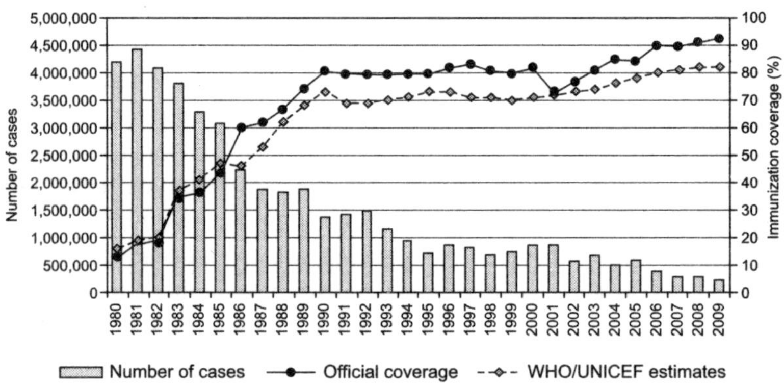

* *Source*: WHO/IVB database 2010.

Transmission

The highly contagious virus is spread by coughing and sneezing, close personal contact or direct contact with infected nasal or throat secretions. The virus remains active and contagious in the air or on infected surfaces for up to two hours. An infected person from four days prior to the onset of the rash to four days after the rash erupts can transmit it. Measles outbreaks can result in epidemics that cause many deaths, especially among young, malnourished children. In countries where measles has been largely eliminated, cases imported from other countries remain an important source of infection.

Prevention and treatment

Severe complications from measles can be avoided though supportive care that ensures good nutrition, adequate fluid intake and treatment of dehydration with WHO-recommended oral dehydration solution. This solution replaces fluids and other essential elements that are lost through diarrhoea or vomiting. Antibiotics should be prescribed to treat eye and ear infections, and pneumonia. All children in developing countries diagnosed with measles should receive two doses of Vitamin A supplements, given 24 hours apart. This can help prevent eye damage and blindness. Vitamin A supplements have been shown to reduce the number of deaths from measles by 50 per cent.

Routine measles vaccination for children combined with mass immunization campaigns in countries with high case and death rates are key public health strategies to reduce global measles deaths. The measles vaccine has been in use for over 40 years. It is safe, effective and inexpensive. The measles vaccine is often incorporated with rubella and/or mumps vaccines in countries where these illnesses are problems. It is equally effective in the single or combined form. Two doses of the vaccine are recommended to ensure immunity, as about 15 per cent of vaccinated children fail to develop immunity from the first dose.

Other points to be kept in mind for prevention are:

1. The child suffering from measles should be kept away from other children to check the spread of the disease.
2. The room of the patient should be kept warm and ventilated.
3. The patient should be guarded against cold.

If immediate precautions are not taken, it may cause bronchitis and pneumonia, infection of the ear and eye and in certain serious cases kidneys and heart may also be affected.

GLOBAL HEALTH RESPONSE

The fourth Millennium Development Goal (MDG 4) aims to reduce the under-five mortality rate by two-thirds between 1990 and 2015. Recognizing the potential of measles vaccination to reduce child mortality, and given that measles vaccination coverage can be considered a marker of access to child health services, routine measles vaccination coverage has been selected as an indicator of progress towards achieving MDG 4. The Measles Initiative is a collaborative effort of WHO, UNICEF, the American Red Cross, the United States Centers for Disease Control and Prevention, and the United Nations Foundation. The Initiative, together with other public and private partners, plays a key role in advancing the global measles strategy. This strategy includes:

- Strong routine immunization for children by their first birthday.
- A 'second opportunity' for measles immunization through mass vaccination campaigns, to ensure that all children receive at least one dose.
- Effective surveillance in all countries to quickly recognize and respond to measles outbreaks.
- Better treatment of measles cases, to include Vitamin A supplements, antibiotics if needed, and supportive care that prevent complications.

(More information on measles on http://www.emedicinehealth.com/measles/page3_em.htm)

2. *Smallpox*

Smallpox is an infection caused by the ***variola*** (say: vair-ee-oh-luh) virus. Smallpox gets its name from the pus-filled blisters (or pocks) that form during the illness. Although the names may sound alike, smallpox is not related to chickenpox, which is a milder disease caused by a different virus. For centuries,

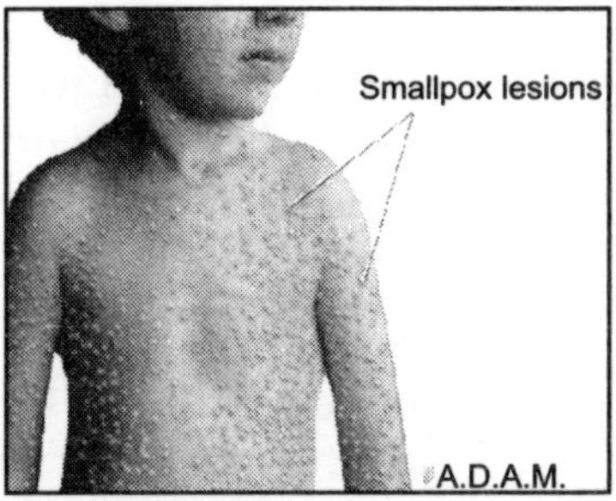

epidemics of smallpox affected people all over the globe, and the disease was often serious. But in 1796, an English doctor named Edward Jenner discovered a way to protect people from getting smallpox, and his experiments eventually led to the development of the first smallpox vaccine. The smallpox vaccine worked so well that there has not been a case of smallpox in the United States since 1949. The United States stopped vaccinating the general population against smallpox in 1972 because the disease was no longer a threat. The world's last known case of smallpox was reported in Africa in 1977. In 1980, the World Health Organization (WHO) announced that smallpox was wiped out—the first (and only) time in history that an infectious disease was declared eliminated from the planet.

Signs and Symptoms

After infection, symptoms may take from 7-17 days to appear for major types of smallpox. The virus begins growing in the bloodstream 72-96 hours after infection, but no obvious symptoms appear immediately.

- People who have contracted smallpox initially develop such symptoms as fever, body aches, headache, chills, and, particularly, backache. Over half of people with smallpox experience chills and vomiting. About 15 per cent become confused.
- A rash appears 48-72 hours after the initial symptoms and turns into virus-filled sores, which later scab over. The process can take up to 2 weeks.
- Just after the rash appears, the virus is highly contagious as it moves into the mucous membranes. The body sheds the cells, and virus particles are released, coughed, or sneezed into the environment. The infected person

can be infectious for up to 3 weeks (until the scabs fall off the rash). Live virus can be present in the scabs. After the scabs or crusts fall off (in 2-4 weeks), a depression or light-skinned scar remains.

- Early in the course of the disease, the rash and pus-filled sores can easily be mistaken for chickenpox. Lesions occur first in the mouth and spread to the face, then to the forearms and hands, and finally to the lower limbs and trunk. In contrast, rash from chickenpox progresses from the arms and legs to the trunk and rarely forms in the armpits, palms, soles, and elbow areas.

Prevention and treatment

1. Medical treatment for smallpox eases its symptoms. This includes replacing fluid lost from fever and skin breakdown. Antibiotics may be needed for secondary skin infections. The infected person is kept in isolation for 17 days or until the scabs fall off.
2. Vaccination is the most effective means of preventing smallpox infection. Vaccination can even be administered up to 4 or 5 days after a person is exposed to the virus. This practice may not completely prevent disease, but probably it will result in a significantly less severe case of the illness.
3. The victim should be immediately isolated. Other children of the same family should be kept indoors.
4. The patient should be kept at a very neat and clean place. His room should be washed with phenyle. The crust fallen from the eruptions of the patient should be kept carefully in a pot containing phenyle.
5. The patient should not be given any salt.
6. No medicine is required. Only proper nursing is needed.
7. Sulphur and leaves of neem tree should be burnt in the room of the patient after he has been removed from there.

3. *Influenza*

Influenza, commonly known as "the flu", is a highly contagious viral infection of the respiratory tract. It is a viral infection that affects mainly the nose, throat, bronchi and, occasionally lungs. The virus is transmitted easily from person to person via droplets and small particles produced when infected people cough or sneeze. Influenza tends to spread rapidly in seasonal epidemics. The illness even has its own season—from November to April, with most cases occurring between late December and early March. Infection usually lasts for about a week, and is characterized by sudden onset of high fever, aching muscles, headache and severe malaise, non-productive cough, sore throat and rhinitis.

Although the flu affects both sexes and all age groups, kids tend to get it more often than adults. Most infected people recover within one to two weeks without requiring medical treatment. However, in the very young, the elderly, and those with other serious medical conditions, infection can lead to severe complications of the underlying condition, pneumonia and death.

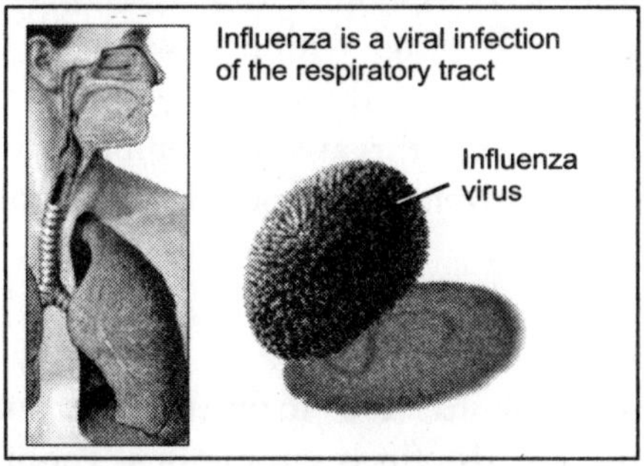

Signs and symptoms

The flu is often confused with the common cold, but flu symptoms are usually more severe than the typical sneezing and stuffiness of a cold.

Symptoms of the flu may include:

- Fever

- Chills
- Headache
- Muscle aches
- Dizziness
- Loss of appetite
- Tiredness
- Cough
- Sore throat
- Running nose
- Nausea or vomiting
- Weakness
- Ear pain
- Diarrhea

Duration

After 5 days, fever and other symptoms have usually disappeared, but a cough and weakness may continue. All symptoms are usually gone within a week or two. However, it is important to treat the flu seriously because it can lead to pneumonia and other life-threatening complications, particularly in infants, senior citizens, and people with long-term health problems.

Contagiousness

Spread by virus-infected droplets that are coughed or sneezed into the air, the flu is contagious. People infected with the flu are contagious from a day before they feel sick until their symptoms have resolved (usually about 1 week for adults, but can be up to 2 weeks for young kids). The flu usually occurs in small outbreaks, but epidemics tend to occur every several years. Epidemics (when the illness spreads rapidly and affects many people in an area at the same time) peak within 2 or 3 weeks after the first cases occur.

The flu vaccine

The flu vaccine usually is offered between September and mid-November, although it may be given at other times of the year. It reduces the average person's chances of catching the flu by up to 80 per cent during flu season. Because the vaccine prevents infection with only a few of the viruses that can cause flu-like symptoms, it is not a guarantee against getting sick. But even if someone who has got the vaccine gets the flu, symptoms usually will be fewer and milder. Flu vaccines are available as a shot or nasal mist. Given as an injection, the flu shot contains killed flu viruses that will not cause the flu, but will prepare the body to fight off infection by the live flu virus. Getting a shot of the killed virus means a person is protected against that particular type of live flu virus if he or she comes into contact with it. The vaccine is updated each year to include the most current strains of the virus.

New vaccines are developed each year to combat rapidly changing influenza viruses

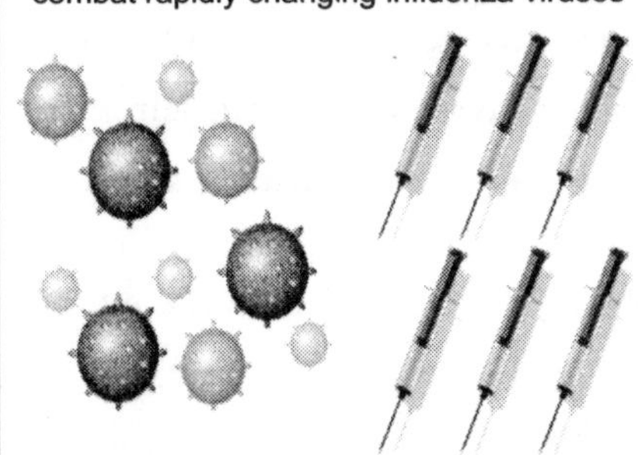

Prevention and treatment

There is no guaranteed way—including being vaccinated—to prevent anyone from getting the flu. Some practical ways to help prevent the spread of the flu are:

- Wash your hands thoroughly and frequently.
- Never pick up used tissues.
- Never share cups and eating utensils.

- Stay home from work or school when you are sick with the flu.
- Cover your mouth and nose with a tissue when you cough or sneeze.

Cases of the flu rarely require specific medical treatment. But some kids with chronic medical conditions may become sicker with the flu and need to be hospitalized, and flu in an infant can also be dangerous. For a severely ill child or one with other special circumstances, a doctor may prescribe an antiviral medicine that can ease flu symptoms, but only if it is given within 48 hours of the onset of the flu.

Some at-home tips can help most otherwise healthy kids cope with the flu. They should drink lots of fluids to prevent dehydration, get plenty of sleep and take it easy, take acetaminophen or ibuprofen to relieve fever and aches and wear layers, since the flu often makes them cold one minute and hot the next.

Some other steps for preventing and treating this disease are:

1. The patient should isolate himself.
2. Inoculation against the disease should be obtained.
3. In order to save others from infection the child-patient should be made to proceed on leave for about eight days.
4. The patient should be given complete rest.
5. He should be saved from cold; otherwise he is likely to catch bronchitis and pneumonia.
6. Food should be protected from flies and vegetables should be washed in potassium permanganate.
7. He should avoid eating exposed articles in the market.
8. The patient should be given boiled water.
9. Cleaning the nose and throat with salt solution is helpful.
10. The medical expert should be immediately consulted for proper treatment.

4. *Tuberculosis*

Tuberculosis (TB) is a contagious disease. Like the common cold, it spreads through the air. Only people who are sick with TB in their lungs are infectious. When infectious people cough, sneeze, talk or spit, they propel TB germs, known as bacilli into the air. A person needs only to inhale a small number of these to be infected. Left untreated, each person with active TB disease will infect on average between 10 and 15 people every year. But people infected with TB bacilli will not necessarily become sick with the disease. The immune system "walls off" the TB bacilli which, protected by a thick waxy coat, can lie dormant for years. When someone's immune system is weakened, the chances of becoming sick are greater. Overall, one-third of the world's population is currently infected with the TB bacillus. 5-10 per cent of people who are infected with TB bacilli (but who are not infected with HIV) become sick or infectious at some time during their life.

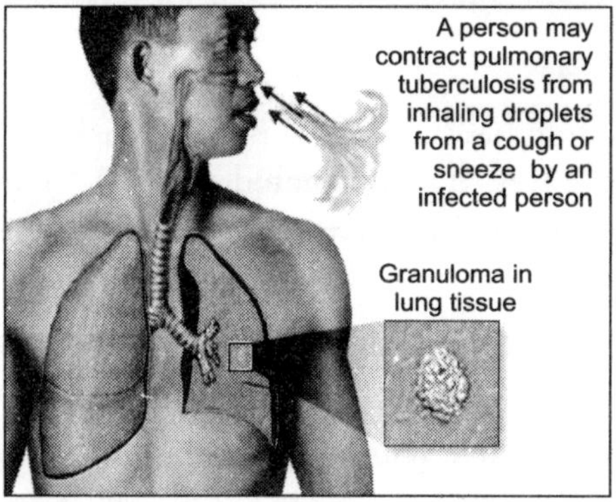

Causes of tuberculosis

Various causes of the spread of tuberculosis are:

1. Lack of fresh air and light
2. Addiction to alcohol
3. Bad food and poor diet
4. Deficiency of vitamins and food in the body
5. Infected eatables and drinks
6. Lack of rest and sleep

7. Heredity
8. Early marriage

Global and regional incidence

WHO estimates that the largest number of new TB cases in 2008 occurred in the South-East Asia Region, which accounted for 35 per cent of incident cases globally. However, the estimated incidence rate in sub-Saharan Africa is nearly twice that of the South-East Asia Region with over 350 cases per 1,00,000 populations. An estimated 1.7 million people died from TB in 2009. The highest number of deaths was in the Africa Region. In 2008, the estimated per capita TB incidence was stable or falling in all six WHO regions. However, the slow decline in incidence rates per capita is offset by population growth. Consequently, the number of new cases arising each year is still increasing globally in the WHO regions of Africa, the Eastern Mediterranean and South-East Asia.

Population at risk

Over 8 million new cases of TB occur each year worldwide. In the United States, it is estimated that 10-15 million people are infected with the TB bacteria and 22,000 new cases of TB occur each year.

Anyone can get TB, but certain people are at higher risk, including:

- people who live with individuals who have an active TB infection,
- poor or homeless people,
- foreign-born people from countries that have a high prevalence of TB,
- nursing-home residents and prison inmates,
- alcoholics and intravenous drug users,
- people with diabetes, certain cancers, and HIV infection (the AIDS virus), and
- health-care workers.

There is no strong evidence for a genetically determined (inherited) susceptibility for TB.

Symptoms of tuberculosis

As previously mentioned, TB infection usually occurs initially in the upper part (lobe) of the lungs. The body's immune system, however, can stop the bacteria from continuing to reproduce. Thus, the immune system can make the lung infection inactive (dormant). On the other hand, if the body's immune system cannot contain the TB bacteria, the bacteria will reproduce (become active or reactivate) in the lungs and spread elsewhere in the body.

It may take many months from the time the infection initially gets into the lungs until symptoms develop. The usual symptoms that occur with an active TB infection are a generalized tiredness or weakness, weight loss, fever, and night sweats. If the infection in the lung worsens, then further symptoms can include coughing, chest pain, coughing up of sputum (material from the lungs) and/or blood, and shortness of breath. If the infection spreads beyond the lungs, the symptoms will depend upon the organs involved.

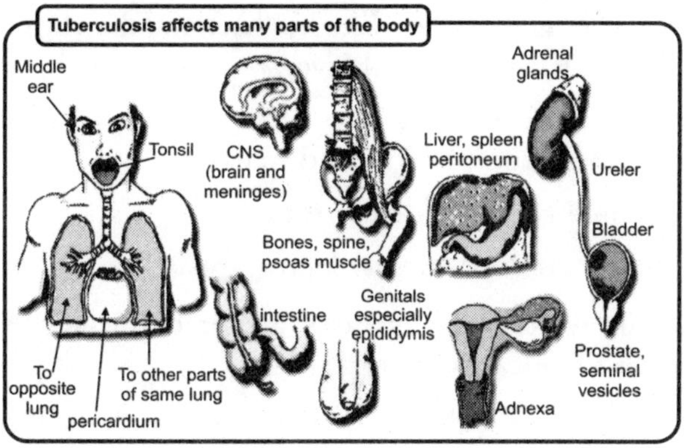

Prevention and treatment

1. *Bacille Calmette Guerin*, also known as BCG, is a vaccine given throughout many parts of the world. It is derived from an atypical *Mycobacterium* but offers

some protection from developing active tuberculosis, especially in infants and children. This vaccination is believed to be important in parts of the world where TB is quite common.

2. One should live in a healthy atmosphere with fresh air and sunlight. The place should be neat and clean and free from dust, dirt and smoke.
3. The patient must be isolated from others.
4. The sputum and the excreta of the patient should be burnt.
5. Rich and nutritive diet is essential.
6. Morning and evening walks are essential for the patient.
7. The patient should avoid hard work and should remain free from worries.
8. In advanced cases it will be advisable to send the patient to some sanitorium where he may get proper atmosphere and medical treatment.

Some other major infectious diseases, which require brief description, are:

1. *Food or waterborne diseases:* bacterial diarrhea, hepatitis A and E, and typhoid fever.
2. *Vector borne diseases:* chikungunya, dengue fever, Japanese encephalitis, and malaria.
3. *Animal contact disease:* rabies.
4. *Water contact disease:* leptospirosis.

Food or waterborne diseases acquired through eating or drinking on the local economy.

Hepatitis A—viral disease that interferes with the functioning of the liver; spread through consumption of food or water contaminated with fecal matter, principally in areas of poor sanitation; victims exhibit fever, jaundice, and diarrhea; 15 per cent of victims will experience prolonged symptoms over 6-9 months; vaccine available.

MANAGING FEAR OF TUBERCULOSIS

The presence of tuberculosis in some societies involves ritualistic processes to be completed in the hope of clearing the ailment. The patient may be imbibed into this form of thinking and prefers to undergo the rituals due to fears of medicine. The fear has its base in poor awareness. The manageability of tuberculosis in these cases involves an understanding and due respect for the cultural mores of the society. The head of the society may be viewed, as the source of wisdom and any hope of educating people must have the concurrence and advocacy of the head. The medical fraternity must assure the immediate family of the presence of rules to prevent the information of tuberculosis being made available to outsiders. At the same time, there may be a need to carry out tests of people who have been in contact with the patient's family. The patient must have the added assurance that the medical fraternity does not inform outsiders of the presence of tuberculosis. The public awareness increases the possibility of a stigma affecting the entire family and information reaching the employer.

A variety of notions about the management of the disease may be broken if international discussions and ideas are shared and implemented. Research on the management of tuberculosis patients to retain the ailment is necessary. The need to return to work, confidentiality regarding the diagnosis due to possibility of loss of employment, rejection by the family and social group are just a few of the fears the diagnosis of tuberculosis brings with it.

A set of necessary processes to ensure minimal direct contact with the tuberculosis patients must be chalked out at a central authority and implemented across health centers. If the patient is to be taken care of in the house, the difficulties of the patient must be made known to the family. The pain, discomfort and loss of appetite that is shown in tuberculosis patients may lead to stressful situations to the other family members. Besides this, regular contact may lead to the spread of the disease in some cases. Family members must get checked for the prevalence of latent tuberculosis in themselves. The loss of acceptance in social circles for the period of the disease and sometimes afterwards leads tuberculosis to a feeling of depression and loneliness. An effective approach to tuberculosis patient care must include an understanding of the emotional state.

(More information on tuberculosis is available on http://www.tuberculosis.net)

Hepatitis E—waterborne viral disease that interferes with the functioning of the liver; most commonly spread through fecal contamination of drinking water; victims exhibit jaundice, fatigue, abdominal pain, and dark coloured urine.

Typhoid fever—bacterial disease spread through contact with food or water contaminated by fecal matter or sewage; victims exhibit sustained high fevers; left untreated, mortality rates can reach 20 per cent.

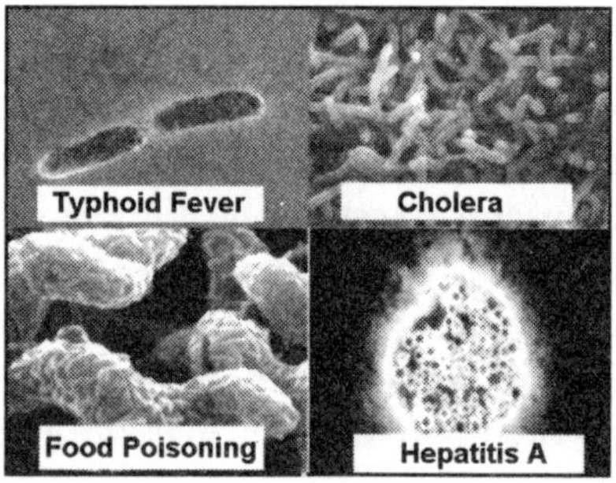

Vector borne diseases acquired through the bite of an infected arthropod:

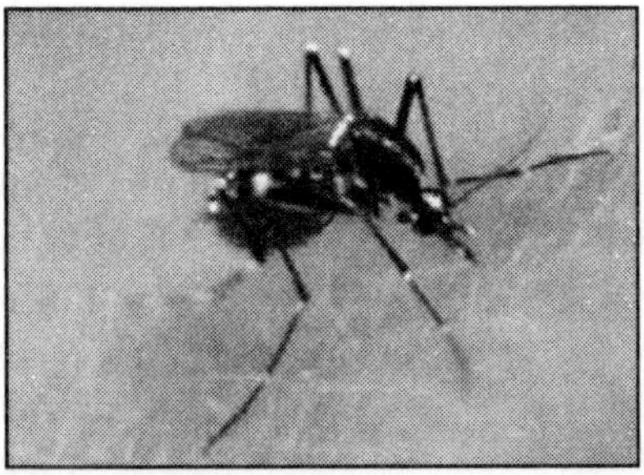

Malaria—caused by single-cell parasitic protozoa *Plasmodium*; transmitted to humans via the bite of the female Anopheles mosquito; parasites multiply in the liver attacking red blood cells resulting in cycles of fever, chills, and sweats accompanied by anemia; death due to damage to vital organs and interruption of blood supply to the brain; endemic in 100, mostly tropical, countries with 90 per cent of cases and the majority of 1.5-2.5 million estimated annual deaths occurring in sub-Saharan Africa.

Dengue fever—mosquito-borne (*Aedes aegypti*) viral disease associated with urban environments; manifests as sudden onset of fever and severe headache; occasionally produces shock and hemorrhage leading to death in 5 per cent of cases.

Yellow fever—mosquito-borne viral disease; severity ranges from influenza-like symptoms to severe hepatitis and hemorrhagic fever; occurs only in tropical South America and sub-Saharan Africa, where most cases are reported; fatality rate is less than 20 per cent.

Japanese Encephalitis—mosquito-borne (*Culex tritaeniorhynchus*) viral disease associated with rural areas in Asia; acute encephalitis can progress to paralysis, coma, and death; fatality rates 30 per cent.

African Trypanosomiasis—caused by the parasitic protozoa *Trypanosoma*; transmitted to humans via the bite of blood-sucking Tsetse flies; infection leads to malaise and irregular fevers and, in advanced cases when the parasites invade the central nervous system, coma and death; endemic in 36 countries of sub-Saharan Africa; cattle and wild animals act as reservoir hosts for the parasites.

Cutaneous Leishmaniasis—caused by the parasitic protozoa *leishmania*; transmitted to humans via the bite of sandflies; results in skin lesions that may become chronic; endemic in 88 countries; 90 per cent of cases occur in Iran, Afghanistan, Syria, Saudi Arabia, Brazil, and Peru; wild and domesticated animals as well as humans can act as reservoirs of infection.

Plague—bacterial disease transmitted by fleas normally associated with rats; person-to-person airborne transmission also possible; recent plague epidemics occurred in areas of Asia, Africa, and South America associated with rural areas or small towns and villages; manifests as fever, headache, and painfully swollen lymph nodes; disease progresses rapidly and without antibiotic treatment leads to pneumonic form with a death rate in excess of 50 per cent.

Chikungunya—mosquito-borne (*Aedes aegypti*) viral disease associated with urban environments, similar to Dengue Fever; characterized by sudden onset of fever, rash, and severe joint pain usually lasting 3-7 days, some cases result in persistent arthritis.

The following table gives in detail the various kinds of infectious diseases, their transmission settings and their affected populations. (*Source*: CIA World Fact book)

Infectious disease category	Important examples	Transmission	Affected populations
Vector-borne diseases (especially with introduction potential)	Rose River virus Dengue fever	Borders and airport	All, if diseases introduced
Congenital and pesinatal infections	Hepatitis B Listeriosis Congenital rubella syndrome Toxoplasmosis Group B streptococcal disease Cytomegalovirus	Maternal and care settings	Pregnant women Neonates

(Contd.)

Blood-borne diseases and those linked to transplants and sharing injecting equipment	Hepatitis C HIV/AIDS HTLV 1&2 CJD Newly recognised blood-borne diseases	Pupulation Health care settings Prisons	All, especially hospitalised injecting drug users
Sexually transmitted Infections	Chlamydia Gonorrhea Syphilis HIV/acquired immune deficiency syndrome HPV HSV Hepatitis B	Population Immigrant populations	All, especially young adults Men who have sex with men
Hospital acquired Infections	MRSA Clostridium difficile Surgical-site infections (SSI) Blood-stream infections (BSI) Device-related infections opportunistic infections	Health care settings	All, expecially elderly
Diseases caused by antibiotics-resistant	Penicillin resistance pneumococci VRE (enterococci) MDRTB PPNG (gonococci) Newly emerging resistance organisms	Human populations Animal populations Health care Veterinary Farming	All, especially hospitalised
Bioterrorism agents	Anthrax Other agents	Population, especially in government facilities	All, especially first responders

Water contact diseases acquired through swimming or wading in freshwater lakes, streams, and rivers.

Leptospirosis—bacterial disease that affects animals and humans; infection occurs through contact with water, food, or soil contaminated by animal urine; symptoms include high fever, severe headache, vomiting, jaundice, and diarrhea; untreated, the disease can result in kidney damage, liver failure, meningitis, or respiratory distress; fatality rates are low but left untreated recovery can take months.

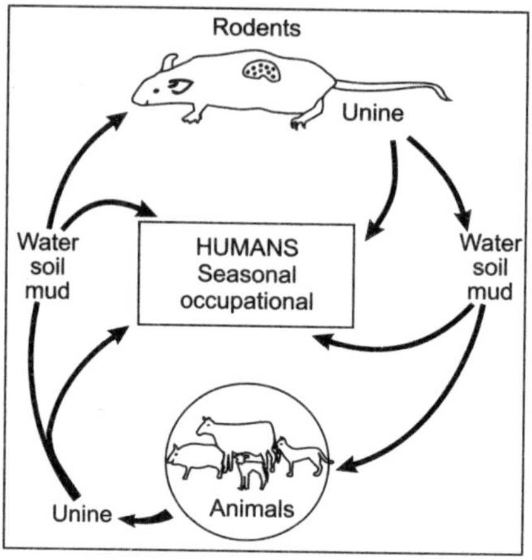

Schistosomiasis—caused by parasitic trematode flatworm *Schistosoma*, freshwater snails act as intermediate host and release larval form of parasite that penetrates the skin of people exposed to contaminated water; worms mature and reproduce in the blood vessels, liver, kidneys, and intestines releasing eggs, which become trapped in tissues triggering an immune response; may manifest as either urinary or intestinal disease resulting in decreased work or learning capacity; mortality, while generally low, may occur in advanced cases usually due to bladder cancer; endemic in 74 developing countries with 80 per cent of infected people living in sub-Saharan Africa; humans act as the reservoir for this parasite.

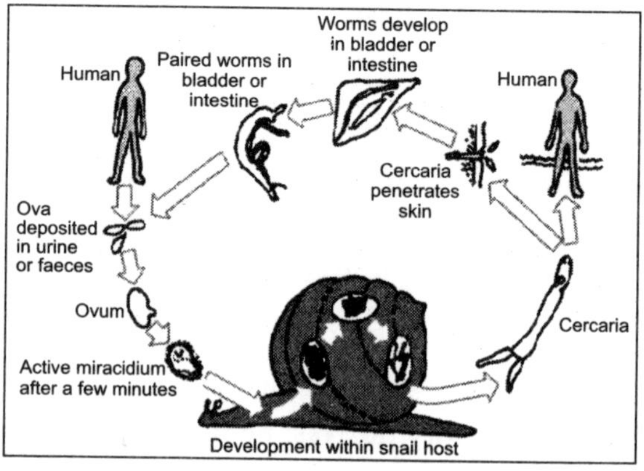

Lassa fever—viral disease carried by rats of the genus *Mastomys*; endemic in portions of West Africa; infection occurs through direct contact with or consumption of food contaminated by rodent urine or fecal matter containing virus particles; fatality rate can reach 50 per cent in epidemic outbreaks.

Animal contact disease acquired through direct contact with local animals:

Rabies—viral disease of mammals usually transmitted through the bite of an infected animal, most commonly dogs; virus affects the central nervous system causing brain alteration and death; symptoms initially are non-specific fever and headache progressing to neurological symptoms; death occurs within days of the onset of symptoms.

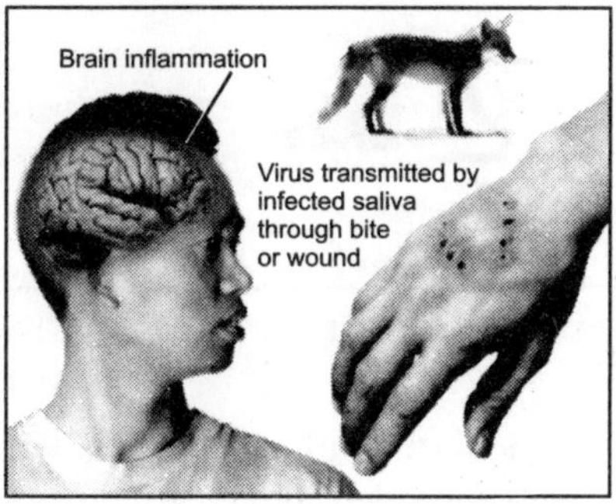

No matter where the wound is, authorities emphasize that the first and most important preventive measure is by cleaning of the site with soap and water, and then go for medical attention. Unlike other immunizations, the rabies vaccine is administered after exposure to the virus. If rabies vaccine treatment is demanded, it should be started immediately after exposure.

14

First Aid and Safety Education

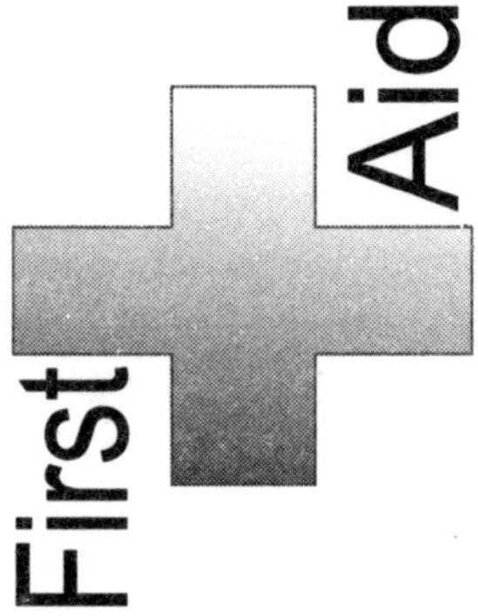

First aid is the immediate and temporary care given to the victim of an accident or sudden illness. Its purpose is to preserve life, assist recovery, prevent aggravation of the condition and preserve the morale of the victim to fight the trouble, until the services of a doctor can be obtained, or during transport to the hospital or the casualty's home. The First Aider's responsibilities end as soon as medical aid is available; but he should stand by after making his report to the Doctor in case he can be of further assistance. First aid is definitely limited to the assistance rendered at the time of emergency with such material, as may be available. It is not intended that the First Aider should take the place of the Doctor and it must be clearly understood that the redressing of injuries and other such after treatment are outside the scope of first aid.

First aid has been practiced ever since the beginning of humanity. Learning first aid is the civic responsibility of every citizen. Methods of first aid have been practiced ever since one person desired to help another in sickness or after an injury. But, an organized worldwide effort at recognizing the importance of first aid came only in the year 1877 with the formation of the St. John Ambulance Association of England named after the great apostle St. John. Over the decades, the importance given to First aid has grown. Mahatma Gandhi was a great supporter of the cause of First aid, and led a band of dedicated Ambulance Corps volunteers in 1906 during the time of the Zulu Rebellion and earlier in 1899 during the Boer war. The expression "First Aider" was not coined till 1894 and was intended to designate any person who has received a certificate from an authorized association that he is qualified to render first hand. The originator of first aid was Esmarch (1823-1908).

Aims of First Aid

The key aims of first aid can be summarized in three key points:

1. *To preserve life*: the overriding aim of all medical care, including first aid, is to save lives.
2. *To promote recovery*: first aid also involves trying to start the recovery process from the illness or injury, and in some cases might involve completing a treatment, such as in the case of applying a plaster to a small wound.
3. *To prevent the worsening of the victim's condition*: this covers both external factors, such as moving a patient away from any cause of harm, and applying first aid techniques to prevent worsening of the condition, such as applying pressure to stop a bleed becoming dangerous.

First aid training also involves the prevention of initial injury and responder safety, and the treatment phases.

Principles of First Aid

1. The first step that a rescuer should take is to examine the victim to know the details of injuries and their nature. This constitutes the diagnosis section of first aid.
2. The next step is to actually perform the first-aid measure or manoeuvre that is deemed appropriate. This constitutes the treatment section of first aid.
3. The third step is to arrange for the casualty to be seen by a qualified doctor or have him shifted to a nearby hospital. This step is in the first aid providers jargon known rather disparagingly as disposal.

Key Skills in First Aid

Certain skills are considered essential to the provision of first aid and are taught ubiquitously. Particularly the "ABC's" of first aid, which focus on critical life-saving intervention, must be rendered before treatment of less serious injuries. ABC stands for Airway, Breathing, and Circulation. All emergency health professionals use the same mnemonic. Attention must first be brought to the airway to ensure it is clear. Obstruction (choking) is a life-threatening emergency. Following evaluation of the airway, a first aid attendant would determine adequacy of breathing and provide rescue breathing if necessary. Assessment of circulation is now not usually carried out for patients who are not breathing, with first aiders now trained to go straight to chest compressions (and thus providing artificial circulation) but pulse checks may be done on less serious patients.

Variations on techniques to evaluate and maintain the ABCs depend on the skill level of the first aider. Once the ABCs are secured, first aiders can begin additional treatments, as required. Some organizations teach the same order of priority using the "3Bs": Breathing, Bleeding, and Bones (or "4Bs": Breathing, Bleeding, Brain, and Bones). While the ABCs and

3Bs are taught to be performed sequentially, certain conditions may require the consideration of two steps simultaneously. This includes the provision of both artificial respiration and chest compressions to someone who is not breathing and has no pulse, and the consideration of cervical spine injuries when ensuring an open airway.

Directions for First Aid

1. Respond quickly to any call for first aid.
2. Give artificial respiration if breathing has stopped—no time should be allowed to lapse.
3. Stop the bleeding, if any.
4. Guard against or treat for shock by moving the victim as little as possible and by handling him gently.
5. Do not attempt too much—do the minimum that is essential to save life, prevent the condition from worsening and help the patient to survive for the time being.
6. Reassure the victim and those around and help lessen anxiety.
7. Do not allow people to crowd around and allow the full benefit of fresh air to the victim.
8. Do not remove clothes unnecessarily.
9. Arrange the removal of the casualty to the nearest doctor or hospital as soon as possible.

First Aid Box

It is the duty of the school to keep a first aid box under the charge of a teacher qualified in first aid. This box should contain absorbent cotton, wool pad, gauze pieces, roller bandages, adhesive plaster, tincture iodine, tincture benzoic, spirit ammonia, scissors, forceps, dettol, burnol, boric acid, soda bicarb, baking soda, antiseptic cream, torch, medicine glass, etc.

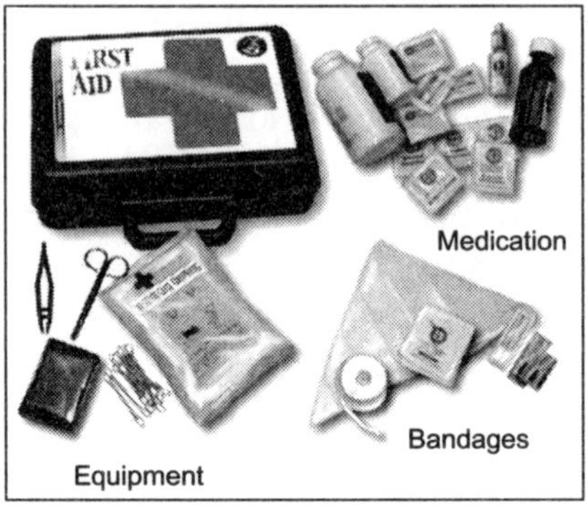

Minor Accidents and their First Aid

Sometimes, accidents like fracture of bones, injuries, burn, sprain, etc. occur in schools while the students are playing, doing woodwork, doing exercise or performing experiments in laboratory. The teacher should possess knowledge of these every-day accidents and render immediate first aid relief. The teacher should not only have knowledge of the above but should be efficient in this job of rendering first aid. Students involved in serious accidents should be sent to medical doctor for proper treatment.

I. Fractures

A fracture is a complete or partial breakage of a bone. Fractures may be:

- Simple, where the broken ends of the bone do not cut open the skin.
- Compound, where the broken end of the bone may be in contact with the external air.
- Complicated, where in addition to the fracture an important internal organ may also be injured. A complicated fracture may also be simple or compound.

Signs and symptoms of a fracture

- Pain at or around the site of the fracture.
- Tenderness (pain on gentle pressure) over the area. It should not be pressed hard.

- Swelling over the area with discolouration.
- Loss of normal movements of the affected part.
- Deformity of the limb may be caused. The limb may lose its normal shape and there may be apparent shortening of the limb.
- If, as in the leg bone, the break is just under the skin, the irregular outline of the bone can be felt easily.
- When one end of the broken bone moves against the other, a crackling sound may be heard. This is called *crepitus* (grating). This should never be elicited by the person giving first aid.
- Unnatural movements may be felt at the site of the fracture. This too should never be elicited by the first-aid provider.

In addition the victim may himself say that he heard the snap of the bone. It is important to compare the injured limb with the normal limb while making an assessment.

Management of fractures

The aims of First Aid here are:

- To prevent further damage.
- To reduce pain.
- To make the patient feel comfortable.
- To get medical aid as soon as possible.
- Fractures often occur along with other injuries. So the rescuer must assess for other injuries and decide which of them requires care on priority. Heavy bleeding is more urgent and requires higher priority care over a fracture.
- If there is no danger to life then temporary attention to the fracture is often sufficient.
- The patient should be handled very gently. All unnecessary movement should be avoided.

- Treatment for shock is necessary, if present.
- If the broken ends of the bones show out, do not wash the wound or apply antiseptics to the end of the bone.
- The fracture should not be handled unnecessarily.
- Never attempt to reduce the fracture or to bring the bones to the normal position.
- Stabilize and support the injured part so that no movement is possible. This stops further injury and helps to control the bleeding.
- Immobilize the fracture area and the joints on both sides of the fracture site (above and below) by using bandages or by using splints wherever available. It is essential that the rescuer be familiar with the use of bandages and splints.

A. Using bandages

Usually it is enough to use the other (uninjured) limb or the body of the victim as the splint. The upper limb can be supported by the body, and the lower limb by the other limb provided that also is not fractured. Most fractures except those of the forearm can be immobilized in this manner:

- Do not apply bandage over the area of the fracture.
- The bandaging should be firm so that there is no movement of the fractured ends but should not be too tight as blood circulation to the affected area could be reduced. If there is further swelling of the injured area, the bandage may be too tight and therefore may need to be loosened.
- Always place padding material between the ankles, knees and other hollows if they have to be tied together so that when the limbs are bound together they are comfortable and steady.
- If the patient is lying down, the bandage should be passed through the natural hollows like the neck, the

lower part of the trunk, knees, just above the ankles, etc., so that the patient's body is not jarred.

- Always tie the knots on the sound side.

B. Using splints

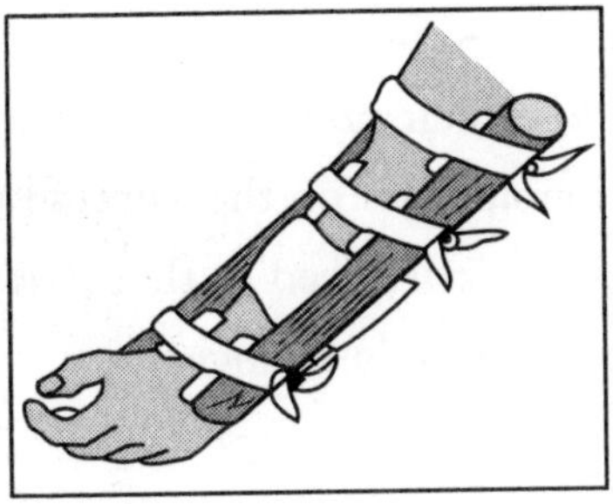

Splints are used only when necessary expertise is there.

- A splint is a rigid piece of wood or plastic material or metal applied to a fractured limb to prevent movement of the broken bone.
- Reasonably wide splints are better than narrow ones.
- Splints should be long enough so that the joints above and below the fractured bones can be made immobile.
- The splints should be well padded with cotton or cloth so as to fit softly on the injured limb.
- Splints are best applied over the clothing.
- In an emergency, splints can be improvised using a walking stick, an umbrella, a piece of wood, a book or even a firmly folded newspaper.
- Use of splints becomes obligatory only when both legs and both thighbones are broken.

Fractures involving the back (vertebral column) require special care. In such cases, the victim should not be allowed to get up. Further, movement must be avoided as much as possible and emergency medical help must be sought.

II. Sprain

Every joint remains in its position as it is bound to ligament fibrous bonds. These joint bonds sometimes either get broken or stretched during a sudden jerk. This condition is called sprain.

Symptoms

1. The joints lose their power of movement.
2. Inflammation appears on the affected part.
3. Severe pain is experienced in that part.
4. The colour of the skin changes.

Treatment

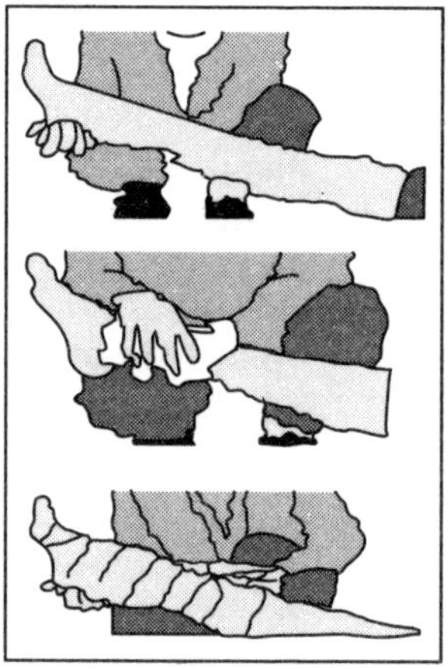

1. The affected parts should be given complete rest and movements should be stopped for some days.
2. The affected part should be thoroughly massaged with mustard oil.
3. The affected part should be tightly bandaged and put in ice water. Use of opium also gives relief.
4. If the above treatment does not give relief, the sprained part should be washed with hot water. This is likely to reduce the pain.
5. The affected part should be tightly bandaged with a water soaked bandage. This fully tightens the affected part. The affected part should not be used for work.

III. Dislocation of Bones

The displacement of a bone from its joint is called the dislocation of bone. Generally knee, elbow, shoulder, lower jaw or feet bones get dislocated.

Symptoms

1. Dislocation of bone causes severe pain.
2. The affected part gets swollen.
3. The affected part loses its power of functioning.
4. The part is deformed.
5. The part becomes motionless.

Treatment

1. This part should be tightened with a cold water-soaked bandage.
2. If the cold water-soaked bandage neither does nor relieve the pain, the affected part should be fomented.
3. If even the fomentation does not prove of any use in relieving the pain, a doctor should be consulted.

IV. Wounds

Wound is caused when body nerves break down and cause bleeding. Disease spreading germs and other poisonous matters enter the body through wounds.

Treatment

The first aid rendered to a wound has two objects: stoppage of bleeding and stopping the poisonous matter to enter the body.

1. The treatment for stopping bleeding should be attempted for stopping the flow of blood from a wound.
2. The coagulate blood on the wound should not be disturbed as a precaution against contagion.
3. The wound should be cleaned with lukewarm water in order to remove the dirt, etc. The wound should then, be allowed to dry for sometime. When it dries, gauze dipped in tincture iodine or spirit should be placed on the wound.

4. A bandage should be tightened over the wound when gauze dipped in tincture iodine or spirit has been placed over it after it has been cleaned with clean and warm water. This protects the wound from germs. Gauze or a pad is most suitable for this purpose.

V. Bleeding

Bleeding is one of the commonest causes of death in accidents. It is caused by the rupture of blood vessels due to the severity of the injury. There are two types of bleeding: external bleeding which is obvious and apparent and internal bleeding where the bleeding is not apparent at the outset but may manifest itself later in the form of bleeding from the nose, ear, lungs or stomach.

Signs and symptoms of bleeding

- The patient may feel faint and even collapse.
- The skin becomes cold and clammy.
- The pulse becomes rapid and weak.
- Breathing becomes shallow and the patient may gasp for air and sigh deeply.
- Profuse sweating may occur.
- Thirst may be prominent.

Identifying the source of bleeding

Bleeding may occur from the arteries, veins or capillaries or from combinations of the three. It can be identified by the following characteristics:

- Bleeding from the arteries is bright red and comes out in jets or spurts, which correspond to the beating of the heart. This kind of bleeding is very dangerous and may cause death quickly.
- Bleeding from the veins is dark in colour and often flows out in a continuous stream.

- Bleeding from capillaries is steady, slow ooze. In an acute situation, especially if on the surface of the body, it is less worrying than an arterial or veinous bleeding.

Managing external bleeding

- Bring the sides of the wound together and press firmly.
- Place the patient in a comfortable position and raise the injured part (if no bone fracture is suspected).
- If the pressure points are known at the appropriate locations then press on them firmly for 10-15 minutes.
- Apply a clean pad larger than the wound and press it firmly with the palm until the bleeding lessens and finally stops.
- If the bleeding continues, do not remove the original dressing but add more pads.
- Finally bandage firmly but not too tightly.
- Treat for shock.
- Shift the patient to a hospital as soon as possible.

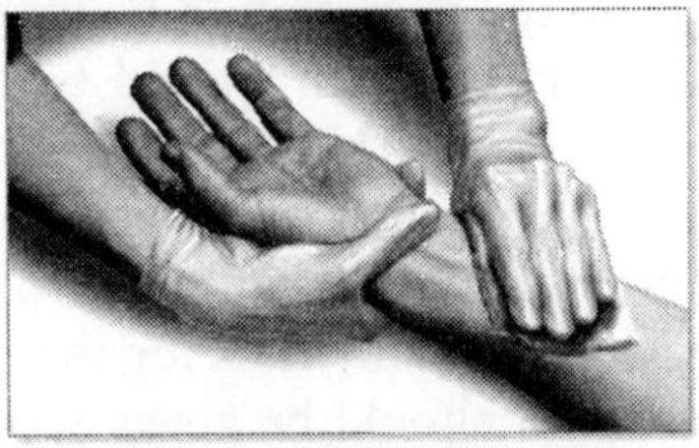

Apply direct pressure on external wounds with sterile cloth or your hand, maintaining pressure until bleeding stops

Managing internal bleeding

- Lay the patient down with the head low. Raise his legs using pillows.
- Keep the patient calm and relaxed with reassurance. Do not allow the patient to move.
- Maintain the body heat with blankets, rugs or coats.

- Do not give anything to eat.
- Do not apply hot water bottles or ice bags to the chest or abdomen. This may make things worse.
- Arrange for the patient to be shifted to the hospital at the earliest.

VI. Nose Bleeding

An injury caused to the nose or a boil causes rupture of blood capillaries of the nose. Consequently, bleeding starts. Sometimes, strong sneeze also injures the blood capillaries with the result that bleeding starts.

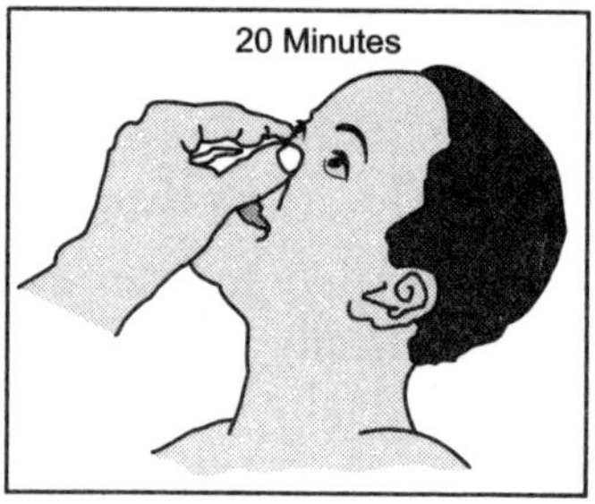

Treatment

Children bleeding from the nose should be made to sit on a chair with head hanging backward. They should sit in the direction of blowing air. Raising of both hands above the head also helps. By so doing, the flow of blood towards head slows down. The clothes on the neck should be loosened, and a cold-water soaked pad of clean cloth should be placed behind the neck or on the nose bone. The feet of the patient should be placed in hot water. He should neither be allowed to sneeze nor breathe through mouth. Alum solution in cold water may also be used. If these treatments fail, a doctor should immediately be consulted and treatment should be given accordingly.

VII. Dealing with Infection

Infection in wounds is caused by dirt and any material contaminated with germs that get into the wound. These micro-organisms may come from:

- The object that caused the wound.
- The skin of the person.
- The clothes of the person.

- The hands of the First-Aider.
- Dirty Dressings.
- Contaminated Water.
- Surrounding Air.

Ways to prevent infections in wounds

- Wash your hands thoroughly with soap and water.
- Clean the external wound with plenty of good clean drinking water.
- Dry the area surrounding the wound gently with dry sterile gauze or freshly laundered handkerchief or dhoti and cover the wound with sterile gauze if available.
- Do not let the cotton come into contact with the wound.
- If you wish to spread antiseptic over the wound, ensure that it is not mixed with water.
- Bandage the wound.

VIII. Bruises

An injury, pressure or a fall causes the blood vessels beneath the skin to break as the result of which the injured part turns blue. Pain is felt in the spot that has turned blue. Its colour also changes and it swells.

Treatment

1. A cloth soaked in ice cold water applied to the injured place gives relief.
2. Fomentation is also beneficial.
3. The injured part should be given sufficient rest.

IX. Insect Stings or Bites

Wounds are sometimes caused through an insect sting or bite. Although only little bleeding takes place, but there is a likelihood of poison spreading in the body.

Treatment

1. Sometimes, the sting is left at the place where the insect strikes. The sting should be taken out with the help of a forcep or a disinfected needle and blood allowed to flow for sometime. Later on, the wound should be cleaned with clean warm water and soap and mercury iodine applied over it.
2. Applying ammonia, spirit or a strong solution of soda bicarbonate at the affected part also reduces pain.

X. Unconsciousness

A man turns unconscious due to the effect of some poison, sun-stroke or heat stroke, too much bleeding from the head, serious mental shock due to injury on head, hurt and hysteria, epilepsy of unconsciousness caused by profuse bleeding.

XI. Poison

Substances which when taken into the body cause damage to health or death are called poisons. Poisons can get into the body either by swallowing, by inhalation, by injection, or by contact with the skin.

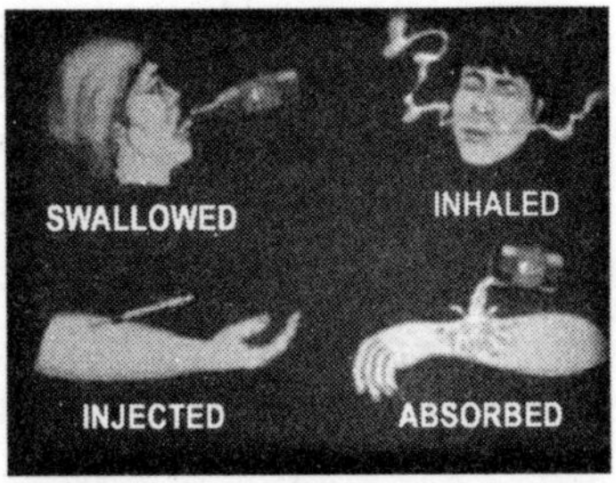

Management

- Removing the patient to the hospital or a doctor is the highest priority and needs to be done as quickly as possible.
- Preserve the packets or bottles of the suspected poison and also any of the vomitus, sputum, etc. for the doctor to examine.
- If the patient is unconscious, do not induce vomiting.
- Make the patient lie on his back on a hard, flat bed without any pillow and turn the head to one side. As there is no pressure on the stomach and the gullet is horizontal, the vomited matter will not get into the air passages. This is also a good posture for giving artificial respiration if needed.
- Sometimes when there is excess vomiting the three quarter-prone position (when the patient is made to lie on his side with one leg stretched and the other bent at the knee and the thigh) will make things easier for the patient.
- If the breathing is very slow or has stopped, start artificial respiration and continue till the doctor comes.
- If the patient is conscious, and the poison is not a corrosive, aid vomiting by tickling the back of the throat or make him drink tepid water mixed with two table spoonfuls of common salt for one tumbler of water.
- When the poison is a corrosive do not induce vomiting. Signs of corrosive poisoning include grayish white or yellowish burn patches around the lips and mouth.

- Certain poisons need to be diluted by giving large quantities of cold water (iced, if possible). This will dilute the irritant and delay the absorption and will replace the fluid lost by vomiting. However, this should be done only for some poisons and not as a general rule (See table below).
- For certain poisons soothing drinks like milk, egg beaten and mixed with water is good for the purpose.
- For several poisons specific antidotes are available and it is essential that one seeks information about these antidotes.

Some common poisons and the first aid for them

Poison	Source	First Aid
Arsenic	Rat Poisons, Weed Killers	Induce vomiting and give soothing drinks.
Aspirin	Aspirin Tablets	Induce vomiting. Drink of soda bicarbonate (one tsp. to a tumbler of water) to be given. Strong coffee or tea may be given.
Carbon-Monoxide	Charcoal Stove, Gas Stove,	Exhaust gases of cars apply artificial respiration. Give Oxygen.
Sleeping Tablets	Chemists	Induce Vomiting. Give Magnesium Sulphate (2 tsp. in water). Give hot coffee. Keep the patient awake.
Mercury	Calomel, Teething Powders, Mercury	Give white of egg in water. Later give milk. Then induce vomiting.
Lead	Paints, Hair Dyes, Pencils	Induce vomiting. Then give Magnesium Sulphate in water.
Opium and Morphia	Hospitals, Some Chemical Mixtures, Opium addicts	Put a few crystals of Potassium Permanganate in a tumbler of water and give as a drink. Give hot coffee. Keep the patient awake.

(Contd...)

Petrol, Paraffin, Kerosene	Houses, Garages, Oil Industry	Induce Vomiting. Give a large quantity of water or tender coconut. Liquid Paraffin if available is preferable to water in cases of kerosene oil poisoning.
Phosphorous	Rat Poisons and Match Heads	Induce vomiting. Give a large quantity of water or tender coconut. Never give oils as they will dissolve the phosphorous and increase the effect of the poison.
Prussic Acid	Photography or Electro-plating Industries, Oil of Bitter Almonds, Tender Bamboo shoots	Emergency. Act at once. Induce vomiting. Begin artificial.
Strychnine	Some Vermin Killers	Induce vomiting if there are no spasms. If breathing is irregular or has stopped, give artificial respiration.
Follidol	Bug Killers and Cockroach	Killers induce vomiting. Give water or tender coconut. Start artificial respiration if required.

In all the cases it is essential to get the patient to a doctor or hospital as soon as possible.

XII. Sunstroke or Heat Stroke

During the summer season sunstroke or heat stroke is caused due to the exposure in bright sunshine. Both these conditions are caused by too high a temperature in the atmosphere, but the signs and symptoms are quite different. Humid surroundings also add to the problems. Loss of body fluids and salt is an important factor complicating heat-related problems. This produces restlessness headache and giddiness. The person feels like vomiting and his temperature rises high. His respiration increases and he feels thirsty. His face turns red and sometimes he becomes unconscious.

Signs and Symptoms

Heat Exhaustion	Heat Stroke
Headache, Dizziness, Nausea, Vomiting and occasionally Abdominal Cramps	Occurs suddenly but may follow untreated exhaustion.
Unconsciousness follows	Unconsciousness rapid but may come after headache.
Face is pale and pulse becomes weak	Pulse is full and bounding. Face becomes flushed. Skin is hot and dry.
Temperature mormal or slightly high	Temperature rises rapidly, sometimes more than 107°F.
Symptoms of shock	Death may occur if temperature is not controlled.

Treatment

The first treatment of such a person suffering from sunstroke is to reduce the temperature. His clothes should, therefore, be loosened and he should be kept in a cool place. His head and neck should be washed with cold water and ice be placed over his head and neck. This gives sufficient relief to the victim. The patient should be given cold water to drink. If all this treatment does not reduce his suffering, sandal paste can be applied on his body. If even this fails to give relief he should be taken to a physician for proper treatment.

XIII. Foreign Matters

Sometimes foreign matters enter into children's ear, nose or throat, which though do not give much trouble at the time, should immediately be taken out. Generally, people try to take them out with the help of crude instruments by their own hands, which are not used for doing such delicate jobs. The results sometimes are very serious. This should never be done under any circumstances; instead a physician should be consulted.

Small insects, dust particles or thin blades of grass sometimes fall in the eyes while the child is playing, walking or running. This is very painful. Efforts should immediately be made to remove them. The victim should repeatedly open and close his eyes in clean water. Washing the eye with water or boric acid is also helpful. Blowing the air from the mouth into the eye also proves useful and relieves the pain. If the foreign matter is in the upper lid, the upper eyelid should be stretched over the lower one. This will enable the eyelashes of the lower lid to remove that substance. This process should continue till the matter is removed.

Sometimes flies, small seeds, insects or blades of grass, etc. enter the ear, which besides being painful also produces deafness. This causes swelling in the ear. There is always a fear of this swelling reaching the brain as well. In this condition putting some oil in the ear is very helpful. If it fails the child should be taken to an ear specialist.

Sometimes some foreign matter enters the nose of the child and creates trouble. In such conditions, the child should be made to smell things that produce sneezing. The nostril that is inhaling air should be closed and efforts should be made to sneeze through the blocked nostril. If these methods fail, a doctor should be approached. An obstruction created into the throat by foreign matter also creates a troublesome situation. The face turns blue, throat is choked, eyes appear to be coming out of the sockets and the victim turns senseless. In this condition efforts should be made to remove the obstruction by putting the finger in the throat. This will cause vomiting and the obstructing matter would come out. If all this fails, artificial respiration should be resorted to. A physician should immediately be called and the victim should be made to stand on his head by raising his legs towards the sky.

XIV. Drowning

A person becomes unconscious when he drowns in water because the water enters the windpipe creating obstruction in his respiration. He feels cold. In this condition efforts should be made to bring him to senses. Immediate help of a doctor should be sought. All the tight fitting clothes of the drowned man should be loosened carefully. His legs should be raised upwards for taking out the water from his body. Artificial respiration should be continued till he begins to breathe air of his own accord. When the victim regains breathing he should be covered with blanket and hot water rubber bottles be placed by his sides. If he is able to drink, hot drinks like tea or coffee should be given to him.

XV. Burns and Scalds

Burns are injuries that result from dry heat like fire/flames, pieces of hot metal, contact with live wires, etc. Scalds are caused by moist heat due to boiling water, steam, oil, tar, etc. Chemical burns are caused by strong acids like Sulphuric or Nitric acid or by strong alkalies like caustic soda. The instantaneous flash of intense heat given off by a nuclear explosion causes nuclear burns. It causes burns on the skins of people several miles away.

Degrees of Burn

The degree of burns indicates the degree of damage to the tissues. There are three degrees of burns. They are:

- First Degree Burns: The skin is reddened.
- Second Degree Burns: There are blisters on the skin.
- Third Degree Burns: There is destruction of deeper tissues with scarring.

The danger from burns depends more on the extent of the burns than on the degree. Superficial burns over a large area are more dangerous than complete charring of a part of a limb. On any one person, different parts of the body may show varying degree of burns. Burns are dangerous because:

- They can very quickly lead to shock in the immediate period following the burn due to loss of excessive fluids from the body.
- They produce intense pain.
- They lead to infection in the affected area.

- When they heal they leave scars behind, which are disfiguring and can restrict movements.

Symptoms

The skin turns red when it burns or scalds. There is unbearable pain and the clothes stick to the burnt spot. The burning sensation caused by the formation of blisters is extremely painful. Sometimes, besides the skin, the flesh below it too, is burnt. Severe burning produces shock as the result of which one may die. His face turns yellow; he feels cold, his respiration and heart beating slow down due to shock.

Treatment

1. The clothes from the burnt spot should be removed carefully. The cloth should be cut if it sticks to the wound. Some kind of oil should be applied over the burnt spot.
2. A solution containing a spoon of soda bi-carbonate in about a pound of water should be applied on burnt places with the help of cotton or piece of clean cloth.
3. The burnt spot should be put in water having body temperature.
4. Blisters should not be opened, because by so doing there is a possibility of catching contagion.
5. Tannic acid jelly ointment should be applied over the wound. It produces cooling effect and cures the destroyed tissues. Iodex or Repento ointment too is useful.
6. After applying these ointments, clean cotton should be placed over the wounds and it should be bandaged.
7. Efforts should be made to overcome the shock. The patient should be kept warm by covering him with blankets and by keeping hot-water bottle besides him. He should be given hot milk, tea, coffee or half a glass of clean water with a spoon of ammonium carbonate or the solution of vanishing salt.

8. Solution of soda-bicarbonate applied over the wounds through gauze also relieves pain in the case of acid burns.
9. Vinegar of lemon juice solution made in water proves beneficial in the case of burns caused by alkaline.
10. The person should immediately lie down on the floor when the clothes catch fire and he should continue to roll till the fire is extinguished completely. The fire also extinguishes if the victim is covered by a piece of blanket.

Management of minor burns and scalds

1. Clean the area gently with clean water.
2. Submerge the burnt area in cold water.
3. Do not apply cotton wool directly over the burnt area.
4. Do not apply any greasy substance.
5. Give the patient warm drinks.

Management of chemical burns

1. Wash off the chemical with a large quantity of water by using a shower as quickly as possible. This flooding with water will wash away much of the irritants.
2. Cut out contaminated clothing.
3. Do not touch the burnt area.
4. Treat as for burns.

Conclusion

Since it is not surprising that teachers spend most of their time with children, teachers' knowledge of what actions to take in times of minor or major injuries is crucial to students' safety. Although most if not all schools have a nurse or other first aid qualified personnel on site, injuries can happen at anytime and any place, and may require the teacher to act alone.

All students have the right to learn in a safe and protective school environment. Preventing unintentional injuries at school would help improve the learning environment. Although it is not mandatory by law for all teachers to have first aid training, the fact remains that teachers are surrounded by children for a significant amount of time, and some teachers may actually find themselves in the situation where other means of intervention is required. Preventing injuries by providing a safe educational environment is of prime concern to teachers. Teachers should be well prepared to act when students are injured.

The focus of health and safety in the school as a workplace is on the prevention of illnesses and injuries. Where an injury or illness does occur, first aid facilities that are adequate for the immediate treatment of injuries and illnesses that may arise in a school are provided. In particular in an emergency, all staff has a duty of care to provide assistance if a person requires immediate attention and no staff member trained in first aid is available. Staff is to use common sense that in an emergency, while they should not act beyond their capabilities and qualifications, they are expected to do what they can to prevent the condition worsening while awaiting medical services. Schools are required to have a member of staff who is the holder of a current first aid certificate issued after successful completion of an approved first aid course.

Role of Teachers in Health Education and Administration

15

Health education has become a focal point during the last few years as our nation has worked toward reaching specific health goals for the citizens of our country. The emphasis on health education has, in turn, led to an increased awareness of the need for effective health educators. In order to be effective, an educator must concentrate not only on academic preparation but also on personal qualifications. Personal qualifications of an educator are important because of the significant emphasis placed on the teacher's behaviour and attitudes. Teaching health is unlike teaching any other topic in the curriculum. However, in health education, the teacher may never know whether a student actually applies a health concept in her life.

Children's health and learning are unquestionably linked. Healthy children are more able to learn and achieve academic success. Schools are often described as being ideal environments for teaching children about health because they provide access to large numbers of children, are staffed by professionally trained educators and nurses, and frequently offer services that promote health, such as nutrition programmes and health centers. According to one study comparing students at low and high risk for food insufficiency, students who were undernourished scored lower on math tests, were more likely to have been suspended from school, and had more problems getting along with others (Alaimo, Olson, and Frongillo, 2001). Conversely, schools that offer physical education and health education produce students with higher scores on tests of reading, writing, and mathematics; higher grade point averages; and better attendance than comparable schools without an emphasis on health (Improving Academic Performance, 2000).

Teachers play an important role in fostering the intellectual and social development of children during their formative years. The education that students acquire is key in determining the future of those students. Whether in elementary or high schools or in private or public schools, teachers provide the tools and the environment for their students to develop into responsible adults. Every teacher in the school is a health teacher, regardless of what discipline she is actually teaching. This implies that regardless of the subject matter the teacher is teaching, she is making an impact on the students through her behaviour. In other words, the teacher is on the display before her students and she has the opportunity to portray a positive health image through his/her behaviour. The teacher has an excellent opportunity to become a good health role model by practicing safe and healthy habits. Students need to be emphasized that they cannot become healthy passively. Involving them in active learning opportunities, in which they are allowed to clarify their values and are taught how to make a wise decision, will personalize their health education. The students will be better able to make their own responsible choices for healthful behaviour.

The teacher has a very active role to play in the School Health Service programme. He comes into contact with the children so often that he is likely to be the first person to notice functional signs of diseases, which appear before physical signs. He finds that certain pupil cannot see from a distance what is written on the board, some are found sleepy, some have running nose, and some pupils remain absent from the school quite often. Such defects may be pointed to the school physician as early as possible because these have a positive correlation with the scholastic achievement of the child.

The teacher should know the signs of different diseases, incubation period after exposure, the duration of communicability and the means of transmission. Children suffering from communicable diseases should not be allowed to attend the class. In this respect, cooperation of the parents must be obtained. The teacher has the added responsibility of reflecting health teaching in a positive way. Both the physical and mental health of the teacher must be good for both have a strong effect upon the developing personalities with whom the teacher comes into extended contact. The health practices and attitudes acquired by the pupils, the quality of the human relationships and the 'emotional climate' that exists in the room are almost without exception reflections of the behaviour and example of the teacher. The teacher consequently owes it to himself as well as also his pupils to assume responsibility for maintaining his best physical condition.

Hindrances in Teacher Preparation in Health

Several factors may account for poor preparation of teachers in health:

- *Lack of time in the teacher education curriculum*: The increased demands placed on teacher education programmes to produce teachers who are competent in numerous subject areas, as well as proficient in classroom management, technology, and multicultural education, results in fewer hours to devote to subjects seen as less important, such as health.
- *Emphasis on standardized testing*: Teacher education programmes must produce teachers who are able to prepare students to take state-mandated standardized tests in math, reading, science, social studies, and several other areas. Subjects like health, for which standardized testing is rare, may be de-emphasized in favour of devoting more time to subjects that are tested.
- *Lack of comfort*: Health education includes many sensitive and controversial topics. Teacher education faculty may find it difficult to overcome their own discomfort with these topics and fail to prepare student teachers adequately to address such topics.

Barriers to Successful Health Teaching

Elementary and secondary education majors in most colleges receive very little instruction in health content and in methodology that specifically relates to health instruction. Because the schoolteacher must teach many subjects, most college programmes emphasize methods and materials instead of specific subject areas. This puts the teacher at a distinct disadvantage, because teaching health requires a different methodology than the teaching of other subjects. Teaching content alone is not sufficient in health education. Students may be able to pass a paper and pencil test on health knowledge, but this does not ensure that the student will put that knowledge into practice. This is known as a health behaviour gap, which refers to the discrepancy between personal health knowledge and general health behaviour.

Health instruction requires an active involvement of the student in the learning process that is, students must be given opportunities to experience situations in which they focus their values and make decisions regarding health behaviour. Again this teaching process is no guarantee that every student will make a healthy decision in each case, but it will more effectively help the student learn the concept being taught as well as apply the concept to her lifestyle. To overcome these specific barriers, prospective health educators should take as many courses as possible that emphasize health content and health instruction.

Effective health instruction is hindered by the tremendous wealth of health information. Health education is by its nature interdisciplinary; it borrows from not only educational theory but also many social sciences, such as psychology and sociology; as well as physical science, biology and even religion. It is difficult enough for a health education specialist to stay current in health, much less the elementary teacher who must master several other subject areas. This barrier is compounded by the fact that health information is changing constantly—the results of new studies related to health information appear virtually every day. The teacher has an obligation to follow these new developments. One way to do this is to attend educational seminars and workshops.

Another barrier to effective health instruction is the fact that so many issues in health education are controversial. Such issues sometimes offend the students and parents and polarize the students. The more controversial the topic, the more emotional the students become about the issue. Thus, there is greater likelihood of dissension and ill feelings among the students. This can disrupt the optimal teaching-learning environment that is necessary in health instruction.

Finally, administrators sometimes place a low priority on health education by allowing other activities to substitute for health instruction, or by not placing health education in the curriculum at all. One way to overcome this problem is to help other teachers integrate health education with the "three R's".

Professional Preparation of Teachers

Teachers who will be providing health education need to have teacher health literacy. This is defined as, "the capacity to obtain, interpret, and understand basic health information and services, with the competence to use such information and services in ways that enhance the learning of health concepts and skills by school students" (Peterson et al., 2001). Although standards for professional training of health educators have been set in the past, school health education has been criticized as being ineffective. This is largely the result of poorly prepared teachers. Ideally, a secondary school health teacher should be a specialist, but this is not feasible when so many subjects have to be taught. Therefore, the secondary teachers are forced to teach subjects like health with less professional preparation.

Health is different from other subjects in that the content comes from a variety of sources and is not limited to one distinct discipline. Also, the behavioural outcomes desired of the student in a health class differ markedly from those with other subjects. Because these outcomes are not easily measured, a health teacher should have specific training in making empirical observations that indicate whether the desired outcomes are being acquired. A course dealing with the personal health of the individual is desirable. In this course, prospective teachers learn more about their own personal behaviour. Further a base course in first aid and emergency is very helpful.

According to the National Task Force on the Preparation and Practice of Health Educators, the prospective health teacher should be sufficiently prepared through a course of study to be able to:

1. Assess individual and community needs for health education.
2. Plan effective health education programmes.
3. Implement health programmes.
4. Evaluate the effectiveness of health education programmes.
5. Coordinate provision of health education services.

6. Act as a resource person of health education.
7. Communicate health and health education needs, concerns and resources.

Personal Qualities of Teachers

There are many influences on a child, such as the media and peer pressure that may be detrimental. Teachers should be positive role models because they are an important factor in students' health behaviour development. Social learning theory supports the premise that educators who model good health behaviour may have a positive impact on their students and may help their students make good choices regarding health behaviour. The health teacher should know oneself, her motivation and her energy, be open-minded, be secure and develop one's own self-concept, always look for new ideas and model programmes, work with goals and objectives—be aware of one's direction, keep the curriculum up to date, be aware that one's own lifestyle is open to public scrutiny and must see the students as the central focus of one's energy, effort and enthusiasm.

Working with students and parents

One of the teacher's responsibilities is counselling the students in health related matters. Counselling should be straightforward and free of moral judgement, preaching or scare tactics. In the role of a counsellor, the teacher must develop good listening and communication skills. Also teachers need to show genuine empathy toward a student's problem. When the teacher is highly empathetic, the students tend to develop a more positive attitude toward self and tend to utilize their abilities more fully in school achievement. Personal interaction between a teacher and her students is critical and each child should feel free to experience uniqueness. A teacher can help make this possible by accepting the child as he or she is.

No matter how concerned a teacher is about a student's problem, she must recognize the limitations of her ability to help. If she cannot provide effective counselling or if she realizes that more help is necessary, she should refer the student to another teacher or an administrator. The student may also require additional guidance beyond the initial crisis counselling the teacher can supply, so teachers should be familiar with available services in the school or community in order to refer the student to the most appropriate one. Most teachers are not professionally trained in counselling, nor are they expected to replace those who are. A teacher's personal attributes are as important as her knowledge of the subject. Some of the teacher's responsibilities in a school as far as health matters of students are concerned are:

1. *Personal cleanliness*

The daily inspection of the students' cleanliness by the teacher in the morning is very helpful in enforcing personal cleanliness. A rapid survey may be made daily and cleanliness competition may be introduced among the students.

2. *Development of habits*

Correct habits of breathing and feeding should be introduced among the children. A wise teacher will also pay adequate attention to classroom habits like posture, etc.

3. *Physical exercises*

A variety of programmes of physical activities will be provided so that the students may choose suitable physical exercises for themselves.

4. *Vaccination and inoculation*

The students should be regularly vaccinated and inoculated through proper arrangements by the school.

5. *Medical inspection and follow-up work*

Regular and thorough medical examination should be arranged and its follow-up taken seriously.

6. *Training in first-aid*

The students should be given training in first-aid in times of emergency.

7. *Better human relations*

The children should be educated to do their best for the betterment of the health of their friends, relatives, neighbours and the whole community.

8. *Special methods of teaching health*

The school should arrange for special methods of teaching health in the form of health posters, health projects and health weeks, health book, films and film strips, excursions, health clubs, health counselling and follow up, healthy environment, radio, etc.

Teachers also need to be aware of the children with special health needs and stress to all students that each of them is unique and that they should strive to coexist with each other regardless of the differences. It is very important for teachers to encourage positive behaviour from the special students, by emphasizing what they can do rather than what they cannot do; to find a talent that each student has and encourage development of the same to foster student's feeling of self-worth and to look for every circumstances in which the special student can be included in social activities with other students. These positive actions will both help special students to adjust to the regular classroom and encourage other students to accept them.

Teachers should always notify a student's parents when illness or serious deviation from normal health occurs. School policy should be followed when parents are notified. Some schools require teachers to contact parents through the administrative offices. A good policy is to ensure that a member of the school administration is present at any parent-teacher conference. The third party can clear up any confusion in communication and can serve as an arbitrator in case of misunderstandings. The teacher needs to explain the parents the significance of the child's health condition and encourage them to obtain needed care for the child. If the parent asks for guidance in seeking care, a teacher or administrator can refer the person to the proper agency.

Working with other teachers and school administration

One of the major responsibilities of the health teacher is to keep the other teachers informed of health matters related to the community and students. This information will assist the other faculty members in understanding their students and also help them recognize the need for health education in the school. Teachers should also attempt to become involved in textbook selection committees so that they can look not only for sound, up-to-date content but also eliminate textbooks that propagate stereotypes. The primary responsibility of the educator is to plan the health education curriculum and make recommendations to the administration regarding the health education programme within the school. The teacher can help interpret and implement any state requirement for the health curriculum and make suggestions concerning the health service programme and health environment. The teacher should keep the administration informed about a child's progress in school after returning from an illness.

Working with the school clinic and outside agencies

Because of the daily observations of each child in class, the health educator can help the school nurse understand the health behaviour of students and assist the nurse in various aspects of the screening programme by helping conduct preliminary screening in the classroom, preparing students for screening tests to reduce their anxiety and referring students who are in particular need of screening. One objective of health educators should be to promote health education and awareness in the community, so that they can help volunteer organizations to educate the community in health matters. Also they should be involved with the local public health department and cooperate with department staff members in providing services to the students and community.

Role of Teachers in Promoting Adolescent Health

Teachers are among the most important influences in the lives of school-aged children, yet relatively the emphasis has been placed on examining the potential role general academic teachers may play in facilitating adolescent health promotion efforts, according to a study conducted by researchers at Columbia University's Mailman School of Public Health and published in the *Journal of School Health*. The study results indicate that teachers provide valuable information to school personnel about what health issues are important to adolescents, in particular, because they hear feedback from adolescents on a daily basis. "We found that teachers agreed that schools were an important venue for discussing and providing health messages", says Alwyn T. Cohall, MD, Associate Professor of clinical Socio Medical Sciences, and Director of the Harlem Health Promotion Center and lead author. "However they expressed concern about their ability to handle mental health, behavioural health, and reproductive health problems, and desire additional staff development workshops to address these needs."

More than half (52%) of those surveyed overheard student discussions about health once a week or more in classrooms, hallways, canteens and playgrounds. Seventy per cent of teachers stated they were actively approached by students one to three times per semester or more with personal problems or health concerns. The survey was conducted among academic teachers and administrators working in four schools in the Northern Manhattan community of New York City. These schools had a cumulative enrollment of approximately 4,600 students, and an active school-based health clinic on site, providing a wide range of free physical and mental health services to students during school hours, including primary and reproductive healthcare. The teachers surveyed believe that schools are an appropriate place for discussion and dissemination of health information. Yet, the data indicates that fewer than 20 per cent of the teachers had provided formal classroom material on a health topic such as nutrition (19.8%), tobacco, drugs or alcohol (19.0%), reproductive health (17.2%), mental health (15%), less than 8 per cent planned to provide such material in the future.

In general, teachers described themselves as being reasonably comfortable addressing many of these problems. They were less comfortable discussing problems at home, emotional or mental health and medical problems or illness. Sixty-three per cent of teachers surveyed indicated they had referred a student to the school-based clinic, suggesting that teachers play an important role in facilitating care for youth. The findings suggest the need for closer and more consistent interactions between school-based clinic staff and school personnel throughout the year, and points out the need for further research to develop cost-effective and time efficient strategies to enhance the health literacy of all school personnel.

Regular classroom teachers are the backbone of school health instruction, particularly at the elementary and secondary level. Thus, colleges and universities can directly impact the quality of health instruction in our public schools by addressing key standards for health education and incorporating important health concepts into their teacher preparation curriculum.

Schools have a fundamental role in the development of a health literate population. Classroom based health education, as both an individual discipline and a component of coordinated school health programmes is the nucleus for the development of health literacy in today's children and adolescents. Emphasizing essential 21st century skills in the instruction practice and assessment that takes place in the health education classrooms will likely lead to improved health literacy.

Section–III

Mental Health, Hygiene and Education

Understanding Normality and Abnormality

16

The definition of the word abnormal is simple enough: "deviating from the norm". However, applying this to psychology poses a complex problem: what is normal? Whose norm? For what age? For what culture? Some would simply classify what is "good" as normal and what is "bad" as abnormal, but this is a vague and narrow definition and brings up many of the same questions for the definition of "good" as does the definition for "normal". There are many more ways of determining a more objective reference point.

What we consider normal and what we consider abnormal, disturbed or psychopathological obviously has great importance for clinical psychology and psychiatry. Yet there is no clear consensus as to the definition of normality against which particular types of deviant or disordered behaviour can be considered normal.

Normality, as health, refers to a reasonable rather than an optimal state of functioning and is defined by the absence of manifest pathology.

> Health in a positive sense consists in the capacity of the organism to maintain a balance in which it may be reasonably free of undue pain, discomfort, disability or limitation of action including social capacity.

The commonplace men and women who exhibit at least ordinary competence in self-management and get along reasonably well with themselves and their associates constitute the normal or average group. The great majority of the general populations are normal people. Clearly, a person can be called normal if he is not sick, if he is average, if he confirms to social norms, or if he approximates an ideally mature, healthy or fully functioning personality. Behaviour according to Shoben (1957) is normal to the extent that it expresses man's most unique capacities for symbolization and social involvement.

Indeed, one can view a kind of continuum ranging from the grossly disturbed to the conventionally adequate to the creatively mature and we often do this in clinical practice as in ordinary social life. Thus, one way of defining abnormality is statistical deviation. Most human characteristics are nicely distributed along a smooth bell-shaped curve.

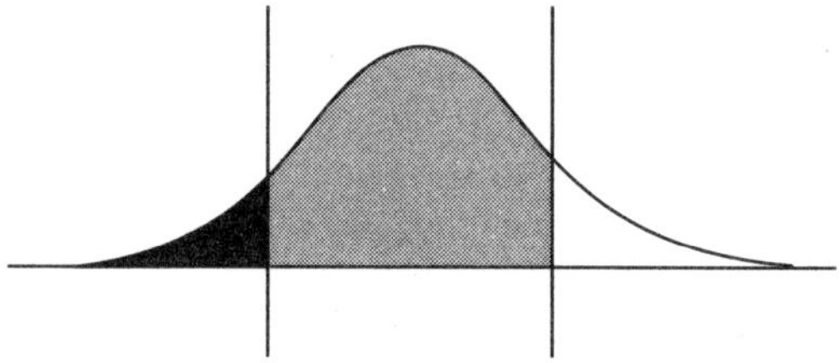

Those who stray too far from the average on this curve are then considered abnormal. This definition, however, has its problems. It does not recognize valuable derivations, such as genius, nor does it recognize common but maladaptive behaviour like smoking and drinking. Nonetheless, this method is both objective and scientific.

The Superior and the Abnormal

Scattered through the rank and file histories there would be found a smaller group of individuals who deviate from the normal in a favourable or healthy direction. In contrast to the mediocrity of the normal group, these individuals are definitely superior in intelligence, personality, social adjustment and emotional stability. These superior men and women not only lead wholesome, successful lives themselves but also often contribute to the welfare and happiness of others through their inventions, achievements and personal influences. Almost about 10 per cent of the general population is classed as superior individuals.

There can be found a small group of equally spectacular and unusual cases that deviate from the normal in an unfavourable or pathological direction. Included in this abnormal group would be individuals marked by limited intelligence, emotional instability, personality disorganization and character defects, who, for the most part, lead wretched personal lives and social misfits or liabilities. These abnormal deviants constitute 10 per cent of the general population.

A very simple idea that can be used to classify abnormal behaviour is personal distress. Basically, if a person is content with their life, then they are of no concern to the mental health field. However, if a person's thoughts or behaviours are causing them personal discomfort or unhappiness, then they will be considered abnormal. The most common criterion for defining abnormality, however, is maladaptiveness. There are two aspects of maladaptive behaviour:

1. Maladaptive to one's self—inability to reach goals, to adapt to the demands of life, and
2. Maladaptive to society—interferes, disrupts social group functioning.

This type of definition allows much flexibility. It provides room for conforming behaviour to society's norms as well as deviant behaviour as long as it is not self-damaging. It makes abnormal the relative term it needs to be, dependent upon each individual's life and circumstances. There are certain categories of behaviour that suggest the presence of psychological disorders which are, in one way or another, maladaptive in that they threaten the well-being of the individual. These categories include long periods of discomfort, impaired functioning, bizarre behaviour, and disruptive behaviour.

Long periods of discomfort

Everyone experiences some kind of psychological discomfort during his or her life. This could be anything as simple as worrying about a math test to grieving the death of a loved one.

This distress, however, is related to real, related, or threatened events and passes away with time. When such distressing feelings, however, persist for an extended period of time and seem to be unrelated to events surrounding the person, they would be considered abnormal and could suggest a psychological disorder.

Impaired functioning

Here, again, there must be made a distinction between simply a passing period of inefficiency and prolonged inefficiency, which seems unexplainable. For instance, a very brilliant person who consistently fails in classes or someone who constantly changes jobs for no reason.

Bizarre behaviour

There are many things people do that others would find strange. The various type of piercing that younger generation of today do and their style of dress may seem bizarre to adults, but their motivations are not hard to understand, which keeps them from being considered clinically abnormal. Bizarre behaviour that has no rational basis, however, seems to indicate that the individual is confused. The psychoses frequently bring on hallucinations (baseless sensory perceptions) or delusions (beliefs which are patently false yet held as truth by the individual).

Disruptive behaviour

Disruptive behaviour means impulsive, apparently uncontrollable behaviour that disrupts the lives of others or deprives them of their human rights on a regular basis. This type of behaviour is characteristic of a severe psychological disorder. An example of this is the antisocial personality disorder.

All of these types of behaviour are maladaptive because they directly affect the well-being of the individual and those around them, and block the growth and fulfillment of the individual's potential.

Perceptions of normality and abnormality differ between cultures, subcultures, and individuals and change over time. The extreme selfishness of a child is accepted as normal; in an adult such selfishness would be regarded as abnormal. Men holding hands are normal in some societies, in others it is regarded as abnormal. For a person to be quiet and withdrawn may be normal for that individual. For a person to be noisy and active may be normal for that individual. If the individual's behaviour changes then, for that person, the behaviour may be abnormal. Thus, every society has certain standards or norms of behaviour that it expects. Such things as the way we dress, politeness, and bad language are subject to certain rules. However, social norms are different in different societies. Ideas of what is normal and abnormal also change over time. Therefore, we have to take account of all the factors relating to an individual before 'Labelling' their behaviour abnormal.

Characteristics of a Normal Person

As now we understand, normality means different things to different people at different times in different settings. If, as a soldier, we shoot someone in wartime we may receive a medal; if we shoot someone in peacetime we will be put in a prison. If we lose our job and someone close to us dies then it is normal for us to be unhappy and depressed. In fact if we were not unhappy and depressed it would be abnormal. Therefore, we have to look at emotions and behaviour in the context in which they occur. Following are some of the characteristics of a mentally normal person:

1. *Efficient perception of reality*

They have a realistic view of their strengths and weaknesses. They know what they can do and what they cannot do. They have a realistic perception of what is happening around them and their reactions to those events.

2. *Self -knowledge*

They have an understanding of why they do things and why they have certain emotions. None of us has complete insight into our feelings and behaviour but normal people have more insight than the mentally ill.

3. *Ability to control behaviour*

Occasionally normal people may act impulsively, i.e., without thinking but normally they can control drives such as aggression or sexuality.

4. *Self-esteem*

They know their own value and feel happy with their achievements and abilities. They feel accepted by those around them. They may wish that they were more handsome or intelligent but they do not allow these ideas to rule their lives. They know that though they may not be handsome, they have a nice personality or that though they cannot be a university professor they are doing a useful job, which brings in money for their family to live on. Mentally disordered people often feel that they are worthless and not accepted by other people for their feelings of worthlessness and rejection.

5. *Able to form close relationships*

Normal people are able to form close and satisfying friendships and relationships. They are aware of other people's feelings and beliefs and adapt to them. Mentally disordered people often think only of their own problems, and are unable to care about other people's problems; they are often self-centered. Sometimes they do not want to form close friendships because at some time in the past they were emotionally hurt by the breakup of a relationship.

6. *Productivity*

Mentally normal people are able to channel their energies into work and social life. They are enthusiastic about their lives and enjoy activities. Mentally disordered people often feel chronically tired and each day is an obstacle to be suffered, not enjoyed.

The Pathological Personality

In general, the disturbed person can be characterized by the obverse of the traits which describe psychological health. Depending on the extent and type of disturbance, the person lacks voluntary control, ego strength, flexibility and adaptability. He experiences himself as weak among powerful and uncontrollable forces. His self-concept is distorted and unrealistic; he lacks self-esteem or has a vastly exaggerated notion of his worth. He is driven by deficiency motives. Basic drives are either acted out in raw and impulsive actions or inhibited and blocked. Powerful and painful negative affects are more than experiences of joy, love or accomplishment. Despite frequent and rigid defensive maneuvers, crystallized into symptoms, threat is always present and with it, anxiety, actual or potential. Basic psychological functions may be disturbed, perception, learning and memory may be need-determined rather than reality appropriate or they may reflect forms more characteristic of lower developmental levels.

All said it has to be remembered that there is a continuum from the abnormal to normal and that boundaries are indeed hard to define. In terms of the general state of the personality, individuals can be positioned from one pole of complete disorganization and pathology to the other of heroic health. But it is also true that in different situations, in different realms of behaviour, and at different moments any of us, could appear more or less abnormal. The healthy person, fatigued or irritated, may express intense rage or other grossly inappropriate feelings or behaviour. Conversely, even severely disordered people may have long periods in which they function adequately or in particular situations which allow ordered behaviour. In general, it is under conditions of stress, when extreme or unusual demands are made, that the strengths or weaknesses of the personality organization appear most vividly.

Among psychoanalysts, Kubie (1954) has most clearly developed the thesis that the essential difference between normal and neurotic lies in whether behaviour is under conscious control or whether it is automatically determined by unconscious processes. The unconsciously determined act is repetitive, insatiable and impervious to conscious experience because it is directed toward unconscious symbols and goals which by their nature are unattainable. Generalizing these concepts, Kubie argues that a person can be called normal to the extent that his actions are determined by conscious motives.... "we may say that a state of greater health is achieved whenever those areas of life that are dominated by inaccessible unconscious forces are shrunk, so that a larger area of life is dominated by conscious or preconscious forces, which can come to awareness when necessary. This is a reasonable concept of health and a reasonable formulation of the goal of therapy..." (1954, p. 184).

Mental Hygiene and Mental Health

17

Mental hygiene is the science that creates a personality in every individual in society that makes for good adjustment with the environment that attains a proper synthesis between the intellectual, emotional and other aspects and avoids tension and conflict in his conduct with other individuals in society. The aim of mental hygiene is the evolution and development of a properly adjusted and balanced personality. The objectives of mental hygiene can be as follows:

1. Treatment and Remedying of Mental Defects

Defining mental hygiene, Lawrence F. Shaffer (1956) has written that mental hygiene or the science of mental health is concerned with the prevention of inadequate adjustment or with those processes or methods, which adjust the maladjusted individual. Thus, this function of mental hygiene is the curing of mental ailments, defects and imbalances.

2. Preventing of Personality Complications

The creative aspect of hygiene does not exhaust its possibilities. The science prevents all kinds of personality disorders, since all mental diseases originate in them. According to Thomas V. Moore (1944), mental hygiene is that science which studies the human personality and its deviations, from the curative standpoint. In this manner, another objective of mental hygiene is the curing or removal of abnormalities of the personality, since it is only in the absence of such aberration that the individual can be balanced. Abnormality leads to imbalance, all kinds of mental conflicts and disease. Prevention of such diseases take the form both of curing them as well as prevention of further procreation from such parents since diseases are likely to be transmitted through heredity.

3. Safeguard of Mental Health

The most comprehensive function of mental hygiene is the safeguard of mental health. According to D.B. Klein (1944), mental hygiene prevents mental aberrations and advances mental health. Mental hygiene consistently stresses the development or creation of such qualities in the individual as optimism, confidence, cooperation, emotional adjustment and maturity, etc. It points out the means of improving the adaptability and efficiency of individuals.

Thus, mental hygiene has three important aspects: curative, preventive and preservative. In its curative aspect, it indicates ways and means of curing mental deviations, defects and imbalances. Ways and means of preventing them are suggested by it under its preventive function while in its preservative aspect it puts forward rules and suggestions by following which any and every individual can ensure his mental health.

The *Encyclopedia of Modern Education* defines mental hygiene as that approach to human adjustment and achievement, which is related to the prevention of emotional maladjustment and preparation of the individual for skilled working. According to the *Dictionary of Education*, mental hygiene is the science, which studies the principles and practices of preventing mental disorders and promoting mental health. Both the above definitions, though better than others, are yet incomplete since they do not emphasize all the three aspects of mental hygiene. Thus, mental hygiene is that science which studies laws and means of curing and preventing mental diseases, personality disorders and complications; it also discovers creative measures for the balancing, adjustment and healthy development of personality.

Scope of Mental Hygiene

Mental hygiene comprehends the curing of mental defects, diseases and abnormalities as well as the prevention of such abnormalities, beside the active preservation of mental health, balance, pleasure and adjustment, etc., of the individual. Evidently then the scope of mental hygiene is very vast. It comprehends the entire life of the individual. Every individual stands in need of mental health. Young children, men and women experience difficulty in adjusting to new circumstances, which lead to mental complications and difficulties that, in turn, endanger mental health. In old age, when man is past his prime and his energy is on the decrease, mental hygiene is intensely needed by them. Besides, children and some adults in the prime of life also require mental hygiene since their mental balance is disturbed and personality disordered for some or the other reason. The list of sufferers is completed by persons who have already lost their mental balance, who are prey to mental defects, diseases and aberrations. They require mental treatment and cure.

Apart from the curative and preventive aspects of mental hygiene, it is also important to describe its preservative aspect. Every healthy individual require mental hygiene as they stand to benefit by its preservative function. In other words, people who are healthy from the mental standpoint are also in need of mental hygiene. In practical life, there is no individual who can be declared completely healthy. Secondly, even if he is healthy at one moment there is no guarantee that he will continue in the same state of health. Man's adjustment to the environment is not a static condition but rather a gradual dynamic process. The question of adjustment is forever present before the individual since man's condition is forever changing somewhat. Hence, there is no saying when an individual, who is at present manifesting the most perfect adjustment, may have cause to loose his mental balance. Consequently, he requires mental hygiene to see to it that he is not deprived of his mental bliss and happiness.

Thus, it is evident that the scope of mental hygiene is not limited to age since it is required by young, old, adolescent, man, woman, the healthy and the unhealthy alike. Its sphere extends from the home to school, factory, office, shop, society, in fact everywhere. It is needed in all human relationships and activities.

Importance of Mental Hygiene

Description of the meaning and scope of mental hygiene also helps to clarify its value. Its value and efficacy consists not only in the curing and preventing of mental health in the individual fortunately blessed with it; it is of value for young, old, healthy, insane, in fact for everyone. Hence, the requirement of mental hygiene in every sphere of human life—home, school playground—has its value.

Yet, this does not imply that mental hygiene possesses the same value in every sphere. Just as physical hygiene is required most by the diseased individual or one who is potentially diseased, mental hygiene is most needed by an individual whose mind is already disturbed or by one who is likely to be deprived of his reason, one who is under such strain that there is a likelihood of his collapsing under it. Mentally diseased individuals include unbalanced, eccentric and disturbed individuals as well as those who are actually insane. Similarly, in normal course of human life, mental hygiene is required, wherever there are human relationships, yet it is most essentially needed in the home and the schools since these are the two institutions, which are the greatest preservatives of mental health. Hence, a complete comprehension of the value of mental hygiene can come only when one has understood its importance for the school and the home, as well as for mentally diseased persons, adolescents, senile people and corrupt persons.

Mental hygiene in the family

Psychologists are of the opinion that the influences that mould the personality of a child during the first five or six years of his life determine his conduct throughout his future existence. It is in the family that the child learns to express, control and refine or modify his emotions, thought, feelings and impressions. It is in the family that he develops the qualities of affection, sympathy, brotherhood, etc. His conduct towards his equals, his juniors and his seniors is moulded and formed in the family. Hence, if some situation or circumstance in the family affects him adversely his mental health is apt to suffer. Hence, it is evident that if the mental health of the future citizens of a nation is to be ensured, it is essential that mental hygiene be introduced into the family. It is not only as a child, but also as husband and father, wife and mother, that one is under family influence. Family as an institution is with an individual from life to death. Mental disease or ill health in even one member of the family has its repercussion on the other members. Hence it becomes important to safeguard the mental health in the family, as it is to prevent and cure mental imbalance if it is present there. Without this, the peace and calm of the family life becomes ephemeral and elusive.

Mental hygiene in school

After the family, another institution that casts important influence upon the child's development is the school. In school the personality is influenced by his teachers and friends. It is in the school that he learns lessons of self-dependence, self-confidence and reliance. He is compelled to conduct himself desirably towards all on his own initiative. And in this effort, it is only natural that he finds frustrations that endanger the balance of his personality with mental difficulties and complexes. Mental hygiene in school is important for preventing such unhealthy development and for preserving mental health.

Mental hygiene in adolescence

Undoubtedly, mental hygiene is important throughout an individual's life, but it assumes greatest importance during adolescence. Adolescence is the most volatile stage in the development of personality. Mental, physical and every other kind of development takes place during this stage. Young boys and girls manifest signs of approaching adulthood. The physical development is accompanied by mental development, due to which they do not appreciate being treated as children. They prefer to be treated as adults. Imagination and emotionality are running high while the adolescent is passing through this period. Interest in the other sex manifests itself in many peculiar fashions and curiosity concerning sex increases very much. The adolescent is also anxious about his future and his livelihood, regarding which he develops ambitions and dreams constantly. Thus, keeping all these intricacies in mind it becomes quite evident that there is greatest need for preventing mental quirks and imbalances and for ensuring mental health of adolescents.

In old age, keeping a sane outlook on life becomes something of a problem; hence the old people have much to gain from mental hygiene, its ways and means. Another class of men and women who stand to gain much from this science is that of the corrupt and evil—alcoholics, criminals, prostitutes and other anti-social elements. Many of their mental problems can be solved through the ways and means suggested by mental hygiene. Thus, mental hygiene is an integral part of human welfare and life. It finds application everywhere, although reaping of the greatest possible benefit from it depends upon the skill of the person using it and the ability with which he can control the circumstances.

Mental hygiene is a science. It makes a study of the ways, means and rules that preserve mental health, prevent mental disturbance and cure mental diseases. Hence mental hygiene can benefit every sphere of life such as personal, family, social, national and international relationships, interrelations between various classes, sexes, age levels, colours, communities, races and peoples. This is the value of mental hygiene and it is not influenced by the very little benefit that is derived from it in practice. Being a science it is neutral, and in no position to bestow gifts and benefits upon people of its own accord. It is for man to reap a rich harvest from it. Its value does not deteriorate if man chooses to neglect it, since its value is proved and beyond doubt.

Principles of Mental Hygiene

Mental hygiene is one of the movements which has become very important in modern times; just as people are keen on preserving their physical health similarly people must preserve their mental health by adhering to principles of mental hygiene. The aim of mental hygiene is to preserve mental health. There are various principles of mental hygiene. Some of them are:

- One of the ways of preserving mental health is to develop positive attitude towards life. Instead of running away from reality one has to face the challenges boldly.
- Another way of preserving mental health is not to worry too much about anything which happens in life. One has to take life as it comes.
- Most of the psychologists suggest catharsis as one of the means to preserve mental health. Catharsis is unburdening to narrate one's difficulties to his/her trust worthy friends.
- Another principle says that it is better to overcome conflict which occurs within the psychological system.

Thus, these are various principles of mental hygiene which are aimed at preserving mental health.

Understanding Mental Health

Mental health is a phrase used to explain either a level of cognitive or emotional well-being or a lack of a mental disorder. From perspectives of the discipline of positive psychology or holism mental strength may consist of an individual's capability to take pleasure in life and obtain a balance between life activities and hard work to achieve psychological resilience. The World Health Organization defines mental health as "a condition of well-being in which the person realizes his or her own abilities, can handle with the usual stresses of life, can work effectively and fruitfully, and is intelligent to make an involvement to his or her area". It was formerly stated that there was no one "official" explanation of mental health. Subjective assessments, cultural differences, and competing qualified theories all concern how "mental health" is defined.

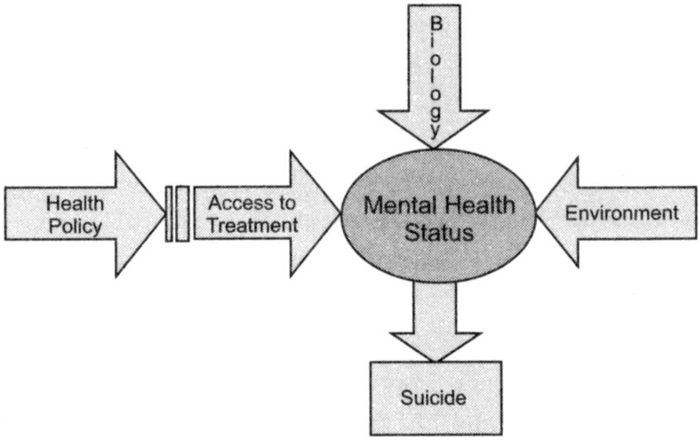

Mental health can be socially constructed and socially defined; that is, dissimilar professions, societies, communities, and cultures have very unlike ways of conceptualizing its personality and causes, determining what is psychologically healthy, and deciding what interventions are suitable. Thus, unlike professionals will have dissimilar cultural and religious backgrounds and experiences, which may impact the tactic applied throughout treatment.

Research has exposed that there is stigma attached to mental sickness. In the United Kingdom, the Royal College of Psychiatrists organized the function *Changing Minds* (1998-2003) to facilitate decrease stigma. Mental health can be seen as a range, where an individual's mental health may have numerous dissimilar probable values. Mental wellness is usually viewed as a positive characteristic, such that a person can attain superior levels of mental health, even if they do not have any diagnosable mental health situation. This explanation of mental health highlights emotional well-being, the capability to live a full and inspired life, and the flexibility to deal with life's inevitable challenges. Many beneficial systems and self-help books propose methods and philosophies indicating strategies and techniques considered as useful for advance civilizing the mental wellness of or else healthy people. Positive psychology is gradually more outstanding in mental health.

Mental health is a term used to describe how well the individual is adjusted to the demands and opportunities of life. Satisfactory adjustment does not mean the absence of maladjustments but is characteristic of behaviour, which is both constructive, and adaptive, that is sufficiently effective in meeting the needs of the individual and socially acceptable. The ideal of mental health is complex and comprehensive, it is unlikely that it will ever be achieved completely, but it has certainly done great good in reducing the incidence of mental disease and ailments.

Mental Health is among the more important public health issues (Herman, 1969). In view of the Alma Ata Declaration, the goal being health for all by 2000 AD, defining health as physical, mental and social well-being, A.V. Shah (1982) has expressed that Mental Health is "the most essential and inseparable component of health...an integrated component of public health and social welfare programs...". The emphasis is on prevention of disease as well as maintenance and prevention of health in the community (Michael, 1982).

Mental health may be better understood by its comparison with physical health. A person is said to be physically healthy when his body is functioning well and he is free from pains and troubles. Similarly a person is in good mental health when his mind or personality is functioning effectively and he is free from emotional disturbances. In general he enjoys life and any unhappiness he has can be understandably explained. He is self-confident, hopeful about himself and his opportunities though he may have temporary setbacks and discouragements. He has a few intimate and close friends, maintain cordial relations with a number of people whom he meets and generally gets along with all those with whom he comes in contact in life and work. He is able to meet his problems without much disturbance, and his fears and anxieties are normal. He keeps an equable temper and when roused expresses his anger in a socially acceptable way. He is concerned about his health but not hyper-anxious about it. He has emotional maturity, balance and equilibrium. He not only understands himself, his merits and abilities, his handicaps and disabilities, but also accepts them and makes the most of his mental and physical capacity.

Greater emphasis is placed on the psychosocial and socio-cultural factors. The sociological and socio pathological views provide ample support to the contributions of psychosocial and interpersonal variables with regard to the mental health of individuals. Further, the rapid social changes occurring in societies seem to have driven man to face competition in his day-to-day life irrespective of whether his abilities or his social conditions permit it or not. Another important aspect is that in the modern world, as a result of greater use of technological and mechanized ways and the political machinery, man has become a stranger not only in relation to others but also in relation to himself. This has contributed to the failure of the individual to live up to the expectation of relevant others as well as to live up to one's own potentialities. This in turn has led to feelings of helplessness, powerlessness, meaninglessness, anxiety and insecurity. This being the rule rather than the exception in the contemporary world, many individuals are considered to be at potential mental health risks.

The social criteria for mental health include determination of how closely a person resemble others in his behaviour, how well he gets along and is liked by others, how much he contributes to and supports his social group and how much he confirms to the approved codes, laws or ideals of his society or social group. When applying individual criteria, we are concerned with the person himself and his attitudes, such as his happiness, ability to withstand psychological stress, assumption of personal responsibility, and the integration of his personality, favourable or realistic self-perceptions and self-actualization. Functional criteria involve the ability of the person to cope with and to master environmental stresses and demands efficiently, productively and maturely. The overall condition of one's mental health is usually determined by assessing the degree to which a person displays behaviours typical of the criteria, conceived as having these positive or negative or desirable vs. undesirable characteristics.

Defining Mental Health

In a book entitled *Mental Hygiene in Public Health*, P.V. Lewkan has written that a "mentally healthy individual is one who is himself satisfied, lives peacefully with his neighbours, makes healthy citizens of his children, and even after performing these fundamental duties has enough energy to do something of benefit to society. Possessing mental health, an individual can adjust properly to his environment, and can make the best effort for his own, his family's and his society's progress and betterment."

In the *Human Mind*, K.A. Menninger (1945) opined, "let us define mental health as the adjustment of human beings to the world and to each other with a maximum of effectiveness and happiness. It is the ability to maintain an even temper, an alert intelligence, socially considerate behaviour and a happy disposition."

The chief characteristic of mental health, thus it is evident, is 'adjustment'. The greater the degree of successful adjustment, the greater will be the mental health of the individual. Lesser mental health will lead to lesser adjustment and greater conflict. The healthy individual can interpret any new situation and adapt himself to suit it. He maintains a healthy and benevolent attitude towards life. He is aware that difficulties visit everyone in life so that running away from them is cowardice. This can be solved only by squarely facing up to them with courage.

In the year 1953 the WHO defined health as a 'complete state of physical, mental and social well-being and not merely the absence of disease or infirmity.' It is related to the promotion of well-being, the prevention of mental disorders, and the treatment and rehabilitation of people affected by mental disorders. This marked a major shift in the emphasis regarding the concept of health. This was necessitated by two reasons. Firstly, somewhere along the long history of the evolution of medical sciences, perhaps as a consequence of an overemphasis for restating the truth-health is a positive state of well-being. Secondly, another basic truth regarding the nature of man, as a bio-psycho-social being, seemed to be forgotten. Therefore, the mental and social aspect of health has to be re-emphasized in the WHO definition of health.

The simplest definition of mental health is peace within and harmony with others. The WHO expert Committee defines mental health as the "capacity in an individual to form harmonious relations with others and to participate in or contribute constructively to changes in the social environment". The different constituent parts of our personality should work in harmony so that an individual faces life situations rationally, successfully and happily. Mental health comprises the well-being of both the intellectual and emotional components of the mind. Mental health is the balance between all aspects of life-social, physical, spiritual and emotional. It impacts on how we manage our surroundings and make choices in our lives—clearly it is an integral part of our overall health. Mental health is far more than the absence of mental illness and has to do with many aspects of our lives including, how we feel about ourselves, how we feel about others and how we are able to meet the demands of life. In the larger context, mental health is the other name of quality of life.

Hadfield (1952) considers that "in general terms we may say that mental health is the full harmonious functioning of the whole personality". There are various urges, impulses, motives, tendencies, interests, attitudes, etc. in human beings, some of which are in born and some are acquired. When these urges are allowed to function harmoniously in coordination with each other and getting full expression, we have a personality, which we may call as wholesome and which is essential for healthy mental life. However, the coordination of these potentialities and dispositions (innate and acquired) is possible only when they are directed towards a common end or goal. So the three requirements of mental health as suggested by Hadfield are: (1) full expression, (2) harmonization, and (3) the direction to a common end of our native and required potentialities. These have been discussed in detail in the Box given on the next page for a better comprehension.

From the above definitions we can draw the following characteristics of mental health:

- Ability to accept themselves, others and nature, having positive self-concepts and relating well to people and the environment.
- Ability to form close relationships with others and display kindness, patience and compassion for others.
- Perceiving the world as it really is and people as they really are. With this perception the person can solve problems because they are able to make decisions pertaining to reality rather than fantasy.
- Ability to appreciate and enjoy life; optimism prevails as they interact and respond to people, places and daily happenings.

HADFIELD'S THREE REQUIREMENTS OF MENTAL HEALTH

Full Expression

Full expression is considered necessary for our biological adoption in life and to the development of strong will and character. The native urges, etc., if repressed, deform the personality of the individual. The individual becomes inefficient, weak willed and of feeble character. Thus, for good mental health repressions are to be totally avoided, otherwise, undue suppression leads to psycho-neurotic conditions where these urges, etc. find their outlet in abnormal behaviour.

Harmonization

The potentialities have different aims and functions to perform which are often in conflict with one another. For example rage comes in conflict with sex, fear with ambition and rage as a whole. In case, the potentialities whether of rage, sex or ambition, function completely but independently of the rest of the personality and its ends, they create mental disorders and the mind becomes disturbed which ultimately results in the breakdown of the personality. Thus, the harmonization and coordination of all these tendencies is necessary to the health of the mind.

The Common End

The third criterion for good mental health is the common end. The harmonization of various potentialities into a unified whole is not possible unless and until they are directed towards a common end. If there are different aims and purposes to achieve which are in conflict with each other, then harmonization will not take place.

Mental health is thus a dynamic functioning of the whole organism. It brings a harmony of movement in the organism to achieve an end, which results in completeness and fulfillment.

- Using a variety of approaches as they perform tasks or solve problems.
- Being independent and relying on personal standards of values and norms.

What is a Mental Challenge?

Along with understanding the concept of mental health it becomes absolutely necessary to understand the meaning of mental challenge. A mental challenge is any disease or condition affecting the brain that influences the way a person thinks, feels, behaves and/or relates to others and to his or her surroundings. Examples of Mental Challenges include Depression/Bipolar disorder, Anxiety disorder, Schizophrenia, Obsessive-compulsive disorder, Stress disorder, Social phobia, Eating disorders (anorexia, bulimia or over-eating) and Addiction.

According to the *DSM* (*Diagnostic Statistical Manual*), fourth edition, text revised (the *DSM-IV-TR*), the term *mental disorder* is unfortunate because it implies that a mental disorder is separate from a physical illness, when actually, according to the American Psychiatric Association (APA), researchers and scientists now know that that distinction is not a clear one to make. The APA argues that "there is much 'physical' in 'mental disorders' and much 'mental' in 'physical disorders'," and continues to use the term "mental disorders" because a better term has not yet been found. The APA defines a mental disorder as "a clinically significant behavioural or psychological syndrome or pattern that occurs in an individual and that is associated with present distress or disability or with a significantly increased risk of suffering death, pain, disability, or an important loss of freedom".

BARE FACTS ABOUT MENTAL HEALTH (WHO)

- 450 million people worldwide are affected by mental, neurological or behavioural problems at any time. About 873,000 people die by suicide every year. Mental illnesses are common to all countries and cause immense suffering. People with these disorders are often selected to social isolation, poor quality of life and increased mortality. These disorders are the cause of staggering economic and social costs.
- One in four patients visiting a health service have at least one mental, neurological or behavioural disorder but most of these disorders are neither diagnosed nor treated.
- Mental illnesses affect and are affected by chronic conditions such as cancer, heart and cardiovascular diseases, diabetes and HIV AIDS. Untreated, they bring about unhealthy behaviour, noncompliance with prescribed medical regimens, diminished immune functioning, and poor prognosis.
- Cost-effective treatments exist for most disorders and, if correctly applied, could enable most of those affected to become flourishing members of society.
- Barriers to effective treatment of mental illness include lack of recognition of the seriousness of mental illness and lack of understanding about the benefits of services. Policymakers, insurance companies, health and labour policies, and the public at large—all discriminate between physical and mental problems.
- Most middle and low-income countries devote less than 1 per cent of their health expenditure to mental health. Consequently mental health policies, legislation, community care facilities, and treatments for people with mental illness are not given the priority they deserve.

Although the exact cause of most mental challenges is not known, it is becoming clear through research that many of these conditions are caused by a combination of genetic, biological, psychological and environmental factors. One thing is for sure, mental challenges are not the result of personal weakness, a character defect or poor upbringing, and recovery from a mental challenge is not simply a matter of will and self-discipline.

Symptoms of mental challenges can include:

- Confused thinking.
- Long-lasting sadness or irritability.
- Extreme highs and lows in mood.
- Excessive fear, worrying or anxiety.
- Social or family withdrawal.
- Dramatic changes in eating or sleeping habits.
- Strong feelings of anger.
- Delusions or hallucinations (seeing or hearing things that are not really there).
- Increasing inability to cope with daily problems and activities.
- Thoughts of suicide.
- Denial of obvious problems.
- Many unexplained physical problems.
- Abuse of drugs and/or alcohol.

Maintaining mental health involves:

- *Attention to lifestyle*—if we are doing too much or too little in our lives, mental health can suffer. We need a good balance between work or study and leisure pursuits.
- *Social contact*—having contact with others whose company we enjoy, whether at school, work, at home or as a member of a club, helps to develop social interaction.

- *Reviewing our lives from time to time*—this involves considering what our aims and goals in life are and whether we are taking steps to achieve them. Problems can arise when we feel that life is not satisfying and fulfilling.
- *Awareness of how mind and body interact*—just as our state of mental health can affect our physical health, the reverse is also true. If diet, sleep and exercise are neglected and inadequate, not only our bodies will suffer but also our minds.
- *Having people in our lives we trust*—it is important to have someone to go to with our problems and worries, such as friends, teachers or family members.
- *Awareness of what can go wrong*—just be conscious of what can go wrong. Realize that tiredness and irritability, if ignored, might lead to more serious stress-related problems.
- *Taking steps to resolve problems*—be aware of problems and seek help if necessary.

Who is Mentally Healthy

There are many erroneous notions regarding the concept of a mentally healthy person. By a mentally healthy person, people usually mean a person who has a biological efficiency or is able to carry on nicely in society or is of good morals, etc. Mental health aims at these also but it differs from this concept in this sense that it is considered necessary that an efficient person or asocial person or amoral person is in every case mentally healthy. On the other hand, it is believed that a person who is mentally healthy will be efficient, social and moral.

There are persons who are efficient in their work, make tons of money in every sense, appear successful persons in life, yet these persons may not always be mentally healthy in the sense that they may be unhappy, worried and troubled. Often it has been seen that such people develop neurosis. On the other hand, there are people who work, utilizing all their energies and powers in the pursuit of some goals and ends; their will power is strong and they pursue their goals with confidence. Therefore people—who are confident, engage in work with energy, and engage in the pursuit of goals and ends—are mentally healthy.

A mentally healthy person is social because he confirms to the laws and customs of the community in which he lives and through which he finds the fullest development and satisfaction of his personality and the greatest measure of freedom. If there is a man who directs and coordinates the impulses of his personality on the basis of certain aims, ideals and purposes in life, he will be mentally healthy and moral in the strict sense of the word. The mentally healthy, may be correctly defined as that individual whose all potentialities whether innate or acquired are fully developed and harmonized with one another by being directed to a common end, aim or purpose.

Viewpoints of Renowned Psychologists

Many psychologists have reported a number of characteristics of a mentally healthy person. Hurlock mentions the characteristics of a well-adjusted person as having realistic goals consistent with age and abilities, acceptance of responsibility, expression of appropriate emotions and the ability to relate to others. Carl Rogers defines a healthy personality as one that shows acceptance of feelings, self-esteem, relating well to others, living fully in the present, continuing to learn, openness to new ideas and ability to make independent decisions and creativity.

Erick Erickson believes that persons with a healthy personality trust others and themselves, are capable of taking on responsibility, are capable of controlling themselves and feel that they can control themselves, are competent and industrious, have a clear, integrated identity, can develop intimate, trusting relationship with others, can guide others to grow or be creative in other ways, have ego integrity and accept themselves as they are.

Jahoda (1958) states that positive mental health is shown in:

1. *Attitude towards the self*: they include the accessibility of the self to consciousness; the correctness of the self-concept; its relation to the sense of destiny and the acceptance by the individual of his own self.

2. *Growth, development and self-actualization*: the extent to which the individual utilizes his abilities, his orientation towards the future and his investment in living.

3. *Integration*: the extent to which the psychic forces are balanced; a unifying outlook on life and a resistance to stress.

4. *Autonomy*: the aim here is to ascertain whether the self-reliant person is able to decide with relative ease and speed what suits his own needs best.

5. *Perception of reality*: a relative freedom from need-distortion and the existence of empathy.

6. *Environmental mastery*: under this heading is listed ability to love, work and play; adequacy in interpersonal relationships; meeting situational requirements; adaptation and adjustment; and efficiency in problem-solving.

Behaviour according to Shoben (1956) is normal to the extent that it expresses man's most unique capacities for symbolization and social involvement. Among his criteria of the fully functioning person, Rogers (1963) emphasizes the capacity for awareness and openness to experience. Maslow (1954) notes that 'self-actualizing' people also are invariably creative, in the sense of giving whatever they do, a personal and distinctive quality.

Gordon Allport (1961) describes the 'mature personality' in terms of soundness of health, as having six salient qualities:

1. *Extension of the sense of self*: this involves authentic participation in important spheres of human endeavour, beyond immediate self-interest.

2. *Warm relating to others*: because of self-extension, the mature person is more capable of intimacy but also of respect and compassion.

3. *Emotional security (self-acceptance)*: this is reflected both in frustration, tolerance and in trust.

4. *Realistic perception, skills and assignments*: this includes not only accurate judgement, but also the capacity to be problem-centered and to loose oneself in one's work.

5. *Self-objectification, i.e. insight and humour*: To know oneself and to laugh at oneself requires mature detachment and

6. *A unifying philosophy of life*: the mature person has a sense of direction and purpose and a broad personal philosophy.

Overall, then, through the overlapping concepts and alternate terms, a coherent picture of the healthy, mature personality emerges. Developmentally, the healthy person is highly differentiated and well integrated. There is a strong sense of personal identity, realistic self-esteem, detachment and sensitivity to self and others. He has a sense of competence and actual competencies in psychological functioning (i.e. learning, memory and problem-solving). His ego is strong, his behaviour is flexible and adaptable and there is considerable stress tolerance. Coping devices are more evident than defenses. With a secure sense of being and value, he can be compassionate, sympathetic and loving towards others. Conscience and values are coherent, conscious and well integrated. Finally, the healthy personality is comfortable with himself and valued by others.

This is not to suggest that such a person is without conflicts, worries or anxiety. Because of high ideals and self-confidence, he can overreach and know failures and frustration. He can hurt others and know guilt. As anyone, he is capable of foolish, thoughtless and self-defeating acts. In his spontaneity and desire for experience in a readiness to accept challenges "because it's there", defeat and despair are predictable risks. But what distinguishes the healthy personality is that these do not lead to defensive retreat, hostile anger or face saving maneuvers. Instead adversity is counteracted as possible, but above all it is the basis for further learning and wisdom. It is in the capacity to continue growth, rather than being without pain or suffering, that the healthy person is best defined.

Mental Health of the Child

According to a WHO report, at least three per cent of school children suffer from mental illnesses such as depression, suicidal thoughts, psychosis, serious attention problems or obsessive-compulsive disorder. Nearly one in five children and adolescents will have an emotional or behavioural disorder sometime during youth. The need is mostly to look at the health programme as a 'health issue' and not as an illness, Dr Shetty said. "As a first step children should be encouraged to share their negative thoughts with their parents, siblings, teachers, etc. so that one knows what goes on in a young mind and deal accordingly."

"An ideal starter for a teacher is to break the concept of favouritism and reach out to reclusive students. In fact the idea is instead of counsellors, teachers and parents be effective counsellors for children", he observed. Principal Veena Sethi from Marble Arts School, Oshiwara maintained that with nuclear working families, children are increasingly becoming the latch-key-door generation so badly in need of interaction. In its manual on mental health in schools, the WHO has identified three main elements of a health promoting school—the formal curriculum, the school ethos (physical and social environment) and the relationship between school, home and the surrounding community.

At home

Early years of life are the most significant for acquiring adjustment patterns and mental health. The young child is ignorant and dependent on parents, he has limited resources to meet the problems and difficulties of life, and therefore he needs all the encouragement, sympathy and understanding parents and teachers can give him. What anxieties and conflicts he experiences and what adjustments he makes in the initial stages set the patterns or adjustments in later life.

Research has suggested that lack of security and affection, and an overcharged atmosphere in the home bring about severe stress and anxiety in the infant. The effect of separation from or loss of mother in early childhood has been specifically studied and investigations report very damaging effects on personality development. Among the responses observed in such children are apathy, lack of initiative, lack of interest in things and people, withdrawal, prolonged immobility and refusal to walk. Largely parents, siblings and neighbours make up the early social environment of children and relations with them are marked by intimacy and emotional acceptance. Any disturbance in this relation resulting from quarrel with brothers and sisters and rebuke from parents leads to disturbances in behaviour. As the child grows he may become less attractive physically and socially; there may be displacement in family affection due to the birth of other children; he may quarrel, excite jealousy by being too bright, or fall ill; he may be temporarily rejected by his social environment. Such fluctuations in emotional relationships may cause behaviour disturbances and unwholesome adjustments.

At school

The school is second only to the home in its influence on the personality and emotional development of the child. Teachers replace parents and classmates take the place of brothers, sisters and neighbours. Very often this social circle of the school provides for the fulfillment of emotional needs neglected in the home. School experiences give them strength, self-confidence and stability. They learn and do things, individually and in groups; they may develop habits to overcome their frustrations and failures or at least to tolerate them; they may sublimate their destructive and hostile impulses into socially acceptable channels. With increase in knowledge and understanding their capacity to achieve desirable adjustments and security may also increase.

But the school may turn out to be a source of constant trouble, worry and anxiety. At each stage of education young people have different worries. In the first place children in school worry about being successful in their studies. They may be anxious to get to school in time, to master their lessons, and to obtain marks and reports which will bring them approval and praise both in the school and at home. Schools as they are at present are either indifferent to pupil progress or too worried about it. In either case they spread frustration, tension and anxiety. Disabilities and deprivation in education may cause mental ill health by producing feelings of inadequacy, frustration and inferiority. An average pupil has some difficulty in some subject or subjects, and when instead of receiving helpful and sympathetic attention he receives insults, taunts and rebukes, it affects his mental health. Teachers may have been trained to teach but they are not adequately equipped to guide effective and sound adjustments. And certainly a good many of them are not themselves well adjusted to their job and do not know how to help and guide young people in their difficulties and problems.

In Indian schools the amount of wastage and stagnation at each stage is considerable, and is largely the result of maladjustments to school programmes and teachers. Other school conditions too may promote premature school—leaving, repeated failure or disgust with the school. But at present our schools have absolutely no programme of helping and guiding young pupils to make suitable and healthful adjustments to school work.

Identified Problems in School

Some studies made in the West repeatedly emphasize that two great hazards to mental health in school children are unsuitable curricula and failure to recognize and provide for individual differences. These findings hold good in the case of Indian schools with much greater force. In the vast majority of primary schools untrained teachers teach by the chalk and the rod, and the provision of recreational, constructive and creative activities is conspicuous by its absence, and children are taught *en masse* without any regard to differences in their abilities, interests and aptitudes. The teachers do not know even the concept of mental health and the status of mental health is important in influencing the mental health of the child.

There is no nation-wide systematic programme for counselling and guidance, which may promote self-regard, self-acceptance, self-respect and self-understanding among the students. The home and the school should help to promote and build a favourable self-concept among children and to cultivate among them an attitude of meeting their problems and difficulties in a frank, direct and realistic manner so as to eliminate worry, anxiety and tension. In schools and classrooms where an atmosphere of quiet, diligent and constructive work prevails, the problems of mental health are reduced to a minimum. To that end the teacher himself/herself should not have signs of worry, keep rivalry and competition within limits, encourage sportsmanship, and distribute his attention and recognition evenly among the class. Many situations in the classroom, which fill students with over concern and excessive emotional tension, can be eased by a sense of humour and a sporting approach. But this, however, does not mean that the teacher should soft-pedal everything in the class. Pupils should be concerned about their duties and responsibilities, else they will not accomplish much. Absence of worry leads to indifference and negligence, reasonable worry makes for diligence and determination and leads to successful and satisfying experience.

Conclusion

In brief, thus, mental health is assured if children and young people are encouraged to fulfil their basic urges and needs in an effective and socially acceptable ways, are able to meet reality in its face instead of denying it and by providing them with an emotional support, sympathetic attitude and understanding atmosphere.

Childhood: Needs and Development

18

When a child is born he comes from a completely secure, comfortable, supportive and safe environment of the mother's womb into a strange, threatening and to him hostile environment. It is the first major separation of the child's life and it is by far the most traumatic that he will experience during the course of many separations in his lifetime. He is dragged from a place where he feels safe and secure into a world where he will feel vulnerable and threatened. The child born into today's world has much to contend with and his parent will have the single greatest influence on what becomes of him. It is the parents who, almost single-handedly, determine both the physical and psychological makeup of the child.

It is true that today's child is faced with a different set of life circumstances than his parents, but it is also true that because he is a product of his own time, he has the capability to develop the required set of coping skills. Over-protection tends to destroy the need for the child to call on his coping skills and therefore, through lack of awareness of the range of coping skills that he has, as well as lack of the use of these skills, they become dormant and eventually extinct. Overprotection is rooted in the feelings of inadequacy and dissatisfaction with the 'self' of the parents or teacher, which causes the person to feel threatened by the presence of competence and confidence in others, and makes it difficult for him to accept these traits in others. As a result, he may unconsciously seek to prevent these positive traits from growing, developing and being used. It is this unconscious but powerful drive in the adult to maintain his own negative self-view that fights against what it perceives as the threat of seeing competence and confidence in others.

But the child today, while having the innate capabilities to cope with his particular life circumstances, has a quite different set of life situations to those which his parents and his teachers had. The role of the adult should be to facilitate the growth of the child's latent capabilities, rather than to impose his own skills. It is important for the teachers and parents to understand the needs and development of the child to help him to be an effective child.

What is Child Development

Child development is a process every child goes through. This process involves learning and mastering skills like sitting, walking, talking, skipping, and tying shoes. Children learn these skills, called developmental milestones*, during predictable time periods. Children develop skills in five main areas of development:

*A developmental milestone is a skill that a child acquires within a specific time frame. For instance, one developmental milestone is learning to walk. Most children learn this skill or developmental milestone between the ages of 9 and 15 months. Milestones develop in a sequential fashion. This means that a child will need to develop some skills before he or she can develop new skills. For example, children must first learn to crawl and to pull up to a standing position before they are able to walk. Each milestone that a child acquires builds on the last milestone developed. Our brains are not fully developed at birth. In fact, a baby's brain weighs about one quarter (1/4) of what an adult's brain weighs. The brain grows very rapidly during the first several years of life. During this time, the child learns all sorts of new skills.

1. *Cognitive development*

This is the child's ability to learn and solve problems. For example, this includes a two-month-old baby learning to explore the environment with hands or eyes or a five-year-old learning how to do simple math problems.

2. *Social and emotional development*

This is the child's ability to interact with others, including helping themselves and self-control. Examples of this type of development would include: a six-week-old baby smiling, a ten-month-old baby waving bye-bye, or a five-year-old boy knowing how to take turns in games at school.

3. *Speech and language development*

This is the child's ability to understand and use language. For example, this includes a 12-month-old baby saying his first words, two-year-old naming parts of her body, or a five-year-old learning to say "feet" instead of "foots".

4. *Fine motor skill development*

This is the child's ability to use small muscles, specifically their hands and fingers, to pick up small objects, hold a spoon, turn pages in a book, or use a crayon to draw.

5. *Gross motor skill development*

This is the child's ability to use large muscles. For example, a six-month-old baby learns how to sit up with some support, a 12-month-old baby learns to pull up to a stand holding onto furniture, and a five-year-old learns to skip.

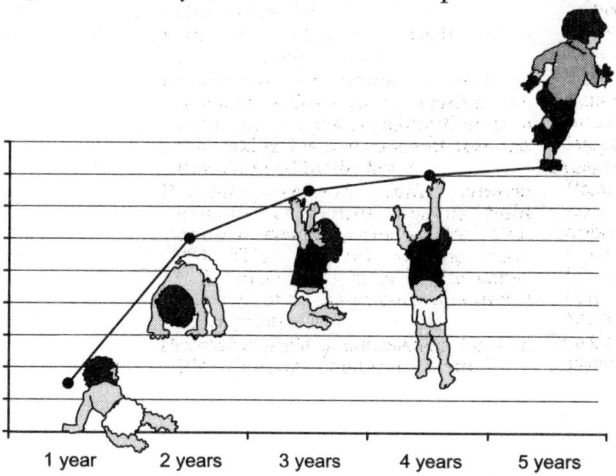

Middle childhood (ages of approximately 6-10 years) is a period of time when children enter the larger culture, primarily through schooling and develop the intellectual and social skills they need to function effectively outside their family environment. Children spend more and more time with non-family members, including peers and teachers. They spend less time under supervision of parents, more under supervision of teachers and other adults, such as coaches, youth group leaders, or teachers. Consequently, they spend more time with peers outside the immediate influence of parents and become more concerned with social expectations of peers and adults. With increased freedom, children feel greater demands to be "good", show respect, and accommodate to social demands of situations, such as the classroom or non-familial social settings. With increasing social experience and the development of new intellectual skills, children:

- Master fundamental skills considered important by culture, such as reading and arithmetic;
- Develop self-awareness, such as knowing how to go about learning;
- Develop skills in consciously planning, coordinating, and evaluating progress, and modifying plans, based on self-evaluation;
- Develop abilities to reflect on themselves and understand that others have different points of view.

School age child (6-12 yrs) should be:

- moving in strong, coordinated manner
- using complex sentences
- becoming more aware of body, possibly developing secondary sex characteristics
- focusing attention for longer periods of time

Under these external pressures, many children begin to lose confidence in themselves and may not find their interests in music, science, sports, or other areas encouraged. Out-of-school programmes can provide a safety-net for middle-children to "...safely explore independence, peer relationships, and leadership...". Science centers, children's museums, youth centers, and other such informal environments can provide children opportunities to learn without external evaluations and chances for children to control their own experiences and learning.

Mental Health Needs of Children: The Extent of the Problem

One out of every five children has a diagnosable mental, emotional, or behavioural disorder. Up to one in ten children suffer from a serious emotional disturbance. However, seventy per cent of children with a diagnosable disorder do not receive

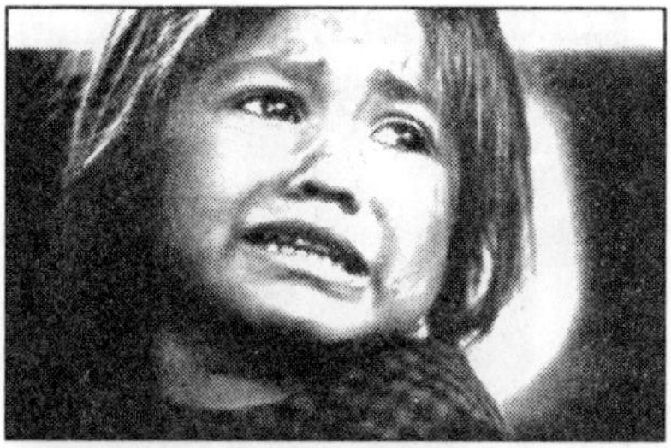

mental health services. In the *National Action Agenda for Children's Mental Health*, the U.S. Surgeon General warns that the nation is facing a public crisis in caring for children and adolescents with behavioural, psychological, and emotional problems. Estimates show that of the children who are receiving mental health services, 70-80 per cent receives mental health care within the school.

Recent data not only points to exceptionally high levels of unmet need, but also to ethnic and racial disparities. Children in minority populations are less likely to have access to mental health services, and the care they receive is often of poorer quality. In addition to children identified with diagnosable mental health disorders, there are a large number of children at risk for future problems or who may need help for a behavioural, emotional or mental disorder. In many low-income populations the per cent of children who are at risk for a mental health problem is greater than 50 per cent. One study found that 32 per cent of children living in poverty, children had diagnosable mental health impairments. By combining the 50 per cent who are at risk and the 32 per cent with diagnosable disorders, there are a great number of low-income children in need of mental health services. Yet, these children are in a population that often has less access to health services than wealthier peer groups and are even less likely to receive needed mental health care.

Need of the Child to Grow and Thrive

A child's development is shaped by many influences, including genetic makeup, early interactions with parents orother caregivers, socio-economic factors, and early childhood

experiences in the family, at school, and in the community. The fact is that who we are and where we come from has a huge impact on our health, well-being, competence and ability to relate to others and cope with the world around us.

All children need an environment that is hospitable and nurturing in order to develop well. However, children are not born "blank slates", on which the environment alone creates an imprint. Children are born with a temperament; that is, whether they are calm or irritable, whether they are easily settled or fussy. There are also genetic factors that influence such things as a child's capacity to learn the social use of language, to play, to regulate his/her emotions, and to interact with adults and peers.

What is crucial is the interaction between the child's inborn strengths and weaknesses and how the parents or caregivers respond to their infant's needs. If the child is temperamentally difficult to handle then the parents can learn how to interact in ways that will limit the child's distress and promote strong affectional bonds between them. If the child is at risk for developing language problems, then those responsible for his or her care can modify the way they interact with the child, providing an environment of enriched language that is also accepting and not harshly critical.

Healthy child development is not solely the responsibility of individual parents. If children need to grow up to be able to reach their full potential, then all those who are in contact with them must be committed to providing more than the bare minimum to achieve that goal. Teachers, neighbours, community members, and government all have to take action to meet the needs of children and help supply the healthy environment known through scientific and social research to produce the best outcomes in our children. Some important needs at childhood are:

Physical well-being

For physical well-being children need:

- *Food security*—families need sufficient money to buy nutritious food that is available on a daily basis.
- *Secure shelter*—as a bare minimum, housing should provide protection from weather conditions, have lighting and heating, have no safety or health hazards, and be affordable without undue strain on family income.
- *Good health behaviours*—children should be able to get adequate sleep and exercise, receive up-to-date immunizations, and have access to medical care, including preventive care.

Emotional well-being

For development of good mental health, children need:

- Love, praise, and positive regard from trusted family members and other adults.
- Children thrive on affection and loving attention, praise, and encouragement. Children should be given the opportunity to explore the arts, be exposed to a wide variety of educational and cultural activities, and learn manual skills, so that they can realize their talents. The environment must change in order to accommodate the range of skills, abilities, difficulties and impairments that children demonstrate all through their development.
- To have boundaries set on their behaviour and to be monitored and supervised when at play or at leisure.
- Acceptance for who they are at home, school, and in the community. Love and positive regard should not be conditional on their parents' or teachers' wants and

needs. Children have a range of skills that need to be challenged in order to grow. They should not be criticized because they cannot be consistently good at everything they try.

- Loving guidance and discipline. Children who are given boundaries, who are treated fairly, and given good guidance about their behaviour, generally develop good self-regard and are more likely to be respectful of others. On the other hand, children who are treated harshly and frequently criticized tend to develop behaviour, mood or relationship problems that can persist into and throughout adult life.

Thinking and learning ability

How a person perceives, thinks, and gains an understanding of his or her world is termed "cognitive development". It refers to our ability to think and learn and includes such things as awareness and judgement, information processing, intelligence, language development, and memory. To help children's cognitive development, they need:

- encouragement of exploration,
- mentoring in basic skills,
- celebration of developmental advances,
- guided rehearsal and extension of new skills,
- protection from inappropriate disapproval, teasing or punishment, and
- a rich and responsive language environment.

Mental Disorders Affecting Children and Youth

Children and adolescents are affected by a wide spectrum of mental health disorders. Mental health disorders in this population can range from mild to severe conditions. Often a child may have more than one disorder. As seen in Table 1, mental health disorders are widespread in the child and adolescent population, yet the majority of children and adolescents with mental health disorders are not receiving treatment. The following

are of some of the more common mental, emotional and behavioural disorders that affect children and youth.

Common Mental Health Disorders and the Number of Children and Youth Affected

Disorder	Number of Children/Youth Affected
Anxiety	8 to 10 out of 100
Conduct	7 out of 100
Depression	6 out of 100
Learning	5 out of 100
Attention	5 out of 100
Eating	1 out of 150
Substance Abuse	Not known

CMHS, Mental, emotional, and behavior disorders in children and adolescents. Center for Mental Health Services. www.mentalhealth.org/publications/allpubs/CA-0006/default.asp

12-month Prevalence for Children (8 to 15 years)

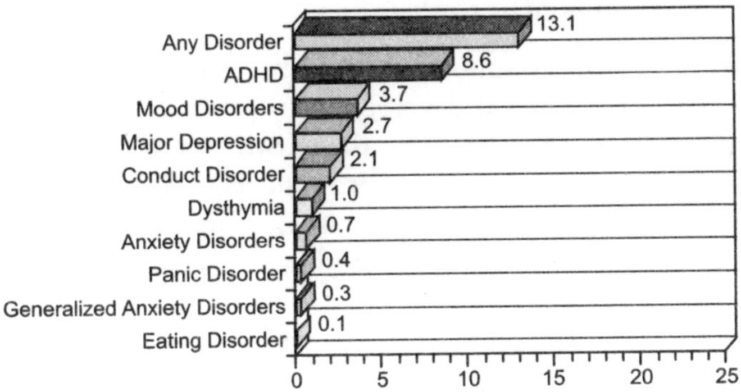

Data Courtesy of CDC

The centers for Disease Control and Prevention's National Health and Nutrition Examination Survey (NHANES) includes prevalence data for children ages 8 to 15; a slightly younger age range than the data from the NCS–A chart above. These data show that approximately 13 per cent of children ages 8 to 15 had a diagnosable mental disorder within the previous year. The most common disorder among this age group is attention-deficit/hyperactivity disorder (ADHD), which affects 8.5 per cent of this population. This is followed by mood disorders broadly at 3.7 per cent, and major depressive disorder specifically at 2.7 per cent.

There are a great diversity of childhood disorder forms and causes. Some of these disorders are primarily disorders of the brain, while others are more behavioural in nature. Brain-based disorders are caused by neuro chemical problems or structural abnormalities of the brain. They can be innate (i.e., appearing at or shortly after birth); or they may result from a physical stress such as illness or injury, or an emotional stress, such as trauma or loss. Behavioural problems, on the other hand, are outward signs of difficulty displayed at home, at school, or among friends in an otherwise physically healthy child. Like brain-based problems, behavioral problems may also result from physical or emotional stress. Brain-based disorders such as ADHD clearly impact a child's behaviour in school and at home, and *vice versa*, many disorders previously thought to be primarily behavioural in nature have turned out to have a biological component to them.

Despite how common they may be, childhood disorders are not part of the normal developmental process that children are expected to go through. The diagnostic criteria for childhood mental disorders require that children's behaviour and/or development deviates from normal age—appropriate behaviour and/or development, so understanding normal child development is important.

Common childhood mental illnesses and developmental disorders include Depression, Bipolar Disorder and Anxiety Disorders, Autism and similar Pervasive Developmental Disorders

(PDD), Attention Deficit and Hyperactivity Disorder (ADHD), Learning Disabilities, Adjustment Disorders, Oppositional Defiant Disorder, and Conduct Disorder. The first three of these disorders are not strictly childhood disorders, but instead, affect both children and adults. Since some of these disorders are common in children and adolescents, some disorders are explained in this chapter and some have been explained in the next chapter in context of the adolescents.

Major depression

Depression is more than just "feeling blue" or having a bad day. And it is different from feelings of grief or sorrow that follow a major loss, such as a death in the family. It is not a personal weakness or a character flaw. Children and teens with clinical depression cannot simply "snap out of it". Depression is a serious health problem that affects feelings, thoughts and actions, and can appear as a physical illness. As many as one in eight teens and one in 33 children have clinical depression. Fortunately, depression in youth is treatable.

It is not strictly a childhood disorder, but children do become depressed. Major depression is diagnosed in children of all ages, but appears to increase significantly throughout adolescence. By age 18, prevalence rates appear to be 20 per cent, with depression found in girls more often than boys.

Anxiety disorders

These are the most common mental illnesses among youngsters today, with prevalence rates ranging between 10 per cent and 20 per cent. Children with anxiety disorders are more likely to develop (or to continue experiencing) anxiety disorders in adulthood, and have an increased risk of developing major depression, attempting suicide, and being hospitalized for mental illnesses. One particular type of anxiety disorder, Obsessive-Compulsive Disorder (a combination of obsessions, or intrusive, repetitive, unwanted thoughts; and compulsions, or anxiety-reducing behaviour such as repeated checking or counting) is found in about 5 per cent of children and adolescents.

Autism and pervasive developmental disorders

The term pervasive developmental disorders (PDDs) refer to a group of developmental conditions that involve delayed or impaired communication and social skills, behaviours, and cognitive skills (learning). Because autism is the best known of the PDDs, the disorders also are known as autism spectrum disorders (ASDs). PDDs include Asperger syndrome and two less common conditions, childhood disintegrative disorder and Rett syndrome. PDDs usually are diagnosed during infancy, toddler hood, or early childhood.

Autism is one of the mental, emotional, and behavioural disorders that appears in early childhood. Autistic children may have a serious lifelong disability. However, with appropriate treatment and training, some autistic children can develop certain aspects of independence in their lives. Parents should support their autistic children in developing those skills that use their strengths so they will feel good about themselves. Signs of ASDs are usually recognizable before a child is 3 years old. However, symptoms can range from severe to so subtle that they seem to be normal aspects of childhood development. For that reason, it can take a few years for an ASD to be fully identified. That's why the American Academy of Pediatrics (AAP) recommends pediatricians look for early signs that suggest the possibility of autism at every visit and formally screen for autism at 18 months and 24 months, and any other time there is a concern. Early signs can include:

- trouble interacting, playing with, or relating to others.
- avoiding eye contact; not looking at people.
- not pointing to objects to call attention to them.
- unusual movements, such as hand flapping, spinning, or tapping.
- delays in developmental milestones or loss of milestones already achieved.
- playing with the same toy in a way that seems odd or repetitive.

- not using or understanding language.
- not exploring surroundings with curiosity or interest.

A child with a suspected ASD should be evaluated by a doctor with expertise in the disorders, such as a pediatric neurologist, developmental pediatrician, pediatric psychiatrist, or pediatric psychologist. Parent questionnaires, educational and cognitive assessments, language assessments, or play and behaviour assessments might be used to help diagnose autism.

Other Developmental and Behavioural Disorders

Although developmental and behavioural disorders are increasingly widespread, they are still poorly understood by most of the society. The lack of knowledge is further compounded by the stigma that often accompanies a diagnosis of a developmental or behavioural disorder. Parents and physicians can educate themselves and others about the range of disorders, as well as the opportunities for treatment and intervention. Whether a child has a developmental delay or disorder, early identification and intervention are essential for achieving the best possible outcome.

The most common developmental disorder is mental retardation. According to the Center for Disease Control and Prevention, more than one out of every 100 school children in the United States has some form of mental retardation. Cerebral palsy is the second most common developmental disorder, followed by autism spectrum disorders.

I. *Attention-Deficit Disorder (ADD)/Attention-Deficit Hyperactivity Disorder (ADHD)*

Attention deficit/hyperactivity disorder (AD/HD) is one of the most common neurobehavioural disorders, characterized by problems with inattentiveness, over-activity, impulsivity, or a combination. It affects as many as one in every 20 children. Although boys are three to four times more likely than girls to experience ADHD, the disorder affects both boys and girls. For these problems to be diagnosed as AD/HD, they must be out of the normal range for the child's age and development. It is usually first diagnosed in childhood and often persists into adulthood. Diagnosis can be made reliably using well-tested diagnostic interview methods. Treatment may include medical, educational, behavioural, and/or psychological interventions. ADHD is a lifelong disorder that can negatively impair many aspects of daily life if not treated, including home, school, work, and interpersonal relationships.

Signs and Symptoms of ADHD

There are three main types of ADHD. One type is characterized by inattentiveness, one type is characterized by hyperactive or impulsive behaviour, and the third type is combined—when children exhibit signs of both types. Symptoms are often unnoticed until a child enters school. To be diagnosed with ADHD, a child must show symptoms in at least two settings, such as home and school, and the symptoms must interfere with the child's ability to function at home or school for at least six months. Specialists have agreed that at least six symptoms from the following lists must be present for an accurate diagnosis, and symptoms must begin by the age of 7.

Signs of inattentive behaviour

- Has difficulty in following instructions.
- Has difficulty in focusing on tasks.
- Loses things at school and at home.
- Forgets things often.
- Becomes easily distracted or has difficulty in listening.
- Lacks attention to detail, makes careless mistakes or is disorganized.
- Fails to complete homework or tasks.

Signs of hyperactive behaviour

- Is fidgety.
- Leaves seat when shouldn't.

- Runs or climbs inappropriately.
- Talks excessively.
- Difficulty in playing quietly.
- Always on the go.
- Blurts out answers.
- Has trouble waiting turn.
- Interrupts.

The presence of some symptoms, however, does not confirm a diagnosis of ADHD. Just because a child has a lot of energy or difficulty paying attention in school does not mean the child has ADHD. An accurate diagnosis relies on the presence of a range of symptoms and difficulties that prevent the child from performing at an appropriate level for his or her age and intelligence level. Teachers often first observe these issues, and their input should be considered seriously.

Symptoms of ADHD can make school difficult for a child with the disorder. Although most children with ADHD have normal or above-normal intelligence, 40 to 60 per cent have serious learning difficulties. Many others have specific problems with schoolwork or maintaining good grades, and face particular challenges with assignments and tests that require focused attention or lengthy writing, or have time limits. On a social level, children with ADHD often have trouble developing meaningful relationships with peers and family members. Other children may find it frustrating to play with a child who has ADHD, because classic symptoms include difficulty following rules, waiting one's turn or excessive talking.

Other disorders that commonly occur with ADHD

Children and adolescents with ADHD are more likely than children without the disorder to suffer from other mental disorders. About one-half of all young people with ADHD have oppositional defiant disorder; about one-quarter have an anxiety disorder; as many as one-third have depression; and one-fifth has bipolar disorder. Adolescents with untreated ADHD are at risk for substance abuse disorders. Research shows that young people treated for ADHD have lower rates of substance abuse than children who go untreated.

Researchers believe that biology and genes play a large role in the development of ADHD. In fact, 30 to 40 per cent of children diagnosed with ADHD have relatives with the same disorder. Brain scans reveal that the brains of children with ADHD differ from those of children without the disorder. Children with ADHD are thought to have problems with the part of the brain that controls the organization and direction of thought and behaviour. Children with symptoms of ADHD should be referred to and evaluated by a mental health professional who specializes in treating children, unless your primary care doctor has experience in treating this disorder. The diagnostic evaluation should include behavioural observation in the classroom and at home. A comprehensive treatment plan should be developed with the family, and, whenever possible, the child should be involved in making treatment decisions. Educational testing should be performed when learning disabilities are present.

Treatment for ADHD is effective for most children. Early identification, diagnosis and treatment help children reach their full potential. The most effective treatments for ADHD include a combination of medication, behavioural therapy, and parental support and education. Nine out of 10 children respond to medication, and 50 per cent of children who do not respond to an initial medication will respond to a second. When ADHD co-occurs with another disorder, such as depression or anxiety, a combination of medication and psychotherapy is shown to be particularly effective. Although the value of medication has been well-documented, parents should feel free to discuss any concerns about medication use with their child's doctor.

II. *Bipolar disorder*

Many children, and especially adolescents, experience mood swings as a normal part of growing up, but when these feelings persist and interfere with a child's ability to function in daily life, bipolar disorder could be the cause. Bipolar disorder, also known as manic-depression, is a mood disorder marked by extreme changes in mood, energy levels and behaviour. It is characterized by a variation of moods that fluctuate between a manic phase of elation, hyperactivity and hyper-imagination, and a depressive phase of inhibition, slowness to conceive ideas and move, and anxiety or sadness. Symptoms can begin in early childhood but usually emerge in adolescence or adulthood. Until recently, young people were rarely diagnosed with this disorder. Yet up to one-third of the 3.4 million children and teens with depression in the United States may actually be experiencing the early onset of bipolar disorder, according to the American Academy of Child and Adolescent Psychiatry. Doctors now recognize and treat the disorder in young people, but it is still an under-recognized illness.

Children with bipolar disorder usually alternate rapidly between extremely high moods (mania) and low moods (depression). These mood shifts can produce irritability with periods of wellness between episodes, or the young person may feel both extremes at the same time. Parents who have children with the disorder often describe them as unpredictable, alternating between aggressive or silly and withdrawn. Children with bipolar disorder are at a greater risk for anxiety disorders and attention-deficit hyperactivity disorder. These "co-occurring" disorders complicate diagnosis of bipolar disorder and contribute to the lack of recognition of the illness in children.

Bipolar disorder is treatable. Early identification, diagnosis, and treatment will help children reach their full potential. Children who exhibit signs of bipolar disorder should be evaluated by a mental health professional who specializes in treating children. The evaluation may include consultation with a child psychiatrist, psychological testing, and medical tests to rule out an underlying physical condition that might explain the child's symptoms. A comprehensive treatment plan should include psychotherapy and, in most cases, medication. This plan should be developed with the family, and, whenever possible, the child.

III. *Conduct disorder*

Conduct disorder is a repetitive and persistent pattern of behaviour in children and adolescents in which the rights of others or basic social rules are violated. The child or adolescent usually exhibits these behaviour patterns in a variety of settings—at home, at school, and in social situations—and they cause significant impairment in his or her social, academic, and family functioning.

Behaviours characteristic of conduct disorder include:

- Aggressive behaviour that causes or threatens harm to other people or animals, such as bullying or intimidating others, often initiating physical fights, or being physically cruel to animals.
- Non-aggressive conduct that causes property loss or damage, such as fire-setting or the deliberate destruction of others' property.
- Deceitfulness or theft, such as breaking into someone's house or car, or lying or "conning" others.
- Serious rule violations, such as staying out at night when prohibited, running away from home overnight, or often being truant from school.

Many youth with conduct disorder may have trouble feeling and expressing empathy or remorse and reading social cues. These youth often misinterpret the actions of others as being hostile or aggressive and respond by escalating the situation into conflict. Conduct disorder may also be associated with other difficulties such as substance use, risk-taking behaviour, school problems, and physical injury from accidents or fights.

Conduct disorder is more common among boys than girls, with studies indicating that the rate among boys in the general population ranges from 6 per cent to 16 per cent while the rate among girls ranges from 2 per cent to 9 per cent. Conduct disorder can have its onset early, before the age of 10, or in adolescence. Children who display early-onset conduct disorder are at greater risk for persistent difficulties, however, and they are also more likely to have troubled peer relationships and academic problems. Among both boys and girls, conduct disorder is one of the disorders most frequently diagnosed in mental health settings.

Despite early reports that treatment for this disorder is ineffective, several recent reviews of the literature have identified promising approaches treating children and adolescents with conduct disorder. The most successful approaches intervene as early as possible, are structured and intensive, and address the multiple contexts in which children exhibit problem behaviour, including the family, school, and community. Examples of effective treatment approaches include functional family therapy, multi-systemic therapy, and cognitive behavioural approaches which focus on building skills such as anger management. Pharmacological intervention alone is not sufficient for the treatment of conduct disorder.

IV. *Cerebral palsy*

Cerebral palsy is a disorder caused by damage to the brain that occurs before, during, or shortly following birth. It affects body movement and muscle coordination. Individuals with cerebral palsy may also experience seizures, abnormal speech, hearing and visual impairments, and mental retardation. Children with cerebral palsy may not be able to walk, talk, eat, or play in the same ways as most other children. Cerebral palsy can include milder versions or more severe symptoms, which lead to total dependency. Although cerebral palsy is a lifelong condition, training and therapy can help improve function.

V. *Expressive language disorder*

Expressive language disorder is a developmental disorder where a child will have problems expressing him or herself in speech. Characteristics may include limited vocabulary, difficulty recalling words and producing complex or lengthy sentences. Children with expressive disorder often start speaking late and experience delays acquiring expressive language. Standardized expressive language and non-verbal intellectual tests, and in certain cases functional assessments, should be conducted if an expressive language disorder is suspected. Expressive language disorders may interfere with academics and social communication. Speech therapy and social skills therapies may benefit children affected by this disorder.

VI. *Learning disabilities (LD)*

Learning disabilities are a group of neurological disorders which become evident in childhood and which are characterized by difficulty learning, sorting, and storing information. Usually affected individuals have average or above average intelligence. Children with learning disabilities may have one or more difficulties with skills such as listening, speaking, reading, writing, reasoning, or mathematical abilities that interfere with academic performance, achievement and, in some cases, activities of daily living. Learning disabilities may overlap with other disorders or environmental influences, but are not the direct result of those conditions or influences. Often these disabilities are not identified until a child reaches school age. Some children find learning in a regular classroom difficult and LD classes may be recommended to help them receive more specific and intensive teaching. They may require information to be presented in multiple formats and broken down in manageable chunks before they can completely understand it. Learning disabilities are lifelong, but with proper intervention, training, and strategies, individuals can lead successful, fully functioning lives.

VII. *Seizure disorders*

Seizure disorders are neurological disorders that may cause physical convulsions, minor physical signs, thought disturbances, or a combination of symptoms that are the result of uncontrolled electrical activity in the brain. An individual with a seizure disorder, such as epilepsy, may experience one or more different types and levels of severity of seizure. The condition can develop at any time of life, especially in early childhood, during adolescence and old age. Treatments included seizure-preventing medicines, surgery, ketogenic diet (primarily in children), or electrical stimulation of the vagus nerve, a large nerve leading into the brain. Although seizure medications are not a cure, they control seizures in the majority of people with epilepsy. For some, seizure disorders will be a temporary problem, easily controlled with medication and outgrown after a few years. For others, it may be a lifelong challenge affecting many areas of life.

VIII. *Schizophrenia in children*

Schizophrenia is a medical illness that causes strange thinking, abnormal feelings, and unusual behaviour. It is an uncommon psychiatric illness in children and is hard to recognize in its early phases. The behaviour of children and teens with schizophrenia may differ from that of adults with this illness. Mounting evidence indicates that schizophrenia has neurodevelopment roots. The appearance of schizophrenic symptoms before the age of 12 is rare (less than one-sixtieth as common as the adult-onset type), but studying these cases is important for an understanding of this disorder.

Neurodevelopment damage seems to be greater in childhood schizophrenia than in the adult-onset type. Most schizophrenic children show delays in language and other functions long before their psychotic symptoms (hallucinations, delusions, and disordered thinking) appear, usually at the age of seven or later. In the first years of life, about 30 per cent of these children have transient symptoms of pervasive developmental disorder, such as rocking, posturing, and arm flapping. Childhood home movies indicate uneven motor development, such as unusual crawling, in adult-onset schizophrenic patients. Children with schizophrenia may be even more seriously impaired in this respect, they are also more anxious and disruptive than adult-onset schizophrenic patients were as children.

Early warning signs

- Trouble discerning dreams from reality.
- Seeing things and hearing voices that are not real.
- Confused thinking.
- Vivid and bizarre thoughts and ideas.
- Extreme moodiness.
- Peculiar behaviour.
- Concept that people are "out to get them".
- Behaving younger than chronological age.
- Severe anxiety and fearfulness.
- Confusing television or movies with reality.
- Severe problems in making and keeping friends.

The behaviour of children with this illness may change over time. The schizophrenic psychosis develops gradually in children, without the sudden psychotic break that sometimes occurs in adolescents and adults. Children may begin talking about strange fears and ideas. They may start to cling to parents or say things that do not make sense. Children who used to enjoy relationships with others may become more shy or withdrawn and seem to be in their own world. Early diagnosis and medical treatment are important. Children with the problems and symptoms listed above must have a complete evaluation. These children may need individual treatment plans involving other professionals. A combination of medication and individual therapy, family therapy, and specialized programmes (school, activities, etc.) is often necessary. Psychiatric medication can be helpful for many of the symptoms and problems identified.

IX. *Tourette syndrome*

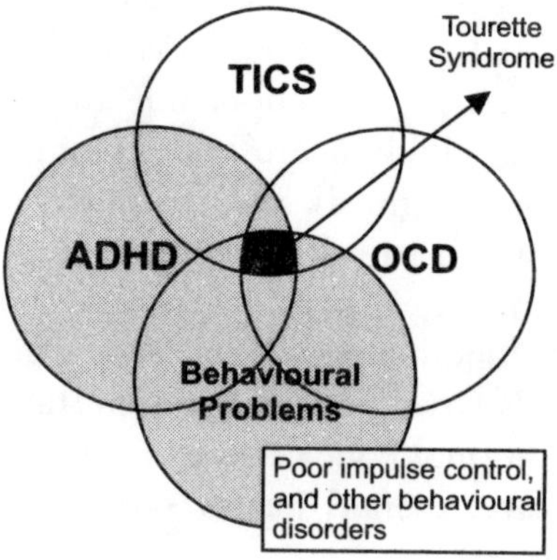

Tourette syndrome is a neurological disorder characterized, in mild form, by recurring involuntary body movements and sounds (called tics) and in advanced cases by large involuntary bodily movements, noises like barks and whistles, and in many instances an uncontrollable urge to utter obscenities. People with Tourette syndrome are often impulsive and have other symptoms of Attention Deficit Disorder. While the average age of onset of Tourette syndrome is 6-7 years old, there are many cases where parents later realized that their child's tics had actually started much younger. In almost all cases, Tourette syndrome emerges before the age of 18, but there are exceptions. The diagnosis is based on patient history, observation, and testing to rule out other conditions. Most cases of TS are thought to be "mild", meaning that the individual does not seek treatment and/or does not experience significant interference in their life from their tics. If tics become problematic, treatment options are available. There are a variety of medications that may provide some relief from the tics and at least one empirically validated non-medication treatment for tics.

(More information on this syndrome can be accessed on http://www.tsa-usa.org/Medical/Faqs.html)

Thus, mental health problems affect children's health, development, and learning capabilities. The extent of mental health problems in children and youth and the importance of getting more help to address these problems have been recognized. Some of the goals include decreasing the number of youth with untreated mental illness, decreasing youth suicides, and decreasing lost days of school due to somatic problems. Mental disorders in children are real, common and treatable. Early identification, diagnosis and treatment of mental health disorders help children to fulfil their potential. Left untreated, children with mental health disorders may have problems at home, and trouble functioning and succeeding in school. Recently some of the schools have realized the importance and provision of many non-traditional education services to children such as primary health care, mental health services, familial support and parenting classes.

Sources of Childhood Stress

Pressures often come from outside sources (such as family, friends, or school), but they can also come from within. The pressure we place on ourselves can be most significant because there is often a discrepancy between what we think we ought to be doing and what we are actually doing in our lives. Stress can affect anyone—even a child—who feels overwhelmed. A 2-year-old child, for example, may be anxious because the parent might not be there to satisfy him or her. In preschoolers, separation from parents is the greatest cause of anxiety.

As children get older, academic and social pressures (especially the quest to fit in) create stress. In addition, well-meaning parents sometimes unwittingly add to the stress in their children's lives. For example, high-achieving parents often have great expectations for their children, who may lack their parents' motivation or capabilities. Parents who push their children to excel in sports or who enroll their children in too many activities may also cause unnecessary stress and frustration if their children don't share their goals. Many professionals feel that a number of children are too busy and do not have time to play creatively or relax after school. Children who begin to complain about the number of activities they are involved in or refuse to go to activities may be signaling to their parents that they are too busy. It is important to talk with the child about how he or she is feeling about after-school activities. If he or she complains, we should talk about the pros and cons of quitting one of the activities. If quitting isn't an option, we must talk about ways that can help the child manage his or her time and responsibilities so that they don't create so much anxiety.

Some of the possible sources of childhood conflict are outlined below. It is important, however, to keep in mind that the source of each child's problem is unique to his/her life.

Causes inside the family

Emotional and behavioural problem among children arise primarily from what happens inside the family.

- How the parents relate to each other.
- How the parents relate to the children.
- Loss of parents through death, separation or divorce.
- Parents' own self-esteem problems.
- Protective behaviours of parents.
- Lack of continuous relationship with mother or mother substitute in the first three years of life.
- Modelling by parents of socially unacceptable behaviours.
- Poor parenting skills.
- Sub-cultural home background whose values, morals and standards differ from these of the larger culture into which children need to fit as they grow up.

Causes within the child

- Poor self-esteem.
- Physical or mental disability.
- Developmental delays.
- Poor knowledge levels.

Causes inside the school

- Fear of the teacher.
- Fear of examinations.
- Fear of performing in class.
- Fear of other students.

Causes outside

- Hostile neighbours.
- Victimization by other children.
- Emotional, physical or sexual abuse and violation by the community.
- Peer group pressure.

Symptoms of Stress in Children

It is not always easy to recognize when the child is stressed out. Short-term behavioural changes, such as mood swings, acting out, changes in sleep patterns, or bedwetting, can be indicators of stress. Some children experience physical effects, including stomachaches and headaches. Others have trouble concentrating or completing schoolwork. Still others become withdrawn or spend a lot of time alone. Younger children may show signs of reacting to stress by picking up new habits like thumb sucking, hair twirling, or nose picking; older children may begin to lie, bully, or defy authority. A child who is stressed out may also have nightmares, difficulty leaving the parents, overreactions to minor problems, and drastic changes in academic performance.

Understanding and Tuning to the Psychological Needs of the Child

Some of the needs of the child may be easily identified simply by looking at the lifestyle and play habits of children. A salient feature of life for children is the unacceptability of being on their own, playing on their own, or working on their own at home or in school. Perhaps this is the result of genuine parental fears about safety, the notion that it is not healthy to be alone, or an overemphasis on the natural affiliative need that all children usually satisfy by joining in with other children. This has become confused with the belief that children always need to have something to do, that they always have to be amused preferably with somebody else or with something other than themselves. Consequently the child never learns—or is never allowed to learn—to be alone or to be happy with his own company. This raises the question for the child: "is my own company not good enough?" which can lead to the child's sense of self being undermined and undervalued.

The development of technologically based forms of communication has led to particular effects on children and relationships. The fact that so many homes have a T.V., a computer, a play station and other types of computer games leads to a number of effects. Children spend increasing amount of time in 'conversation' with their screen, engaging in one-way conversations, thus denying them access to the affective (feeling) give and take which conversation with other person demands. There is no exchange of language, touch or emotion; the child is interacting with a mechanical device, which has no feeling and so gives out no emotional, tactile or human response. Such overabundance of technology-based forms of communications might lead to the child becoming shy and introverted.

Interaction with a computer or computer game, gives immediate gratification of needs and a continuous variety of response. Instant gratification means that the child is immediately given the response that he wants and it presents the child with an unrealistic view of reality. Continuous exposure to technological modes of communication and recreation allows the person the luxury of having a conversation with himself where he has complete control over the questions and the answers. In actual situations when the child does not find responses in accordance with his expectations, there is a possibility of developing mental disturbances like frustration,

An ***introverted person*** is someone who is quiet, thoughtful and enjoys solitude. He is more interested in ideas than in outside things and people. It is not the same as being shy and is in no sense abnormal or 'wrong'. There may be an unconscious fear that there is something wrong with the child who is quiet and introverted and this sometimes results in a desire to have children always playing with their friends. Parents often worry because their child is shy, introverted or reserved and it often happens that such children do suffer in the competition stakes. But shyness or quietness is not in itself a disadvantage. Such children can learn just as effectively as other more outgoing children. They learn in a different way and have different needs, but they do not suffer from any disability and do not need to be 'cured'.

depression and anxiety. Such instant gratifications might also lead to reduce attention span in the child, and a tendency to seek instant satisfaction in real life situations.

Today the child is no better or worse off physically or psychologically in relations to his needs than his parents were. He has the potential and the capability to survive in his environment and the role of the parent and teacher is to enable him to use his latent survival skills.

Need of Parent Different from the Child

Very often the child's needs are confused with the parent's needs. Because a child is a separate person, he will have different needs from other children and from the adults in his life. It is very easy for parents to assume that their child's needs are the same, as their own personal needs. Personal needs are based on the individual psychological, social, emotional and physical makeup of the child. His needs are determined by the kind of person he is, what he is capable of becoming, the environment in which he finds himself and his ability or inability to cope with his environment in a way that does not threaten his view of himself.

When the parent, teacher or any other adult projects their own unconscious needs onto the child, the adult believes that their own needs are the same as the needs of the child, and the child in turn believes these to be his own. Projecting adult needs onto the child means that the adult will only be happy if and when the child achieves what the adult wants for herself. These 'adult' needs would be unsuitable for the child. It also means that the child will never achieve his own ambitions. The parent sees the child as the extension of himself. It follows that the child will be unable to have a separate identity from the parent. This results in what is termed idealization, where the child and parent think so highly of each other, that there is a fusion of identities. As a result, the child becomes stuck at an infantile stage of emotional development and never manages to separate from the parent, never sees himself as separate and never manages to develop an identity which stands on its own separate from that of the parent.

Tuning in to the Child's Needs

The most effective way to both prevent and counteract the dangers of parents and children's needs being fused is by tuning in to the child. Parents' natural desire to be in tune with the child often results in unnecessary interference in their child's life and especially interfering in their arguments and fights. The willingness to allow the child to do things by himself and to face up to problems without parental interference depends on the parents' confidence in themselves and in the child. The natural instinct in parents to protect their young may become over-active when the child starts school. This overprotection may result in:

- The child is not given enough space to grow.
- The child is not allowed to make decisions by himself.
- The child is not allowed to deal with conflict in his own life.
- The child is not allowed to develop confidence in his own judgement.

- The child is prevented from developing a realistic sense of his own capabilities.
- The child is protected from dealing with his own limitations.
- The child may not learn to deal with failure in his or her life.

Parents and teachers can avoid overprotection and get closer to the real needs of the child—thus allowing him to become an effective child—if they tune in to the needs and feelings of the child.

Starting school is the first real opportunity that the child has to survive on his own and however, many parents consciously say that this is what they want, there is an unconscious need to maintain dependency because it makes parents feel wanted. It is important for both parents to be aware of their own needs so that the needs of the child can be clear. In learning to tune in to the child, it is essential to know one's own needs, so that one can separate these from the needs of the child.

Secondly, we need to see our children as 'other people' separate from us physically, emotionally and socially. It is an important 'given' that if we are going to tune in to the child, we first of all accept that child, as a being is separate and different. Above all, if we want to know what the child's needs are we need to give him the space to tell us so. Rather than putting pressure on the child to tell us 'what happened', 'why did you do that?' it is much more informative to allow the child to tell his own story.

Role of the School and Teacher

Although all children develop in their own unique fashion, as a direct result of both hereditary and environmental influences, there is a certain pattern of development that applies to nearly all children. It is crucial for today's educators to have a thorough understanding of that development. Schools today play an important role in the socialization of children and therefore it is critical that teachers know how to best socialize their students. An understanding of basic human developmental stages can be used to gear the teacher's lesson plans in order to maximize the success of students in both the academic and the social realms of their lives. This understanding can also be used to minimize problems in the classroom.

For the teacher, it is usually a case of getting others to pay attention to what he is saying and getting others to listen. One of the basic pre-requisites of the teachers' work is that the children pay attention. This becomes such an important part of the work that listening to what the child is saying may not come easily. If the teacher is to tune in to the child and be aware of his needs, then it is essential that he/she not only listens to what the child is saying verbally, but physically and emotionally as well.

If the teacher can observe the child in class and in the playground, it helps him to gain an insight into the child, which will help in tuning in to his needs. It is through the child's misbehaviour that the teacher will find out most about the child; if a teacher can look at the misbehaviour as a way into the psyche of the child, rather than just something to be eliminated and punished, it can help both teacher and child enormously.

In the same way, the child's moods, tantrums, day dreams and verbal outbursts are windows to the psyche of the child. For a teacher who is under pressure to get the work done, they are most likely to be a nuisance. But if a teacher pays attention to these unconscious messages from the child, he is likely to get closer to the child and to be much more in tune with him. To gain the child's confidence and to allow the teacher to tune in to the child's world, it is helpful if the teacher as a first response takes the child's word seriously and believes until he knows otherwise.

In general a class teacher should watch for:

- The child who says nothing (he/she is communicating in other ways).
- The child who is always looking for attention.

- The child who doesn't play.
- The child who never steps out of line.
- The child who does not want to go home.
- The child who finds it difficult to allow others to have their share of attention.
- The child who is always in a world of his own.

Understanding Adolescents

19

The term 'adolescence' comes from the Latin word *adolescere*, meaning 'to grow' or 'to grow to maturity'. Primitive peoples—as was true also in earlier civilizations—do not consider puberty and adolescence to be distinct periods in the lifespan; the child is regarded as an adult when capable of reproduction. As it is used today, the term adolescence has a broader meaning. It includes mental, emotional and social maturity as well as physical maturity. Piaget has expressed this point of view when he said:

> Psychologically, adolescence is the age when the individual becomes integrated into the society of adults, the age when the child no longer feels that he is below the level of his elders but equal, at least in rights.... This integration into adult society has many affective aspects, more or less linked with puberty.... It also includes very profound intellectual changes.... These intellectual transformations typical of the adolescents' thinking enable him not only to achieve his integration into the social relationships of adults, which is, in fact, the most general characteristic of this period of development.

The Adolescent Years

Adolescence begins when children become sexually mature and end when they reach the age of legal maturity. However, studies of changes in behaviour, attitudes and values throughout adolescence have revealed not only that these changes are more rapid in the early than in the latter part of adolescence but also that the behaviour, attitudes and values in the early part of the period are markedly different from those in the latter part. Adolescence is often described as a phase of life that begins in biology and ends in society (Sharma 1996). It means that physical and biological changes are universal and take place due to maturation but the psychosocial and behavioural manifestations are determined by the meaning given to these changes within a cultural system. The experience of adolescents during teen years would vary considerably according to the cultural and social values of the network of social identities they grow in.

In reality, there are markedly different notions of adolescence in different parts of the world. These stand apart from western account of what does or should happen during this transitional period between childhood and adulthood (Brown et al., 2002). In contemporary India while adolescence is a comparatively new term, the word youth is better known and has been used at the levels of policy formulation and programming (Singh, 1997).

The concept of adolescence as it is commonly understood as a period of *storms and stress* was initiated by G. Stanley Hall of Clark University in the U.S.A. at the turn of the century. Subsequently the Adolescent Psychology with an emphasis on psychological upheaval during this stage dominated the literature for several decades. Erickson (1975) a well-known psychologist, viewed adolescence as a natural period of uprootedness in human life. He also theorized adolescence as a stage of life during which inner identity is to be achieved and called it a period of identity crisis. The crisis term has been used by

Erickson in a developmental sense to connote a 'threat of catastrophe, but a turning point, a crucial period of increased potential' (Erickson, 1968, p. 69).

When people talk about puberty, teenagers and adolescence, the things that come to mind are: raging hormones, cracking voices, budding breasts, menstruation, cranky, rebellious teenagers, sprouting hair, acne and other such characteristics. The onset of puberty is the most obvious sign of 'growing up' physically. To put it more formally, puberty can be defined as "a biological or physiological process characterized by the maturation of the sexual organs and the appearance of secondary sexual characteristics". People often think that puberty and adolescence refer to the same thing. However, they refer to two different aspects of growing up. While puberty covers the physical, adolescence deals with the mental and has been described as a "psychosocial process characterized by mental and social growth, and often extending from puberty to the early 20s and sometimes beyond".

ONSET AND END OF ADOLESCENCE

The interplay of biological changes and social attitude will determine the psychological meaning of puberty for its members. The common themes and assumptions, which are relevant in this context, are:

The onset of puberty marks the beginning of adolescence. There are individual as well as cultural differences in the length of adolescence and in the age of onset and completion. While the physical changes of pubescence signal the beginning of this phase. Sociological criteria such as achievement of adult status and privileges, marriage, the end of education and the beginning of economic independence frequently mark the termination of adolescence. The stage of adolescence is likely to end earlier in primitive cultures and later in technological ones. (Sharma, 1996, p. 25)

Developmental Needs of Adolescents

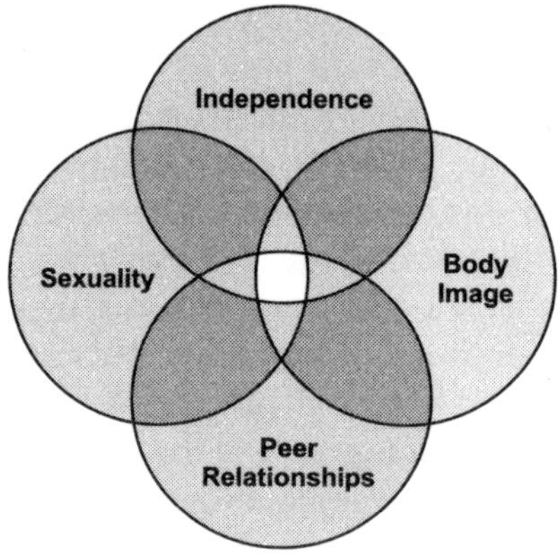

Adolescence is marked as a period of growth spurt and maturation, extent of physical growth is not determined by genetic, heredity factors alone but also on availability of adequate nutrition, micronutrients in the diet and access to health services. Inadequate nutrition during adolescence can have serious consequences throughout reproductive years and beyond. Extra nutritional requirements include increased intake of calcium, iron, iodine, minerals and proteins. Unmet nutritional needs lead to several public health problems such as stunted and retarded growth, impaired mental development, anaemia, complications during pregnancy and low birth weight babies.

Adolescence is also a stage when young people extend relationships beyond their parents and family. It can be very difficult for parents to accept that their 'little' son or daughter is growing up, is starting to form opinions, is wanting to have some independence, and finds hanging out with friends a whole lot more interesting than hanging round with parents. Parents can sometimes be heard speaking about their teenagers in general as "she is sullen and moody", "he is absolutely lazy and selfish", "I can't trust her to be truthful about where she is going", "we have always been so close but now it's as if I'm some stranger", and that "he spends most of his time in bed".

Thus, it is a time of intense influence of peers, and the outside world in the society. A desire to experiment and explore can manifest in a range of behaviours—exploring sexual relationships, alcohol, tobacco and other substances abuse. The anxiety and stress associated with achievement failure, lack of confidence, etc. is likely to lead to depression, anger, violence and other mental health problems. Adolescents as they mature cognitively, the mental functioning process becomes analytic, capable of abstract thinking leading to articulation and independent ideology. These are truly the years of creativity, empathy, and idealism and with bountiful spirit of adventure. Thus, if nurtured properly, undoubtedly youth can be mobilized to contribute significantly to national development.

Unmet needs during this critical period have serious consequences not for the individual alone but for the family, community, society and nation at large. The data available from the reviewed literature on physical growth, nutritional and health status demonstrate that health scenario of a large proportion of adolescents in India is plagued by under nutrition, anaemia, and infectious diseases resulting from poor environmental sanitation and ignorance. While the consequences of poverty do not spare the adolescent boys, the girls come through as the endangered sex (Anand et al. 1999, Chaturvedi et al., 1996, Kanada et al., 1999).

Several studies have indicated that parents rarely provide the desired support to growing adolescents regarding biological and physiological changes as also the meaning attached to these. Youth sexuality stands out as an important aspect, which is inadequately understood; taboos to access information and lack of counselling services make youngsters turn to peers and other sources of information (Abraham, 2000; Abraham and Deshpande, 2001; Sachdev, 1998; Murthy, 1993). We need to be aware that distorted information has consequences related to exploitation, abuse, mental health problems and risk of HIV/ AIDS. Providing awareness services and strengthening capabilities of institutions like family, community and school to act as sources of correct information are thus important and need to be given attention.

Characteristics of Adolescence

As is true of every important period during the lifespan, adolescence has certain characteristics that distinguish it from the periods that preceded it and the periods that will follow it.

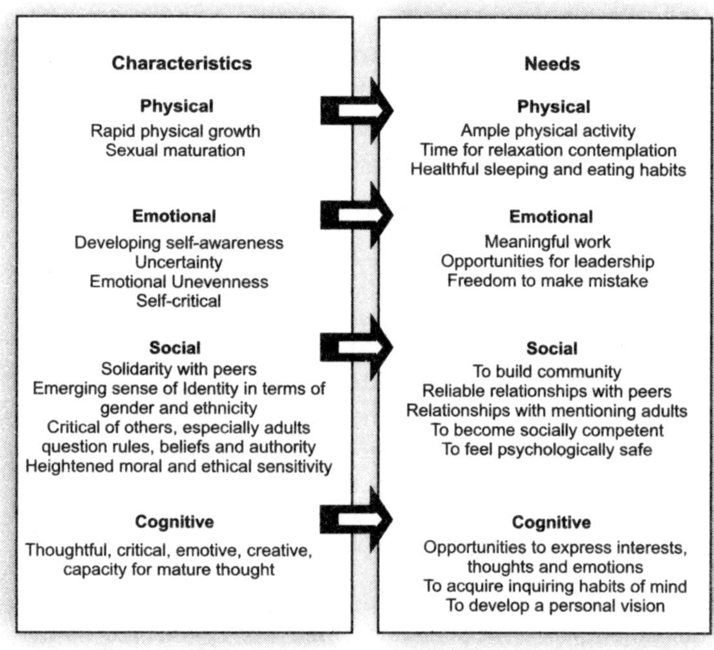

Adolescence is an important period

Adolescence is one of the periods when both the immediate effects and long-term effects are important. Some periods are important for their physical and some for their psychological effects. Adolescence is important for both. Accompanying these rapid and important physical developments, especially during the early adolescent period, rapid mental development occur. These give rise to the need for mental adjustments and the necessity for establishing new attitudes, values and interests.

Adolescence: A time of transition

> Fourteen-year-old Tanmay is driving his parents crazy. A few years ago he was a pleasant, cooperative child but now he's restless, obstinate, defiant and more interested in spending time with his friends than his family.

There are three factors that can help us to understand the erratic, fickle, rebellious, sometimes maddening, frustrating and exasperating behaviour of the adolescent. First, adolescence is a time of rapid biological change. The adolescent is growing to his full adult stature and experiencing new and strange impulses that he doesn't yet know how to handle. Hormones are running wild. Second, adolescence is a transition period between childhood and adulthood. No longer a child, but not yet an adult, the adolescent is caught between the past and the future. Although biologically mature, in that she is capable of sexual reproduction, psychologically and socially she has still not achieved full adult status. Third, the adolescent is not yet a fully productive member of society. Because of the educational demands of our complex, technical and industrial world, young people have to spend many years acquiring the knowledge and skills they will need to find useful employment.

If he is restless and full of energy, it is because of the biological changes that he is undergoing, and because of his anxiety about his uncertain status. If she behaves like a mature, responsible adult one-day, and a spoiled, immature child the next, it is because she is half-child and half-adult. If he likes one thing one moment, and another thing the next moment, or if he wants to be one type of person at one time, and another type of person at another time, it is because he really doesn't yet know what he wants or wants to be. If she is a bit too rebellious, or if she challenges parental values and rules, it is because she is searching for her own principles. Till this period, she has tended to uncritically accept her parent's values but now she feels that she is better equipped intellectually to challenge those beliefs and decide upon her own.

Transition does not mean a break with or a change from what has gone before but rather a passage from one stage of development to another. Children, when they go from childhood to adulthood, must put away childish things and they must also learn new patterns of behaviour and attitudes to replace those they have abandoned. During any transitional period, the individual's status is vague and there is confusion about the roles the individual is expected to play. The adolescent, at this time, is neither a child nor an adult. If adolescents behave like children, they are told to "act their age". If they try to act like adults they are often accused of being "too big for their age" and are reproved for their attempts to act like adults.

Adolescence is a period of change

The rate of change in attitudes and behaviour during adolescence parallels the rate of physical change. During early adolescence, when physical changes are rapid, changes in attitudes and behaviours are also rapid. As physical changes slow down, so do attitudinal and behavioural changes.

There are five almost universal concomitants of the changes that occur during adolescence. The first is heightened emotionality, the intensity of which depends on the rate at which the physical and psychological changes are taking place. Because these changes normally occur more during early adolescence, heightened emotionality is generally more pronounced in early than in late adolescence. Second, the rapid changes that accompany sexual maturity make young adolescents unsure of themselves, of their capacities and of their interests. They have strong feelings of instability, which are often intensified by the ambiguous treatment they receive from parents and teachers.

Third, changes in their bodies, their interests and in the roles the social group expects them to play create new problems. To young adolescents these may seem more numerous and less easily solved than any they have had to face before. Until they have solved their problems to their satisfaction, they will be preoccupied with them and with themselves. Fourth, as interests and behaviour patterns change, so do values. What was important to them as children seems less important to them now that they are near adults. Fifth, most adolescents are ambivalent about changes. While they want and demand independence, they often dread the responsibilities that go with independence and question their ability to cope with these responsibilities.

Adolescence is a problem age

While every age has its problems, those of adolescence are often especially difficult for boys and girls to cope with. There are two reasons for this. First throughout childhood, their problems were met and solved, in part or at least, by parents and teachers. As a result, many adolescents are inexperienced in coping with problems alone. Second, because adolescents want to feel that they are independent, they demand the right of coping with their own problems. Because of their inability to cope with the problems alone as well as they believe they can, many adolescents find that the solutions do not always come up to their expectations.

Adolescence is a time of search for identity

Throughout the gang age of late childhood conformity to group standards is far more important to older children than individuality. Any deviation from the group standard is likely to be a threat to group belonging. In the early years of adolescence, conformity to the group is still important to boys and girls. Gradually, they begin to crave identity and are no longer satisfied to be like their peers in every respect, as they were earlier. Erickson explains:

> The identity the adolescent seems to clarify is who he is, what his role in society is to be. Is he a child or is he an adult? Does he have it in him to be someday a husband and father? Overall, will he be a success or a failure?

One of the ways adolescents try to establish themselves as individuals is by the use of status symbols in the form of cars, clothes and other readily observable material possessions. They hope, in this way to attract attention to themselves and to be recognized as individuals whole, at the same time, maintaining their identity with the peer group.

Adolescence is a dreaded age

As Majeres has pointed out, "many popular beliefs about adolescents have definite evaluative connotations and unfortunately many of them are negative. Acceptance of the cultural stereotype of teenagers as sloppy, unreliable individuals who are inclined toward destructiveness and antisocial behaviour has led many adults who must guide and supervise the lines of young adolescents to dread this responsibility and to be unsympathetic in their attitudes towards and treatment of normal adolescent behaviour.

Popular stereotypes have also influenced the self—concepts and attitudes of adolescents toward themselves. The acceptance of this stereotype and the belief that adults have poor opinions of them make the transition into adulthood difficult. By so doing, it leads to much friction with their parents and places a barrier between them and their parents, which prevents them from turning to their parents for help in solving their problems.

Adolescence is a time of unrealism

Adolescents have a tendency to look at life as bed of roses. They see themselves and others, as they would like them to be rather than as they are. This is especially true of adolescent aspirations. These unrealistic aspirations, not only for themselves but also for their families and friends, are in part, responsible for the heightened emotionality characteristic of early adolescence. The more unrealistic their aspirations are, the more angry, hurt and disappointed they will be when they feel that others have let them down or that they have not lived up to the goals they set for themselves. With increased personal and social experiences and with increased ability to link rationally, older adolescents see themselves, their families and friends and life in general in a more realistic way. As a result, they suffer less from disappointment and disillusionment that they did when they were younger. This is one of the conditions that contribute to the greater happiness of the older adolescent.

Adolescence is the threshold of adulthood

As adolescents approach legal maturity, they are anxious to shed the stereotype of teenagers and to create the impression that they are near-adults. Dressing and acting like adults, they discover, are not always enough. So they begin to concentrate on behaviour that is associated with the adult status—smoking, drinking, using drugs and engaging in sex, for example. They believe that this behaviour will create the image they desire.

Bearing in mind the normal characteristics of adolescents mentioned above, perhaps the following points might be helpful to plan education for children of this age group:

1. *The desire for responsibility*

Adolescents like to manage things for themselves, to organize discussions, arrange demonstrations, to plan and to execute without too much adult assistance.

2. *The tendency to be irresponsible*

At the same time youth likes to feel thoroughly carefree and irresponsible sometimes, and should be able to rely on grown-ups in the background to take responsibility now and again for them.

3. *Impatient for results*

Young people need to feel that the ends for which they are striving can be achieved in a not too distant future. Carelessness, hurry, superficiality are all characteristics of this age, and no amount of scolding or retribution will greatly influence these traits until the child himself recognizes the need for reform.

4. *Enthusiasm*

Adolescents notably are enthusiastic and their zeal should be directed to some worthwhile end. The desire to alleviate distress, to reform, to build a new heaven upon earth is present in almost every young person and this can be harnessed to some purpose. Many valuable lessons in citizenship can be learned if they are made sufficiently practical and appropriate. His/her enthusiasm and interests for diverse areas should always be encouraged, never scorned, even though adolescent tastes may change in few weeks.

5. *Adult interests*

Although the adolescent will be childish, flippant, off-hand, bored and foolish at times, he is very much aware and interested in his approaching adulthood, and his education should seek to give him further information and inspiration concerning more mature interests. Perhaps the most obvious way by which this can be done for the girl is to teach her something about home making and mother craft, personal hygiene and beauty culture. This will normally be of real interest to her and fulfil an obvious need. In the case of boys particularly, the medieval practice of apprenticeship to a craftsman had much to commend it. It is obviously best to learn about a trade or a craft by watching an expert and trying alongside him. Contact with adults, who are themselves artists, craftsmen, and skilled workers of any kind can be very beneficial to young people.

The approach of the teacher to the whole question of further education is of the greatest importance. The young people should be thought of as students striving to discover things for themselves with the aid of experts, rather than pupils whose immature minds need to be moulded or driven.

Emotionality during Adolescence

Traditionally, adolescence has been thought of as a period of 'storm and stresses'—a time of heightened emotional tension resulting from the physical and glandular changes that are taking place. While it is true that growth continues through the early years of adolescence, it does so at a progressively slower rate. The growth that is taking place is primarily a completion of the pattern already set at puberty. The explanations are to be found in the social conditions that surround the adolescent of today. Adolescent emotionality can be attributed mainly to the fact that boys and girls come under social pressures and face new conditions for which they received little if any preparation during childhood.

Not all adolescents by any means go through a period of exaggerated storm and stress. True, most of them do experience emotional instability from time to time, which is a logical consequence of the necessity of making adjustments to new patterns of behaviour and to new social expectations. For example, problems related to love relationships are very real at this time. While the relationship with the opposite sex is moving along smoothly, adolescents are happy, but they become despondent when things begin to go wrong. Similarly, with the end of their schooling, adolescents begin to worry about their future. The emotional patterns of adolescence, while similar to childhood vary somehow. Instead of having temper tantrums, however, adolescents express their anger by sulking, refusing to speak or loudly criticizing those who angered them. Adolescents also become envious of those with more material possessions.

To achieve emotional maturity, adolescents must learn to get a perspective on situations which otherwise would lead to emotional reactions. They can do this best by discussing their problems with others. Their willingness to disclose their attitudes, feelings and personal problems is influenced partly by how secure they feel in their social relationships, partly by how much they like the target person and by how much the target person is willing to disclose to them. In addition, if adolescents are to achieve emotional maturity, they must learn to use emotional catharsis to clear their systems of pent-up emotional energy. This they can do by strenuous physical exercise, in play or work, by laughing or by crying. While all of these provide an outlet for pent-up emotional expressions, social attitudes toward crying are unfavourable, as they are toward laughing, unless the laughter is held in check and occurs only when the social group approves.

Psychological Disturbance in Adolescence

Children now love luxury. They have bad manners, contempt for authority. They show disrespect for elders and love chatter in place of exercise. Children are now tyrants, not the servants of their households.

In *The Adolescent Society*, Coleman infers from a study of several thousand high school students that the modern adolescent is experiencing a marginal existence between childhood and adulthood that requires him to look increasingly to his peers for his rewards and values. Far from becoming prematurely assimilated into adult society, Coleman continues to say that today's adolescents have developed their own teenage subculture, replete with its own terminology, language and standards, all of which contribute to distinctly adolescent personality patterns.

He is 'cut off' from the rest of the society, forced inward towards his own age group, made to carry out his whole social life with others of his own age. With his fellows, he comes to constitute a small society, one that has most of its important interactions within itself, and maintains only a few threads of connection with the outside adult society. Adolescents are excessively egoistic, regarding themselves as the center of the universe and the sole object of interest and yet at no time in later life are they capable of so much self-sacrifice and devotion. They form the most passionate lcve relations only to break them off as abruptly as they began them. On the one hand they throw themselves enthusiastically into the life of the community and on the other, they have an overpowering longing for solitude, sometimes they will work with indefatigable enthusiasm and at other times they are sluggish and apathetic.

Like adults, adolescents can have mental health problems that interfere with the way they think, feel, and act. These problems are real and painful. They can lead to school failure, family conflicts, drug abuse, violence, or suicide. Mental health problems often limit young people's current and future ability to be productive. In addition, these problems can be very costly to families, communities, and the health care system. Sometimes a young person has a mental health problem that severely disrupts his or her ability to function at home, in school, or in the community. This child or adolescent is said to have a "serious emotional disturbance". Usually the impaired emotional, behavioural, and mental functioning continues for a year or more. In some cases, the impairment lasts for a shorter period of time, but its severity is high or life threatening. Many children and adolescents are affected by mental health problems. Studies show that, at any given time, at least one in five children and adolescents may have a mental health problem. At least 1 in 10—or as many as 6 million young people—may have a serious emotional disturbance.

Worldwide up to 20 per cent of children and adolescents suffer from a disabling mental illness (WHR, 2000). Worldwide suicide is the 3rd leading cause of death among adolescents (WHR, 2001). Major depressive disorder (MDD) often has an onset in adolescence, across diverse countries, and is associated with substantial psychosocial impairment and risk of suicide (Weissman, 1999). More adolescents die of suicide than AIDS, cancer, heart disease, obesity, birth defects and lung disease. In 2006-07, 5,857 students took their own life, which works out to a stunning 16 suicides a day, says the National Crime Records Bureau (NCRB). While the global teen suicide rate is 14.5 per 100,000, a 2004 study by the Christian Medical College (CMC), Vellore, reported 148 for girls and 58 for boys in India.

Conduct disorder related behaviours tend to persist into adolescence and adult life through drug abuse, juvenile delinquency, adult crime, antisocial behaviour, marital problems, poor employee relations, unemployment, interpersonal problems, and poor physical health (Patterson, DeBaryshe, and Ramsey,

1989). Weissman et al. (1999) demonstrated in a longitudinal study the poor outcome of adolescent onset major depressive disorder. There was continuity and specificity related to the adolescent onset which continued into adulthood and was associated with high rates of suicide and suicide attempts, increased rates of psychiatric and medical hospitalizations, psychosocial impairment and lower educational achievement.

Geller (2001) reported that children with pre-pubertal major depressive disorder, as adults, had significantly higher rates than a normal comparison group of bi-polar disorder, major depressive disorder, and substance use disorders and were suicidal. Eating disorders are becoming more prevalent and observable across cultures (Becker, 2002). After taking account of confounding factors Woodward and Fergusson (2001) found that significant associations remained between the number of anxiety disorders reported in adolescence and young people's later risks of anxiety disorder, major depression, illicit drug dependence, and failure to attend university.

Context for the Diagnosis of Mental Disorders

In considering the care for children and adolescents with mental disorders the importance of the contextual understanding and context of the disorders must be stressed. This contextual understanding places a special importance on understanding the environment of the child and the adolescent, that is, family, community and nation. Also, specific situations might impact on diagnosing a mental disorder in children and adolescents, such as: exposure to conflict, economic and psychosocial adversity, voluntary and forced migration, effects of AIDS/HIV and the perception of the "rights" of the child and adolescent in a given society. Disorders of mental functioning cannot be seen as static diagnostic labels, but rather must be seen as dynamic responses to social/environmental stressors. This does not imply that those disorders now known to have a biological, presumed genetic component are to be negated. Rather, the weight is given to appreciating the potentially unique impact of environmental factors in the expression of these and other disorders.

Specific Mental Health Problems in Adolescents

Per cent of youth who meet criteria for a mental disorder diagnosis

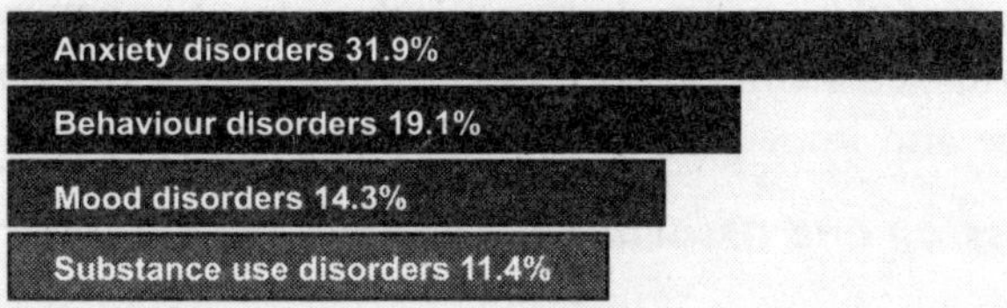

Source: Journal of the American Academy of Child and Adolescent Psychiatry (Vol. 49, No. 10).

Mental disorders and mental health problems seem to have increased considerably among adolescents in the past 20-30 years. In most developed countries young people aged between 10 and 20 years account for 13-15 per cent of the population. The World Health Organization classifies young people as 10-24 year olds, with adolescence (10-19 years) and youth (15-24 years) overlapping within that age range. There were 7.6 million adolescents aged 10-19 years in the United Kingdom in mid-2000, making up 12.7 per cent of the population. Projections suggest that the numbers of adolescents will grow by 8.5 per cent between 1998 and 2011 (http://www.bmj.com/content/330/7488/411.extract).

The rise has been driven by social change, including disruption of family structure, growing youth unemployment and increasing educational and vocational pressures. The identification, treatment and follow up of mental health problems in young people can be complicated. Parents and teachers may dismiss problems as merely reflecting adolescent turmoil. Young people are often very reluctant to seek help, owing to developmental needs about being "normal" at the time when they are exploring identity issues and trying to engage with a peer group.

Variations of mood and temporary deviant behaviours are part of the normal adolescent process. It is normal for young people to feel depressed from time to time and for this mood to last several days. Similarly, many young people will experiment with drugs or 'delinquent' behaviours as part of normal exploration of their own identity. Such normal behaviours can be distinguished from more serious problems by the duration, persistence and impact of the symptoms.

I. *Depression and associated suicide*

Depression is now recognized as a diagnosable disorder in children and adolescents. The magnitude of the association of depression and aggression with suicide remains open to confirmation on a general population basis but are, nevertheless important clinical issue. It is clear that the combination of depression with substance abuse puts children and adolescents at greater risk for suicide. The recognition, evaluation and treatment of depression and related suicidal or self-harming behaviour are the highest priorities in adolescent mental health. Epidemiological studies suggest that at any one time 8 per cent to 10 per cent of adolescents have severe depression. This means that the major burden of assessing and managing adolescent depression falls on primary care practitioners.

Recognizing adolescent depression

Adolescent depression is increasing at an alarming rate. Recent surveys indicate that as many as one in five teens suffers from clinical depression. This is a serious problem that calls for prompt, appropriate treatment. Depression can take several forms, including bipolar disorder (formally called manic-depression), which is a condition that alternates between periods of euphoria and depression.

Depression can be difficult to diagnose in teens because adults may expect teens to act moody. Also, adolescents do not always understand or express their feelings very well. They may not be aware of the symptoms of depression and may not seek help. These symptoms may indicate depression, particularly when they last for more than two weeks:

- Poor performance in school.
- Withdrawal from friends and activities.
- Sadness and hopelessness.
- Lack of enthusiasm, energy or motivation.
- Anger and rage.
- Overreaction to criticism.
- Feelings of being unable to satisfy ideals.
- Poor self-esteem or guilt.
- Indecision, lack of concentration or forgetfulness.
- Restlessness and agitation.
- Changes in eating or sleeping patterns.
- Substance abuse.
- Problems with authority.
- Suicidal thoughts or actions.

Teens may experiment with drugs or alcohol or become sexually promiscuous to avoid feelings of depression. Teens also may express their depression through hostile, aggressive, risk-taking behaviour. But such behaviours only lead to new problems, deeper levels of depression and destroyed relationships with friends, family, law enforcement or school officials.

To evaluate risk of depression properly, young people must be interviewed confidentially and additional information gathered from parents as well as other sources (such as teachers, social workers or youth workers). As well as eliciting symptoms and risk factors for depression, it is essential to assess potential suicide risk in depressed young people. They must be asked about past and present suicidal ideation and self-harming behaviour, past attempts and whether they plan to harm themselves. Asking about suicide reduces rather than increases the risk of suicide.

Treating adolescent depression

It is extremely important that depressed teens receive prompt, professional treatment. Depression is serious and, if left untreated, can worsen to the point of becoming life-threatening. If depressed teens refuse treatment, it may be necessary for family members or other concerned adults to seek professional advice. Therapy can help teens understand why they are depressed and learn how to cope with stressful situations. Depending on the situation, treatment may consist of individual, group or family counselling. Medications that can be prescribed by a psychiatrist may be necessary to help teens feel better. Some of the most common and effective ways to treat depression in adolescents are:

- Psychotherapy provides teens an opportunity to explore events and feelings that are painful or troubling to them. Psychotherapy also teaches them coping skills.
- Cognitive-behavioural therapy helps teens change negative patterns of thinking and behaving.
- Interpersonal therapy focuses on how to develop healthier relationships at home and at school.
- Medication relieves some symptoms of depression and is often prescribed along with therapy.

Antidepressant medications are prescribed to treat children and adolescents with depression. Recent studies indicate that certain selective serotonin re-uptake inhibitors (SSRIs) are safe and efficacious treatments for depression in young people. However, care must be used in prescribing and monitoring all medication. Special forms of psychotherapy, such as cognitive behavioural therapy, have proved effective for adolescents with depression, and current studies are evaluating the effectiveness of individual, family, and group therapies for young people. When depressed adolescents recognize the need for help, they have taken a major step toward recovery. However, few adolescents seek help on their own. They may need encouragement from their friends and support from concerned adults to seek help and follow treatment recommendations.

TREATING THE SUICIDAL ADOLESCENT

The demography and dynamics of adolescent suicidal behaviour identify the major considerations in treating the youngster who has made a suicide attempt. Above all, every such attempt must be taken seriously. Although suicide attempts vary in severity and implications for subsequent suicidal behaviour, even the least serious gesture is intended to communicate something significant to the important people in the youngster's life. It is, therefore, almost inevitable that the failure of others to attach significance to his behaviour will presage additional and increasingly more dangerous self-destructive actions.

Although there is no single explanation for adolescent suicidal behaviour, clinical experience and a wealth of data indicate the most common denominator in both suicide attempters and suicide completers is a depressive constellation of feelings of deprivation, guilt, helplessness and rejection.

It is hoped that family or friends will give an adolescent's suicide attempt sufficient credence to seek professional help, even when the physical consequences do not demand such attention. Then regardless of whether the youngster has ingested a near fatal dose of barbiturates or merely few tablets, the therapist can begin to act on the almost certain knowledge that some otherwise incommunicable distress and some failure in interpersonal relationships have contributed to the youngster's actions.

Another mandatory aspect of treating the suicidal adolescent is the inclusion of the parents in the process. To the extent that an experienced loss of love has participated in the adolescents' suicidal behaviour, the therapist should seek to replace such losses not only by making himself available

(Contd...)

but also by encouraging more positive patterns of family attitudes and interactions. It is vital that the parents too understand the motives for their child's suicide attempt and that the youngster's covert communication be expressed and shared with them openly. The more the suicidal youngster subsequently encounters warm concern, attempts to understand his behaviour, and desired changes in family patterns, the less likely he is to contemplate future suicide behaviour, and these are the considerations that should govern the treatment approach.

II. *Psychosis*

The early identification of psychotic conditions is important for they are not always as obvious as would be thought. Psychoses can result in a host of maladaptive behaviours. The early treatment of psychotic disorders such as schizophrenia not only brings relief to patients, families and society, but also improves the prognosis. Toxic psychoses are treatable when recognized with a dramatic reduction in symptoms and often-rapid return to functioning. It should be noted that medical disorders often associated with psychiatric symptoms, such as diabetes and seizure disorders, might be co-occurring with all the disorders noted above.

III. *Substance use disorders*

Substance use disorders are also significant co-morbid conditions that can alter the course of illness, treatment and outcome, and represent a growing in importance issue in the treatment of children and adolescents. Co-morbid substance use disorders or substance abuse can add dramatically to the degree of morbidity and functional incapacity of the individual, and may influence the type of care provided.

IV. *Learning disabilities*

Learning disability encompasses disorders that affect the way individuals with normal or above normal intelligence receive, store, organize, retrieve and use information. Problems include dyslexia and other specific learning problems involving reading, spelling, writing, reasoning and mathematics. Undiagnosed learning disabilities are a common but manageable cause of young people deciding to leave school at the earliest opportunity. The clinicians' role in these situations is to screen health conditions that may affect performance (such as hearing or vision problems or neurological disorders) and to identify psychosocial and environmental factors that may affect learning abilities (such as family disruption, poor peer relationships or cultural and economic difficulties).

V. *Conduct disorders*

Conduct disorder can be defined as persistently disruptive behaviour in which the young person repeatedly violates the rights of others or age appropriate social norms. It is often preceded by oppositional and defiance in early years and can become more disruptive during adolescence. Symptoms include damage to property, lying or theft, truancy, violations of rules and aggression towards people or animals. Teenagers with a conduct disorder often have concomitant disorders such as depression, suicidal behaviour and poor relationships with peers and adults. Consequences include school problems, school expulsions, academic and vocational failure and problems with the law. Parents and families need support to help them make sure the young person does not stay away from school and severely affected adolescents should be referred to mental health professionals for evaluation and care.

VI. *Attention-deficit/Hyperactivity disorder*

Definition of the symptom complex known as Attention deficit/hyperactivity disorder (ADHD) differ, but severe problems with concentration or attention and/or hyper activity are estimated to affect about 5 per cent of adolescents (Kondo et al.) 6 times as many boys as girls are affected. The main consequences of ADHD are poor academic performance and behavioural problems, although adolescents with ADHD are at substantially higher risk of serious accidents, depression and other psychological problems. About 80 per cent of children with ADHD continue to have the disorder during adolescence and as many as 50 per cent of adolescents still do throughout adulthood. The main differential diagnoses are with behavioural problems secondary to poor parenting or poor school supervision. Milder forms of ADHD can be amenable to simple management strategies. More severe problems may require treatment including educational changes, behavioural programmes, family therapy and individual counselling.

VII. *Anxiety disorders*

Anxiety disorders are relatively common in adolescents and often persist into adulthood. Whereas separation anxiety disorder and autism are more prevalent among younger children, generalized anxiety disorder and panic attacks emerge during adolescence. Generalized anxiety disorder is marked by uncontrolled excessive worrying over every day events accompanied by difficulty in concentrating, irritability, sleep problems and often fatigue. Panic disorders are characterized by recurrent spontaneous panic attacks, often associated with physiological and psychological signs and symptoms. As with other mental health problems in adolescence, anxiety disorders are often accompanied by other conditions, particularly depression. Some other types of anxiety disorders that occur in adolescents are:

(a) Obsessive Compulsive Disorder (OCD) characterized by intrusive, unwanted, repetitive thoughts and rituals performed out of a feeling of urgent need, at least one-third of adult cases begins in childhood;

(b) Panic Disorder characterized by feelings of extreme fear and dread that strike unexpectedly and repeatedly for no apparent reason, often accompanied by intense physical symptoms, such as chest pain, pounding heart, shortness of breath, dizziness, or abdominal distress.

(c) Post Traumatic Stress Disorder (PTSD), a condition that can occur after exposure to a terrifying event, most often characterized by the repeated experience of the ordeal in the form of frightening, intrusive memories, and brings on hyper vigilance and deadening of normal emotions.

As many anxiety disorders during adolescence are accompanied by physical symptoms, careful evaluation is needed—at least a complete medical history and a comprehensive physical examination—to exclude conditions such as hypoglycemic episodes, migraine, seizure and other neurological problems. Treatment may include simple educational strategies, behavioural interventions, cognitive behaviour therapy, family therapy and rarely the use of anxiety tics.

VIII. *Emotional problems*

Over-eating, excessive sleepiness and a persistent over-concern with appearance may be signs of emotional distress. Anxiety may produce phobias and panic attacks. Recent research suggests that even family and friends do not often recognize emotional disorders. At some time, 4 out of 10 adolescents have felt so miserable that they have cried and have wanted to get away from everyone and everything. During their adolescence, more than 1 in 5 teenagers think so little of themselves that life does not seem worth living. In spite of these powerful feelings, depression may not be obvious to other people.

IX. *Sexual problems*

The dramatic physical changes of adolescence can be very worrying to some teenagers, especially to those who are shy and who don't like to ask questions. At the other end of the scale, some express their concern with excessive bragging about sexual ability and experiences. Crushes on someone of the same sex are common in adolescence. Sensitive support, clear guidance and accurate information about these different aspects of sex are essential—from parents, schools, family doctors, and family planning clinics. Most adolescents choose their partners quite carefully. Their lifestyle is more of risk-taking. Adolescents who take risks in one way tend to take risks in other ways as well.

X. *Behaviour problems*

Teenagers and their parents complain about each other's behaviour. Parents often feel they have lost any sort of control or influence over their child. Adolescents want their parents to be clear and consistent about rules and boundaries, but at the same time may resent any restrictions on their growing freedom and ability to decide for themselves. Experience suggests that children are at greater risk of getting into trouble if their parents don't know where they are. So, parents should try to make sure about where they are going and what they are up to.

XI. *School problems*

School phobia also called school refusal is defined as a persistent and irrational fear of going to school. It must be distinguished from a mere dislike of school that is related to issues such as a new teacher, a difficult examination, the class bully or lack of confidence. The phobic adolescent shows an irrational fear of school and may show marked anxiety symptoms when in or near the school. Refusal to go to school can be due to difficulties in separating from parents, being perfectionist and becoming depressed because they can't do as well as they would want to, disturbed family life, with early separation from or death of parent; an established pattern, it may have happened at primary school. Such children often have physical symptoms such as headache or stomachache.

Those who go to school, but then play truant, are usually unhappy at home and frustrated at school. They prefer to spend their days with others who feel the same way. Emotional problems will often affect school work—worry about oneself, or about what is going on at home, makes it difficult to concentrate. Pressure to do well and to pass exams may come from parents or teachers, but adolescents usually want to do well and will push themselves. Excessive nagging can be counter-productive. Exams are important, but they should not be allowed to dominate life or to cause unhappiness.

Bullying can cause all of the above. Around 1 in 10 secondary school children is bullied at some point; about 1 in 20 is bullied every week. Short children are more likely to be bullied. School phobia often occurs alongside social and other phobias and may be quite disabling, leading to failure in school and later vocational failure. Management usually requires involvement of the young person's whole 'system' including parents, siblings and the school. Short-term cognitive behaviour therapy has been shown to be effective.

XII. *Trouble with the law*

Most young people do not break the law, but those who do are usually boys. When they do, it usually only happens once. If a parent doesn't feel that breaking the law is particularly important, it is more likely that their children will offend. Unhappiness or distress can also lead to behaviour that will get them into trouble with the police. It is always worth asking about such feelings if an adolescent is repeatedly getting into trouble.

XIII. *Eating problems*

Weight can be a real problem. If an adolescent is overweight and is criticized or made fun of, he/she is more likely to dislike himself/herself and become depressed. This can lead to inactivity and comfort eating, which worsens the weight problem—dieting can actually aggravate the situation. It is more important to ensure that they feel happy with themselves, fat or thin. Many adolescents follow dieting. Fortunately, few will develop serious eating disorders—only around 1 in 100 teenagers develop anorexia, 1 in 50 have bulimia. However, these are more likely to occur in those who take up serious dieting, think very little of themselves, are under stress and who have been over-weight as a child.

Eating disorders are treatable. The sooner they are diagnosed and treated, the better the outcomes are likely to be. Eating disorders require a comprehensive, long-term treatment plans that usually involves individual or family therapy, and that may include medication and even immediate hospitalization. Unfortunately, many people with eating disorders will not admit they are ill and refuse treatment. Support from family and friends are vital to successful treatment and recovery.

XIV. *Drugs, solvents and alcohol*

Many teenagers experiment with alcohol and illegal drugs. Regular use of drugs or alcohol is much less common. Less than 1 in 100 of 11-12-year olds are regular users, but this increases to 1 in 6 of 15-year olds. Although cannabis has been widely felt to be relatively harmless, there is now good evidence that it can make mental health problems worse in adolescence and can double the risk of developing schizophrenia. Despite publicity about other drugs, alcohol is the most common drug to cause problems for adolescents. One should consider the possibility of drug or alcohol use when sudden or dramatic changes in behaviour are seen in the adolescents.

XV. *Abuse*

Physical, emotional and sexual abuse may occur in adolescence and may cause many of the problems mentioned above. Children or teenagers who are being abused can find someone to talk to. Families with these problems need expert advice and should seek help.

XVI. *Mental illness*

Much less often, changes in behaviour and mood can mark the beginning of more serious psychiatric disorders. Although uncommon, manic depression and schizophrenia may emerge for the first time during adolescent years. Extreme withdrawal may indicate schizophrenia, though there are usually other explanations for such behaviour. Parents who are concerned about these possibilities should see their family doctor.

XVII. *Schizophrenia*

Schizophrenia is a chronic, severe, and disabling brain disorder that affects about 1 per cent of the population during their lifetime. Symptoms include hallucinations, delusions, disordered thinking, and social withdrawal. Schizophrenia appears to be extremely rare in children; more typically, the illness emerges in late adolescence or early adulthood. However, research studies are revealing that various cognitive and social impairments may be evident early in children who later develop schizophrenia. These and other findings may lead to the development of preventive interventions for children. Only in this decade have researchers begun to make significant headway in understanding the origins of schizophrenia. In the emerging picture, genetic factors, which confer susceptibility to schizophrenia, appear to combine with other factors early in life to interfere with normal brain development. These developmental disturbances eventually appear as symptoms of schizophrenia many years later, typically during adolescence or young adulthood. A number of new, effective medications for schizophrenia have been introduced during the past decade (www.nimh.nih.gov).

Causes, Signs and Symptoms

The factors and causes affecting the mental health of children and adolescents have been discussed in detail in the next chapter. Undoubtedly, the problems in children and adolescents can be caused by biology, environment, or a mix of both. Examples of biological causes are genetics, chemical imbalances in the body, and damage to the central nervous system, such as a head injury. There are many environmental factors that can put young people at risk of developing mental health problems. Examples of these factors include exposure to environmental toxins, such as high levels of lead; exposure to violence, such as witnessing or being the victim of physical or sexual abuse; stress related to chronic poverty, discrimination, or other serious hardships; and loss of important people in the lives of young people through death, divorce, or broken relationships.

A variety of signs may point to a possible mental health problem or serious emotional disturbance in a child or adolescent. It is important to pay attention if a child or adolescent is troubled by feeling really sad and hopeless without good reason and the feelings don't go away; is very angry most of the time, cries a lot or overreacts to things; is worthless or guilty a lot; anxious or worried more than other young people; is unable to get over a loss or death of someone important; is extremely fearful—has unexplained fears or more fears than most kids; is constantly concerned about physical problems or physical appearance; and is frightened that his or her mind is controlled or is out of control.

The adolescent experience changes, for example, does much worse in school; loses interest in things usually enjoyed; has unexplained changes in sleeping or eating; avoids friends or family and wants to be alone all the time; daydreams too much and can't get things done; feels life is too hard to handle or considers suicide; and hears voices that cannot be explained. He/she is limited by poor concentration; is not able to sit still or focus attention; worry about being harmed, hurting others, or about doing something "bad"; need to wash, clean things, or perform certain routines hundreds of times a day in order to avoid danger; thoughts that race—almost too fast to follow; and persistent nightmares.

The adolescent behaves in ways that cause problems, for example uses alcohol or other drugs; eats large amounts of food and then makes self vomit, abuses laxatives, or takes enemas to avoid weight gain; continues to diet and/or exercise obsessively although bone-thin; constantly violates the rights of others or breaks the law without regard for other people; and does things that can be life threatening.

If there is concern about the child's or adolescent's mental health, it is important to get help as soon as possible.

20

Behavioural Maladjustment: Factors and Causes

The mental health of children, adolescents and their families is as important as their physical health to their well-being and personal development. While some mental health problems are relatively mild and short-lived, others can cause significant suffering and may even be life threatening. The consequences of failing to address the mental health needs of children and adolescents are extensive. High social and economic costs occur through school failure, disruptive behaviours and inability to develop the social and problem-solving skills that enable young people to become productive and happy members of the society.

Applying a public health approach to mental health is relatively recent. This approach to mental health includes identifying the prevalence of mental health problems and disorders in children, the risk factors, the protective factors and effective interventions. Effective interventions should span the spectrum of mental health, health promotion, prevention of mental health problems, early intervention in the development of mental health problems, and management of existing mental health problems and disorders.

Epidemiology

International studies have estimated the prevalence of mental health problems in children and adolescents to be between 18 and 22 per cent. The Western Australian Child Health Survey found that nearly one in five children and adolescents aged 4 to 16 years (18 per cent) had experienced a mental health problem in the previous six-month period. Of these, 6 to 8 per cent had had more than one type of problem. In common with other disorders, untreated child and adolescent mental health problems may become significant health problems in adulthood. Extensive evidence indicates that prevention and early intervention programmes may reduce later mental health problems and disability and ease the burden suffered by these children, adolescents and their families, with potential cost saving to communities and governments.

Mental health problems affect children and adolescent's health, development, and learning capabilities. When these children first come to the attention of helping agencies they are often at an age when patterns of behaviour are already deeply established and hard to change. Many not only come from disadvantaged background in respect of poverty and poor housing but also experience much adversity as a result of disrupted relationships with the parents or other important people in their lives to offer services when behaviours are entrenched, is too late. It is in the earliest years of life when children are at their most vulnerable. We should be focusing upon supporting families with adolescents and providing preventive services in their earliest years. As Bowlby (1979) insisted, "there is a strong causal relationship between an individual's experiences with his parents and his later capacity to make affectional bonds".

Although a number of researches have already been done on adolescents and their problems but what intrigues is the incidence rate of various mental health problems in children and adolescents who are at a high risk of developing some of the crucial mental disorders and then through a preventive approach help such individuals so that they are better able to adjust in future and live a successful life.

Review of Pattern and Extent of Disorders in Adolescence

International scenario

Emerging evidence continues to point to an increase in the prevalence of mental health problems among adolescents and young adults (Surgeon General's Report, 1999). Whether this increase is due to better diagnosis, an actual increase in prevalence, or both is unknown, but half of all lifetime cases of mental illness are now recognized to begin by the age of 14 and three-quarters by the age of 24 (Kessler et al. 2005). Despite effective treatments, however, there are typically long delays, sometimes decades, between when individuals first experience clinically significant symptoms and when they first seek and receive treatment.

Severe, disabling depression affects approximately 17 per cent of adolescents and young adults nationally (Kashani and Sherman, 1988; Fleming and Offord, 1990; Lewinsohn et al., 1993 and 1994; Kessler and Walters, 1998), while anxiety in its many forms results in significant impairment in approximately 13 per cent of children and adolescents (Shaffer et al. 1996). Other mental illnesses, such as Attention Deficit-Hyperactivity Disorder (which has a prevalence of 3-7 per cent) and Bipolar Mood Disorder (which has a prevalence of over 1 per cent), affect smaller numbers but are ubiquitous amongst children, adolescents, and young adults, causing an untold amount of suffering and lost productivity (DSM-IV; American Psychiatric Association, 1994). Despite the fact that federal government spending on anti-drug measures has increased over ten-fold in the last 15 years, over 50 per cent of high school seniors have experimented with an illicit drug, 23 per cent have used an illicit drug within the past 30 days, and over 30 per cent have been drunk within the past 30 days (Monitoring the Future, 2005). Suicide, the most feared and tragic outcome of mental illness, is the third most common cause of death among adolescents and young adults, preceded only by accidents and homicide (Anderson and Smith, 2003).

Banks (1983) found a case rate of 3.5 per cent in a sample of 200, 17-year olds as a result of individual interviews using the Present State Examination, an instrument designed from the standpoint of adult general psychiatry and solely dependent upon the mental state as determined at interview alone. A considerable number of teenagers have good accounts of subjective affective symptoms in spite of their parents and teachers reporting no observable abnormality. In early adolescence, there is an evident continuity with childhood. A number of children with conduct, emotional or developmental disorders will continue to be affected during their teenage years, their conditions persist. This is particularly true for conduct disorder.

Anti-social behaviour outside the home is at its peak in the mid-teens though the prevalence of different types of offence changes with age, shoplifting being more typical of young offenders and crimes of violence rising proportionally with age (West, 1982). Theft and vandalism are remarkably common among urban teenage boys (Clarks, 1978; Belson, 1975).

Anxiety state, hysteria, hypochodriasis and obsessional disorder may all be seen before puberty but become more frequently recognized during adolescence. The prevalence of depression and depression symptomatology increases markedly after puberty and may rise further during the teens. Para suicide rates also show a dramatic surge, peaking in the late teens. Most depression in adolescence is not, however, bipolar. The rise in the prevalence of neurotic and affective disorder during the teens is the factor largely responsible for the change from male excess among psychiatrically disordered young teenagers to female excess in the late teens.

Anorexia nervosa has been mostly observed at around the age of 17 (Crisp, 1980) and is, perhaps, the only disorder which can be said to have a specific relationship to the adolescent developmental process. Schizophrenia is very rarely diagnosed before puberty but the condition is recognized increasingly throughout the teens. Abuse of a variety of psycho-active substances becomes widespread during adolescence though there is suspicion that the patterns of substance choice vary with age, solvent abuse in the early teens, alcohol and opiates later on.

Indian scenario

Studies conducted in India also somewhat show the same results. Clinic based studies conducted on individual child psychiatric disorders have shown a wide variation in prevalence of behaviour disorders, ranging from 3-36 per cent (36% Bassa, 1962; 13% Chacko, 1964; 3.3% Murthy et al., 1974; 3% Praveen et al., 1988; 4.6% Singh and Gupta, 1970); and neurotic disorders ranging from 3.7-54 per cent (Chacko, 1964; Manchanda and Manchanda, 1978; Nagaraja, 1966; Praveen et al., 1988; Raju et al., 1969; Sharma et al., 1980).

A study conducted on school children by Jiloha and Murthy (1981), reported a prevalence rate of psychiatric disorders in 20.7 per cent adolescents and the common disorders reported were enuresis (8.8%), mental retardation (5.9%), stammering (2.1%) and emotional problems (1.7%). Another study on school children and adolescents conducted by Deivasigamani (1990) reported the prevalence of psychiatric disorders in 33.7 per cent children, and the common disorders were enuresis (14.3%), conduct disorder (11.1%), mental retardation (2.9%) and hyper kinetic syndrome (1.7%).

The drug abuse surveys in school have identified alcohol and tobacco as the most commonly abused drugs in adolescents (Varma et al., 1979). A recent study on drug abuse by Bansal and Banerjee (1993) in child labourers has revealed a higher prevalence (45%) than in school children, and tobacco smoking was found to be the commonest followed by tobacco chewing, snuffing, cannabis and opium. Studies have also been carried out investigating different variables linked to child abuse. For example, Gil (1977) investigated social class and family size, Light (1973: 556-98) investigated unemployment, and Garbarino (1977: 721) investigated social isolation in child abuse.

Every 90 minutes a teenager tries to commit suicide in India. Many of these attempts are half-hearted cries for attention, help and love. But every six hours, one succeeds.

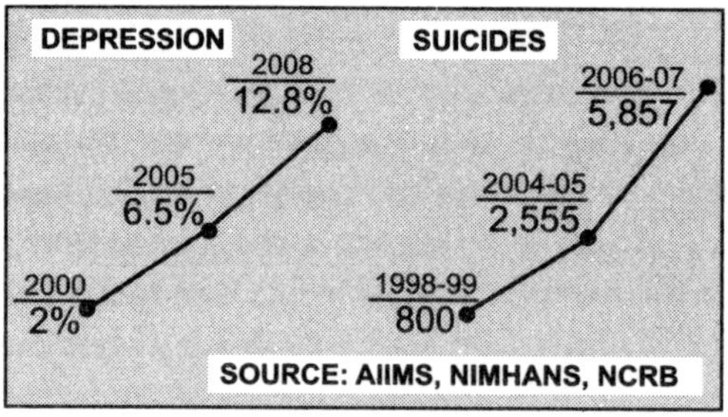

More adolescents die of suicide than AIDS, cancer, heart disease, obesity, birth defects and lung disease. In 2006-07 5,857 students took their own life, which works out to a stunning 16 suicides a day, says the National Crime Records Bureau (NCRB).

While the global teen suicide rate is 14.5 per 100,000, a 2004 study by the Christian Medical College (CMC), Vellore, reported 148 for girls and 58 for boys in India. If globally, suicide is the fourth leading cause of teen deaths, in India it is at number one in some pockets and is the third largest killer all across. Over 150 students ended their lives across the country last month.

Virtually in almost all the societies, as well as in India, boys are considered adventurous, achievement oriented, independent, dominant and aggressive, which contributes to the violent behaviour shown by them and makes them prone to indulge in criminal activities. The sense of insecurity and emotional dependence sometimes predisposes females to become a victim of sexual abuse, which serves as a base for some of them to indulge into criminal behaviours and some of them either forcefully or willingly opt for self-defeating roles such as call girls and prostitutes. In India 10 per cent teenage girls of the country population are sexually active. The increase in number of delinquency has become a major problem these days and requires a strong consideration of the public in general.

Factors Influencing the Development of Mental Health Problems

A number of factors associated with an increased risk for mental health problems in childhood have been identified. Factors associated with a lower risk of mental health problems have also been identified:

Children's Risk Factors and Protective Factors for Development of Mental Health Problems

Type of Factor	Risk Factors	Protective Factors
Environmental	Poverty	Positive peer relationships
	Housing conditions	Social support (elders and peers)
	Unemployment	Family structure and cohesion
	Family size	Positive parent-child relations
	Parent marital status	
	Marital conflict	
	Poor parenting skills	
	Parental psychopathology	
	Exposure to negative life events (e.g. Bereavement, family separation, trauma, family illness), Life transitions (e.g. Change of school)	
Child Characteristics	Genetic influences Biological influences (Prenatal, perinatal and postnatal), Difficult early temperament, Cognitive style, Low IQ Academic failure	Repertoire of coping skills Social skills Strong intellectual skills Cognitive style Academic competence
Social and Economic	Marginalisation Racism	Family or Career employment Family or career income Social status School environment

Many factors acting together are responsible for one's mental health or illness. Occasionally one factor or another may predominate, but even then the wellness or activity of other factors affects how one will respond to events or conditions. At any one time our behaviour depends upon characteristics we have inherited, the stage of our development as accelerated or retarded by metabolic or nutritional factors, physical potentialities and patterns of learned behaviour all acting and reacting in complex, changing systems of environmental stimuli. Some persons who might have physical or psychological susceptibilities to stress might never encounter the conditions that would trigger illness. Others who may be basically stronger might encounter such stress that they become ill. Each person has a breaking point. For some it is less than for others.

Aggressive social behaviour, which typically begins to emerge during childhood, is a key risk factor for progression of externalizing disorders (Brook, Cohen, et al., 1992; Kellam, Ling, et al., 1998; Lipsey and Derzon, 1998; Robins and McEvoy, 1990; Tremblay and Schaal, 1996; Woodward and Fergusson, 1999) and also is a predictor of internalizing disorders (Kaltiala-Heino, Rimpela, et al., 2000; Keenan, Shaw, et al., 1998; Kellam, Brown, et al., 2008). There is now extensive evidence on interventions designed to help families develop practices that prevent the development of aggressive and antisocial behaviour and its associated problems. These interventions focus on providing training in parenting skills.

Seminal research on family interactions by Patterson and colleagues over the past 40 years has shown that harsh and inconsistent parenting practices contribute to aggressive and uncooperative behaviour and that positive involvement with children and positive reinforcement of desirable behaviour contribute to cooperative and prosocial behaviour (e.g., Patterson and Cobb, 1971; Patterson, 1976, 1982). Building on the early parenting interventions by Patterson's group (e.g., Patterson and Gullion, 1968; Patterson, 1969, 1974), a number of programmes have emerged that target parents of children at different developmental stages, including childhood (e.g., Forgatch and DeGarmo, 1999; Webster-Stratton, 1990; Sanders, Markie-Dodds, et al., 2000), early adolescence (e.g. Dishion and Andrews, 1995; Spoth, Goldberg, and Redmond, 1999), and adolescence (Chamberlain, 1990; Henggeler, Clingempeel et al., 2002). All of these programmes teach and encourage parents to (1) use praise and rewards to reinforce desirable behaviour; (2) replace criticism and physical punishment with mild and consistent negative consequences for undesirable behaviour, such as time-out and brief loss of privileges; and (3) increase positive involvement with their children, such as playing with them, reading to them, and listening to them.

The efficacy of interventions focused on parenting skills is well established (see Lochman and van-den-Steenhoven, 2002; Petrie, Bunn, and Byrne, 2007; Prinz and Jones, 2003; Serketich and Dumas, 1996). In addition, several meta-analyses report positive effects of such interventions across a range of child and parent outcomes for parents of young children (Barlow, Coren, and Stewart-Brown, 2002; Lundahl, Nimer, and Parsons, 2006; Serketich and Dumas, 1996; Kaminski, Valle, et al., 2008). Kaminski, Valle, and colleagues (2008) report the greatest effect sizes for programmes that include parent training in creating positive parent-child interactions, increasing effective emotional communication skills, and using time-out and that emphasize parenting consistency. Many parenting programmes have been shown in two or more experimental trials to produce positive behavioural outcomes.

Early adolescence is a developmental period during which the prevalence of substance use, delinquency, and depression begins to rise. There is also evidence of an increase in the rates of teasing and harassment in middle school. Significant physical changes occur with the onset of puberty, along with social changes, including the transition from elementary school to middle school or junior high school, increased concern about peer acceptance (Steinberg, 1999), and increased demand for autonomy (Eccles, Midgley et al., 1993).

Major environmental risk factors that are especially important in early adolescence include family poverty and family conflict, as well as inadequate parental monitoring and deviant peer group formation. A key behavioural risk factor is aggressive social behaviour, which contributes to social rejection and deviant peer group formation (Patterson, DeBaryshe, and Ramsey, 1989). In addition, young people who use cigarettes and alcohol are more likely to use other drugs (Kandel, Johnson et al., 1999). More generally, psychological and behavioural problems tend to be interrelated (Biglan, Brennan, et al., 2004).

Neyes and Kolb (1963) observe that disturbed communication between and adjustments of various psychological and physiological subsystems, rather than either alone, are the main determinants of breakdown. Stresses in interpersonal relations and in the socio-cultural field are no less to be considered than stresses in the biophysical sphere. Behaviour cannot be adequately described in terms of an impersonal disorganization of cellular structure or physiological processes, nor do there seem to be any psychiatric symptoms—except in some cases of toxic organic syndromes, which can be considered as correlates of brain changes, physiological, biochemical or electrical.

Heredity

Except for a few rare mental deficiencies and the psychosis, there is little conclusive evidence for direct single-gene inheritance of mental disorder. Varying degrees of genetic cause have been claimed for several senile diseases, main depressive and evolutional psychosis, homosexuality, and myoclonic epilepsy (Shields and Stater, 1961).

Biological and Physical Factors

Physical defects, such as deformation of the spine, clubbed feet and congenital defects of vision or hearing take their psychological toll in feelings of inferiority, social isolation and negative self-attitudes, thus, reducing a handicapped person's resistance to stress. It is known too that several mental deficiencies are caused by maternal prenatal diseases, such as German measles, birth injuries or endocrine disorders.

Illnesses of any kind sometimes contribute to conflicts and frustrations, already present. Much of the disability in both mental and physical illness is traceable to the hospitalization itself as well as to the disease. Separation from family, worry over finances and loss of wages, plus feelings of helplessness and fear of the illness, all contribute to stress. Any weaknesses already present may become exaggerated. Psychosomatic disorders may accompany, augment or be precipitated by almost any other mental or physical illness and greatly complicate the symptom picture.

Social-learning Experiences

Perhaps the greatest contributor to maladjustment is in the area of socialization. When a child is born into a family, he forms a meaningful relationship first with his mother, then with other members of his family who satisfy his needs and administer rewards and punishments for his behaviour. Through these relationships, systems of punishments and reinforcements and by generalizations of attitudes so formed to others, the child comes to attach certain values to people, to depend upon them and to form conceptions about him from these interactions.

These relationships are the wellspring of the self. If the early family experiences are pleasant and reassuring, the child adjusts and develops well socially, forms wholesome self-attitudes and is able to accomplish various developmental tasks. With a minimum of stress, should any of numerous unfavourable family conditions or child-rearing practices establish fears, conflicts, hostilities or negative self-reactions not only will the person experience intra-family tensions, but also he will be handicapped in future social relationship. These, in turn, affect future self and other adjustments and the stresses amass like a rolling snowball. Frustrations in toilet training, of inconsistent and severe discipline, rejection, indulgence, domination, jealousy of siblings or of a parent, unreasonable demands for perfection, all prevent a child from developing social skills and favourable self-attitudes and thus reduce his ability to cope with frustration and his resilience to stress. Poorly adjusted in his family, the child may lack the skills to adjust well to his peer group and lacking these skills, he may fail to adjust in his school, his work, his marriage and possibly fail in understanding his own children.

Psycho-social Factors

It has been shown that depressed children and adolescents, compared to others in the year before the depression, had experienced more considerable difficulties, such as love problems, negative events in the school situation, and problems in relationships with friends and family. The younger the child is, the heavier is the weight of life's difficulties, which contribute to the cause of depression. This may entail the loss of someone close, a lack of positive feelings of self-worth, lack of experience in accomplishing things (which for example can come up if the child has limited motor skills and/or perception), lack of encouragement (for example if family members are also depressed and more distant), and alcohol abuse in the family.

When it comes to relationships during the formative years, the special relationship children perceived they had with their parents is of major significance in the development of depressive disorders. Studies show that depressed people overall have considered their parents to be emotionally inaccessible and distant. The earliest ages for depression have been significantly lower in people whose parents have also been depressed, who see their parents as reserved and dismissive. An American study shows a strong relationship between depression in teenagers and how they handle a perceived lack of support from parents.

One of the most meaningful factors in the early interaction between parents and children is the bond of affection that is developed between them. Parents' capacity to react emotionally and respond to the child is a natural prerequisite in realizing a secure attachment. When the mother for one reason or another is unavailable or unsupportive, or when her response to the child's signals are inconsistent and unreliable, the child will be insecure. Many studies affirm the relationship between early attachment and later adjustment according to, for example, social capacity. If an infant does not form an attachment to its parents, it can be one of many factors, which contribute to a later depression in that child/teenager.

General Psychological Factors in Health and Diseases

Research has repeatedly yielded evidence that mental and emotional processes are implicated in some way both in good health and in the majority of the physical diseases that afflict humankind.

Health, attitudes and coping resources

The sometimes devastating effects of attitudes of hopelessness and helplessness on organic functioning have long been known, partly through anthropological research on death and similar phenomenon. Today, many surgeons will not undertake a major operation until they are convinced that the patient is reasonably optimistic about the outcome.

Less dramatically, but in many ways of equal or greater importance, the effects of multiple life changes on a variety of illnesses has been amply documented in the research on significant life changes and subsequent health status. In a study of 192 men between the ages of 30 and 60, Payne (1975) found that long-standing physical and psychological health problems were related to larger degrees of life change, even when the changes had been favourable. Evidently, the amount of adjustment required overtaxed the individual's resources.

In other instances, it is the particular nature of the individual's coping resources that is itself suspected. The most familiar example is the Type A behaviour pattern. When certain ordinary frustrations of life, such as having to wait in line, habitually provoke extremes of impatience and inhibited rage, the person is designated 'Type A' and a large body of evidence has established this coping style as a significant risk factor for coronary heart disease. Often it appears that any severe stress serves to pave the way for, precipitate or aggravate a physical disorder in a person already predisposed to it. A person who is allergic to a particular protein may find resistance further lowered by emotional tensions, similarly, where an invading virus has already entered the body—emotional stress may interfere with the body's normal defensive forces or immunological system.

In the like manner, any stress may tend to aggravate and maintain certain specific disorders, such as migraine headaches (Levor et. al., 1986). Day (1951) noted that unhappiness was among the stressors that could lower resistance. The relationship between psychological factors and good health has also been well documented (Jones 1977). Positive emotions seem often to produce certain immunity to physical disease or to be associated with speedy and uncomplicated recoveries when disease does strike. The patient, who believes that the treatment is going to be effective, has a much better chance of showing improvement than does the patient who is neutral or pessimistic—even when the treatment is subsequently shown to have no direct or relevant physiological effects.

Lifestyle as an added factor in health maintenance

Today a great deal of attention is being paid to the role of lifestyle in the development or maintenance of many health problems. Numerous aspects of the way we live are now considered influential in the development of some severe physical health problems—diet—particularly overeating and consuming too many high cholesterol; low fiber foods; lack of exercise, smoking cigarettes, excessive alcohol use, constantly facing high stress situations and just ineffective ways of dealing with day-to-day problems are but a few of the many lifestyle related patterns that are viewed as contributing causes.

Negative thought patterns

Too many pessimistic thoughts, that is to say to interpret events in a negative manner, are thought to be risk factors in developing depression in children and adolescents. It is unclear whether such a negative cognitive lifestyle is a result of negative life events, difficulties and/or sensitivity or a more basic personality trait. Individuals with previous negative experiences can acquire a learned vulnerability, which causes the individual to focus on negative events, and to have a hard time seeing and taking in positive events. It easily becomes a vicious circle where individuals believe they have no influence over their own lives, which leads to helplessness which in turn leads to passiveness, decreased social capacity, hopelessness, and other signs of depression. Such a cognitive style has been shown to give children and adolescents a predisposition to end up in long states of depression (dysphoric states) when the individual is exposed to difficulties, for example, receives poor grades in school or feels rejected by parents.

Symptoms of depression have been proven to be a risk factor for future depressions. Adolescents who reported depressive symptoms were shown to run three times the risk of getting a serious depression within the next few years. Up to 12-31 per cent of young people have been estimated to have such an increased risk. Students with depressive symptoms tend to have a more pessimistic explanation style, i.e. they tend to explain and interpret everyday events in a more negative and less adequate terms, and at the same time assign themselves self-deprecating characteristics. Such an interpretative manner can lead to self-fulfilling prophecies, which support the depressive symptoms.

Nurturing childhood

This refers to familial-child interactions. This also affects the development of mental health. Positive nurturing starts with bonding at childbirth and includes feelings of love, security and acceptance; this will lead to the child positive interactions with parents and siblings. Negative nurturing includes maternal deprivation, parental rejection, sibling rivalry and early communication failures. Individuals exposed to poor nurturing may develop poor self-esteem or poor communication skills. They may also display socially unacceptable behaviour as they seek to meet their basic needs.

Life circumstances

These circumstances can influence one's mental health from birth. Positive experiences are generally emotionally secure and successful in school and establish healthy relationships. Negative circumstances such as poverty, poor physical health, unemployment, abuse, neglect and unresolved childhood loss generally precipitate feelings of hopelessness, helplessness and/or worthlessness. These negative responses place a person at risk for depression, substance abuse or other mental health disorders.

Critical Stages in the Development of Mental Health or Mental Illness

Stage I: Prenatal conditions, early family environment and behavioural developments of the child

Most children are born healthy, but some are born defective or injured. This is the period when the basic influences of heredity and congenital traumas and diseases are asserted and the foundations are laid for social learning and personality. Occasionally adjustment problems of childhood signal the deeper disturbance, but too often such symptoms are dismissed as "nervousness" or are treated as misbehaviours or bad habits and so are left untreated or are met with rejection and discipline. This is sometimes true even for organic difficulties associated with mental deficiency. Needless to say, this is the period of incubation for many mental illnesses, which will flower in later years.

Stage II: Crisis of everyday living asnd development from pre-adolescence throughout the life span

This stage covers problems of early peer group and school relationships and responsibility in family and community living, religion, courtship, marriage and parenthood, occupational choice and satisfaction, economic stability, physical illness, ageing and various other emotional and environmental stresses.

Stage III: Onset of Mental Illness

Difficulties developed in the first two stages culminate in symptoms of mental breakdown. There is rapid deterioration of work habits, family and social relationships and responsibilities and overall personal control in the home and community.

Stage IV: Treatment

The treatment often requires prolonged hospital care and therapy. For milder or earlier cases, outpatient treatment may be given in a psychiatric clinic or general hospital.

Stage V: Rehabilitation of the mental patient

This includes various types of therapy, training and community services, which assist the patient to return to the community, to obtain satisfactory employment, to make adequate social and personal adjustment following treatment and to prevent recurrence of the disorder.

Framework for Mental Health Prevention Services for Children

There is a growing scientific basis to support the practice of prevention in the field of mental health for children. The focus must shift from individual casework to a broader understanding of the biopsychological, socio-economic, cultural and spiritual needs of the communities. By its nature, prevention of mental disorders among children requires the public health approach of developing partnerships among people and agencies in the community.

Provision of high quality services and programmes demands a spectrum of interventions: mental health promotion, prevention, early intervention and treatment. One of the difficulties for implementing promotion and prevention programmes is that their future benefits may seem uncertain or too distant. Clinicians trained in individual casework may therefore be reluctant to change to a public health model.

Many mental illnesses have a long history in the individual, beginning in early childhood and are the result of many interacting factors (as discussed above) of a physical and emotional nature resulting in stress, cloaked by family and friends, many mental illnesses appear only after years of progressive maladaptation to problems of everyday living plus physiological changes some of which are believed to be aggravated or caused by crisis of growing up or ageing, disease and unresolved frustrations.

For this reason, we no longer think of treating disorders only when they appear fully developed, but we search for ways to prevent or to arrest their growth and seek means to restore to normal, responsible and productive living in their homes and communities those who have been treated successfully. The modern emphasis has shifted from concern only for treatment and care of mental illness to more comprehensive attention to a way to develop and to maintain mental health and to promote optimal human functioning.

In a review of the use of evidence-based care for child and adolescent mental health, Kurtz et al. suggested that preventive interventions should be implemented at the earliest possible stages in the development of disorders. Mental health problems in children may impair their social and educational development. This may lead to low self-esteem and poor attainment of positive learning experiences, further compounding their risk of psychological problems. Mental health problems are also associated with an increased risk of youth suicide.

Effective Prevention Programmes

Postnatal depression

The most important issue for promoting the mental health of infants is identifying the family situations that predict later problems. A major risk for infants is postnatal depression in their mothers. Approximately 10 per cent of women after delivery experience a depressive disorder that is severe enough to interfere with their daily functioning. Studies have shown that the care received by infants of such mothers is less responsive, more rejecting and more coercive than that received by controls. This care may affect infant growth and development, and infants may develop a depressed mood style as early as three months of age. Appropriate and effective treatment of postnatal depression at the earliest stages may prevent psychological withdrawal and developmental impairments in the infant.

Behavioural disorders

Behavioural disorders or problems affect a significant number of children. They include a range of challenging behaviours, such as oppositional defiant disorders, and aggressive behaviours. Behavioural problems in childhood may escalate over time and may develop into delinquent and antisocial disorders in adolescents. As these disorders progress they become more difficult to treat and may persist into adulthood. Programmes that promote appropriate parenting for vulnerable families or families at risk can reduce the risks of disruptive behavioural problems in preschool-aged children that may lead to conduct disorders. Improving a parent's sense of competence in parenting and promoting marital communication may lead to improved mental health outcomes for both parents and children.

Primary-school-aged children

Depression has been predicted as one of the major public health problems of the 21st century. Depression currently accounts for almost 11 per cent of the disease burden worldwide: this is expected to rise to 15 per cent by 2020. Prevention of depression in children and adolescents is possible and opportunities first present themselves in childhood. Programmes that improve self-esteem, encourage positive thinking and increase social and problem solving skills can protect children against depression. Such programmes can be provided through a general curriculum format, with the school education system supplying an efficient and systematic environment for their delivery.

Conclusion

A public health framework can also be applied to mental health. The increasing evidence about the prevalence of mental health disorders in children can be combined with advancement in knowledge of effective interventions to promote the mental health of children and adolescents. Prevention and early intervention programmes are crucial to improving mental health outcomes for children. If significant advancements are to be made, then interventions need to target the early stages of mental health problems and disorders as well as the early years of life. Effective interventions work best when delivered in partnership with the many services and organizations involved with children and their families.

21

Education for Mental Health and Hygiene

The scope of mental hygiene is not limited to the work of clinics, or to the diagnosis and treatment of persons who are already maladjusted. In a very real sense, everyone is engaged in mental hygiene whether he intends it or not. In this respect, mental hygiene is like other endeavours that are intimately concerned with human welfare. If all persons who deal with others, especially parents, teachers and employers, were governed by the requirements for mental health there would be fewer unhappy and inadequate personalities for clinicians to treat.

Years back, sick people were bled in a vain attempt to cure their illnesses. Modern medicine recognizes that bleeding is generally futile and usually harmful. But children are beaten and scolded even today because parents still in the dark ages of mental hygiene believe that these are effective ways to control their conduct. Some of mental hygiene is as old as the Bible and has existed as long as there have been kind and understanding persons.

The layman's role in mental hygiene is exactly analogous to the part he plays with respect to physical health. Parents and teachers do not treat serious physical illnesses, but must know how to recognize their presence in order to call a physician in time. In providing proper food, cleanliness, sleep and exercise, on the other hand, the parent has a primary responsibility. As far as severe disorders of personality are concerned, layman needs only to know how to recognize them, to regard them with constructive rather than moralistic attitudes and to seek such expert assistance as may be available. In dealing with everyday situations in which children learn to cope with their life problems, parents and teachers can contribute directly to the growth of effective personalities. Also, just as parents bind up the child's little wounds of physical injury, so they may give some remedial help to the simpler, more common conflicts and anxieties.

The process of growth and development and of learning has been studied in their several aspects and facets. They all help to explain and interpret human behaviour and present a picture of the significant changes, which take place in an individual through successive stages of life. Stress has been laid on physical and intellectual growth and development, and on the acquisition of knowledge and skill, language and creative thinking, but more important than all of them are the personal and social adjustments of the child for they hold the key to his success and happiness in life. In schools it is being increasingly recognized that high academic distinctions, robust physical health and affluent conditions in the home may miserably fail an individual in the attainment of success and happiness in life if he has not learned to accept himself and his world, to get along with people and situations he has to deal with, and to make suitable and healthy adjustments both to himself and to his environment.

That is why, modern schools are stressing the need of such adjustments in their practices and programmes and provide for a large variety of experiences and activities, and even offer guidance that young people may learn to live and work together. The primary responsibility for teaching and cultivating adjustment patterns among young people lies with parents with whom they spend the best part of their formative years and from whom they imbibe thoughts and habits, interests and attitudes, and ways of adjusting to things and persons. Whether their lives will be marked by satisfaction and self-fulfillment or by frustration and self-defeat depends very largely on the foundations of adjustment patterns laid in the early experiences in the home. Very often teachers emphasize that relationships and values acquired in the home are the keystones to adjustments in the school. When children enter school their potentialities for further development are not altogether exhausted, and it is the teacher's privilege, as well as his responsibility, to accept the learner as he is and to help him to gain healthy constructive adjustments within the framework of his social heritage.

Mental Hygiene and Prevention of Mental Disorders

With an increasing knowledge of the causes of personality disturbances, mental hygiene has been mainly concerned with preventive measures. Wise parents and teachers catch the incipient signs and take suitable measures to effect suitable adjustments in the life of the child. Social workers and clinical psychologists offer helpful advice and apply corrective measures for home conditions. Thus many cases that might in course of time become profound neuroses are helped in time to take to normal life. The development of mental hygiene means a new approach and a new responsibility for the class teacher who has not only to teach certain facts and information to the child but also to make sure that he achieves wholesome adjustment. It has revolutionized the idea of discipline. It is no longer believed that discipline can be ensured by ordering about; it has to be understood in the wider perspective of personal adjustments of each individual child.

Many mental hygienists have examined the cult of the curriculum in recent decades. They wonder whether formal education is doing a good job of developing wholesome personalities, whether the average teacher can recognize the beginnings of serious personality disturbance and what the competitive atmosphere of our classroom procedure with its emphasis on marks and promotions might be doing to the pupils, more particularly about the effect of such an atmosphere on the youngsters who fail. The entire school system can be used as a means of training the public in the principles of mental hygiene just as this system has been used for years to promote knowledge of ordinary hygiene.

As might be expected, there has been considerable criticism of the schools for their alleged failure to introduce and abide by mental hygiene teachings. They have been criticized for employing teachers ignorant of such teachings. Students of education have been urged to secure the requisite knowledge by enrolling for courses in mental hygiene. There can be no question of the vigour with which official mental hygiene has tackled official education. The result has been an avalanche of books, articles and lectures on the general theme of mental hygiene in education. It may prove instructive to devote a little attention to this general phase of the mental hygiene movement.

Schools can Promote Mental Health

The school has two responsibilities for mental hygiene. One task is to rid itself of practices that contribute to pupil maladjustment, and to provide resources to discover and help pupils already in difficulties. The school's duties are not limited to such negative virtues however. A greater need is to insure that education will be a positive and constructive influence in the life of every student. All functions of the school, including the curriculum, provision for individual differences, the handling of conduct problems, and individual guidance can be made to contribute to these ends.

The chief mental hygiene tasks of the schools is not so much to prevent actual mental breakdown as to re-enforce and amplify the functions of the ideal home in building up wholesome and socially constructive attitudes. This does not mean that an already crowded curriculum should be burdened with one more subject or the addition of a course in mental hygiene at either the elementary or high school level. The scope of mental hygiene is such that it cannot very well be compressed within the confines of a series of lesson plan or formal school projects.

The mental hygienist is more concerned about the attitudes built up in the child by school experiences—both curricular as well as extra-curricular—than he is with formal academic success. Every teacher has a responsibility for shaping and influencing the child's attitude. Wholesome personality development of every child should be the fundamental educational objective. In terms of such a mental hygiene ideal it is just as important to adjust the school to the child, as it is to have the child to adjust to the school. Mastery of the curriculum should be regarded as a means for enhancing personality development rather than as an end in itself.

Existing curricula should be evaluated on the basis of their efficacy in furthering this goal. It is particularly important to consider their range and flexibility, for an extremely rigid curriculum of narrow consent cannot be adapted to the individual needs of individual students. Many of our so-called educational misfits are causalities of an underlying curriculum. Enlightened school officials have long been aware of this and have already made considerable progress in the difficult and expensive task of fitting the school to the vagaries of the individual child.

Mental Hygiene Hazards in School

School experiences sometimes have a detrimental effect on student's adjustments, whereas they should be constructive and integrative. An example familiar to every teacher is the student who seems unable to learn inspite of adequate mental ability. Scolding, threats of failure, and even well-meaning attempts to help by intensive tutoring, all seem ineffective. Accumulated experience, and the results of some research studies, indicates that three factors contribute to special disabilities in school subjects. The first component is primarily educational. An inflexible school curriculum, which attempts to teach every child in the same way, is not well adapted to individual pupils. A minority of students may fail to learn when taught by methods that are successful, or at least tolerable, for the majority. A second factor is the attachment of anxiety to school in general or to a particular subject because of emotional experiences within the school. The third component, a severe and common one, is the effect of home grown anxieties on school work. The three factors are rarely found in isolation. All three are usually present in some degree, but their relative significance varies from one student to another.

School failure and morale

When school failure is due primarily to shortcomings of the teaching process, straightforward educational treatment is often successful. Educational psychologists have devised diagnostic tests to determine exactly where the progress of learning has gone astray and methods for remedial instruction designed to meet individual needs. At the high school and college levels some students fail because they do not know how to study or how to solve problems independently. They can be helped by individually planned retraining in study methods, but not by mere exhortation and advice. The cure of school disabilities can be a useful tool for mental hygiene. A youngster who is failing in school suffers a loss of self-esteem, and may be goaded by his teachers and parents and ridiculed by his peers. Relieving his academic difficulties reduces his anxiety and makes him free to undertake more constructive adjustments in other areas of living.

School problems that spring from acquired anxieties are perplexing to teachers and of special interest to mental hygiene. Such anxieties may arise from a large variety of causes. Ridicule and overt punishment, experienced in connection with a subject, are the most obvious sources. Somewhat more subtle are perfectionistic attitudes on the part of the teachers and parents. When school difficulties are linked to pervasive conflicts or deep seated anxieties, psychotherapeutic approaches are needed. Play therapy for younger children may relieve anxiety and hence, by reducing the drives for defense or escape, make them again free to learn.

There are two possible evils of the child's handling by the family: one the consequence of pampering and the other the consequence of neglect. These are the evils of overindulgence of the child and of hostile antagonism. The latter causes the child to feel rejected by the family group. He lacks emotional security. These psychological considerations apply to the school community as well. Too much solicitude for his welfare by the teacher may make a child too dependent on others for solving this problem. However, the more common evil is that of the other extreme of not getting enough attention to feel that he is understood and welcomed by the teacher. Failure in schoolwork with expression of disapproval and disappointment by the teacher often induces the youngster to feel that 'teacher doesn't like me'. It is but a short step from the conviction of being disliked to the feeling of being rejected.

One of the crucial mental hygiene opportunities for the teacher is to guide the youngster in wise ways of facing the fact of failure. Individual morale is largely contingent on the possession of healthy techniques of adjusting to failure and a good teacher is one who can help the child develop such techniques. For the child, failure in school can be as momentous as bankruptcy or business failure to businessman. A good portion of the healthy sense of emotional security making for zestful daily living is a function of being able to handle one's routine assignments successfully. School assignments are the child's business obligations. They affect his life largely.

How much emphasis a child's family usually places on his school advancement is very important. As a consequence, he fears the loss of goodwill of his family members. In other words, those whose affectionate approval he craves expect him to handle this school job. Not to be able to live up to the expectation of those who have been good to them and for whose admiration they yearn is hard on them. Even young children soon learn that grown-ups regard school failure as some kind of disgrace. They may even regard it as a stigma on the family reputation. In brief, the youngster is often made to feel guilty because he failed at school. He may even be told that he ought to be ashamed of himself. Shame and self-respect cannot dwell in the same psychological household and morale goes to smash when self-respect crumbles. This is what makes school failure a mental hygiene problem.

Perfectionism as a mental hygiene evil

One of the chief evils of unbridled competitiveness in the classroom is its possible unwholesome influence not merely on the children who fail, but also on those who succeed. This may sound paradoxical, but every mental hygienist and psychiatrist will recognize the danger immediately. It is the danger of becoming a perfectionist. The perfectionist is chronically dissatisfied because he expects too much of himself and of those who chance to come under his direction. Reference is not being made to that individual who sets for himself standards of reasonable accomplishment of a relatively high order. Instead that individual is being referred here who is afraid of making a single mistake, of falling short in a single particular, of being wrong in any respect.

In many respects perfection constitutes an impossible goal. In the classroom very few, if any, teachers deliberately set ridiculous standards. For them the concept of perfection is an outgrowth of the stereotyped rigidity of spelling and arithmetic and similar subjects. To be perfect means to master this sort of conventional curricular content in flawless fashion. Not only must the answers be correct, they must be given within a 'reasonable' time.

Our striving for perfection in school may make for the vicious extreme of the never-ending push for power and prestige. The competition for success runs through the wrap and woof of our society. Our schools reflect and re-enforces this strident competitiveness in the children and adolescents. Perfectionism as an ideal thus easily jeopardizes the psychologist's ideal of the balanced personality. Ambition can be either healthy or morbid. The perfectionist is more likely to lead toward the morbid kind of self-disparaging, never relaxing struggle. Mental health calls for avoidance of these extremes in favour of a balanced mean.

Youngsters ought to be prepared for this critical world. To the extent that perfectionism as an ideal induces them to hope for such brilliant achievement as to avoid all adverse criticism, it constitutes poor preparation. It would be healthier to teach them to expect some sort of criticism by some people as inevitable and to reconcile themselves to this inevitability. Instead of teaching youngsters to strive to be perfect in the sense of dodging all possibility of error and expecting 100 per cent approval of the entire public, it might be better mental hygiene pedagogy to teach them to rest content with accomplishing the best job of which they are capable under given circumstances. They ought also to be taught how to handle criticism in resolute fashion, so that exaggerated fear of criticism will not paralyze action.

Educational goals should be so adjusted for each individual child as to make success a consequence of reasonable effort. There is no fun in reaching easy goals and no fun in struggling for futile objectives. Learning can be made an exciting game when educational tasks are so arranged as to provoke such effort on the part of the learner. To accomplish this end the task must not only come within the scope of the learners' capacity but it must also be short enough to be accomplished within a reasonable length of time.

Love of learning as a mental hygiene value

From one point of view every normal child manifests the beginnings of a love of learning. The endless questions of the little child are indications of this love. He wants to know about stars and why we must die and if dogs can talk and where God lives and a myriad other problems. His is a restless and persistent curiosity. He wants to know these things not in order to pass examinations to impress others with his erudition, to get a job or to earn a degree, but just for fun of finding out. For him learning is not a means to an end, but an end in itself. But all too often our schools mutilate or destroy this alert, joyous curiosity of the child. What should have been nurtured into at least an avocational love of study and reflection and serious reading—the nature equivalent of childish curiosity—is crushed by the Juggernaut of the Curriculum. That is why educators are urging the curriculum be adjusted to the child rather than have the child warped to fit the curriculum.

From the viewpoint of mental hygiene, as a consequence, fostering a love of this sort is one of the chief purposes of a formal education. To tell a student that he has reached the "limit of his educability" is thus poor mental hygiene. The task of educating for mental health thus goes far beyond the confines of the traditional curriculum. It involves far more than mastery of tool subjects or particular content subjects. It calls for the utilization of every agency capable of enabling the child to keep moving from ignorance to knowledge and from knowledge to understanding and from understanding to the wisdom, which culminates in service to others.

Positive Contributions to Mental Hygiene

The role of education is to make positive contributions to the personal adjustments of students. The cure or even the prevention of educational difficulties is not enough. School experiences can help students develop attitudes, insights and skills which enable them to meet life problems more integratively and with a minimum of preventable anxiety. Several modern developments in education have tended to make schools more effective agencies for positive mental hygiene. The changes have been gradual and much still remains to be achieved.

Among recent trends in education, perhaps the most significant for mental hygiene is an increased emphasis on interpersonal relationships. Teachers pay more attention to students as individuals, are more aware of their needs and personalities, and have more respect for them as persons. The ideal of modern teacher is one who teaches students, not subjects. The role of the teacher is as a psychotherapist. The teacher observes and listens to the student's feelings, and communicates an acceptance of them as worthwhile persons. A warm interpersonal relationship breeds confidence, avoids anxiety and promotes sounder learning.

Schools can also contribute to mental hygiene by giving attention to the interpersonal relationships of students with their peers. Learning to live with other people is therefore one of the major tasks of psychological development. The conventional procedures of the classroom have been modified so as to provide for social learning. School clubs, athletic teams, and other extracurricular activities, when examined in terms of mental hygiene, are not educational frills but are means for giving students an opportunity to learn interpersonal adjustments.

Principles governing the improvement of transfer of training have important implications for mental hygiene. School subjects can contribute to mental health when they effectively teach general understandings which are applied to a variety of genuinely relevant situations in the students' lives. By proper adaptation to the abilities and needs of students of various degrees of maturity, values can be achieved at all levels of education. Only when the primary attention is directed to the learner and his needs, and when school subjects are regarded primarily as tools for the development of persons, can education contribute to mental health.

School Psychological Service

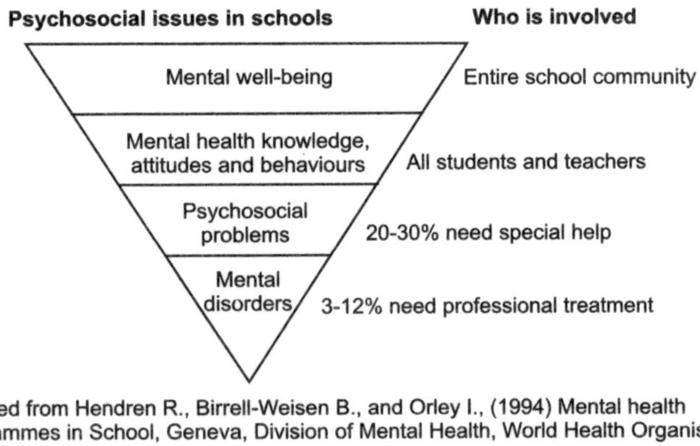

Adapted from Hendren R., Birrell-Weisen B., and Orley I., (1994) Mental health programmes in School, Geneva, Division of Mental Health, World Health Organisations.

It is widely accepted that schools have an important role to play in promoting children's physical health. They organize sports programmes, give guidance on healthy living and, in some countries, provide nutritious meals for their children. Yet many parents and teachers are alarmed by the suggestion that schools also have a role to play in promoting children's mental health. Teachers say: we're educators, not health workers. Parents say: we don't need to worry about mental health, our children are fine. The provision of school mental health services is sometimes shown as an upside down triangle. At the top, every child can benefit from health promotion programmes. Down at the bottom, relatively few children need treatment. The trouble is that many countries concentrate their resources on treating the few, despite the fact that prevention is better and cheaper than cure.

The influence of psychological teaching has been especially evident in the school. The teacher, nowadays, has gained a wider and deeper knowledge of psychology from his training. He recognizes the value of mental tests in helping him to assess the mental ability of his pupils and to know how much or how little to expect from them. He learns also that intellectual ability is not the whole story; physical and mental health is equally important and if he is to do justice to the child, he must remember the importance of physical and emotional factors. He will also be on the lookout for the signs and symptoms of maladjustment and emotional disturbance, as well as for special disabilities and general retardation. He will recognize the importance of consulting the expert, whether physician, psychiatrist or psychologist, when ordinary school methods do not bring about improvement.

But there is another side of the picture. An estimated two-thirds of all young people with mental health problems who need help are not getting it! Most often, children and adolescents' mental health problems are not recognized for what they are—and appropriate help is not sought. The stigma about mental health problems keeps many people from asking for help. Stigma also causes isolation and discrimination for many young people and their families. Punishment is often incorrectly used to try to solve these problems within the home, at school, or in the juvenile justice system.

Good information about children's mental health problems is not available to many people who work with and care for children and adolescents. In addition, culturally competent and child-focused mental health services are not yet available in every community. Sometimes, there is not a good match between the family or problem and the provider or service that is offered.

When a serious emotional disturbance in a child or adolescent goes untreated, it can have grave personal, social, and economic impacts on the child and his or her family. The child may experience major problems interacting with others, fail in school, act out or show violent behaviour, or have additional or more severe mental health problems as an adult. The family may incur high medical bills and the community also pays if the child becomes involved in the juvenile justice system. Most of all the child pays if he or she doesn't get help.

Raising public awareness about children's mental health issues may lead to earlier recognition of possible mental health problems. Identifying these problems when they first appear may help to keep them from getting worse later.

1. *Reducing the child's stress*

How can we help the child cope with stress? Proper rest and good nutrition can help increase the child's coping skills, as can good parenting. The child should be given time each day. Whether he or she needs to talk or just be in the same room with significant other, one should make oneself available. Even as the child gets older, this "quality time" is important. It's really hard for some people to come home after work, get down on the floor, and play with their children or just talk to them about their day—especially if they've had a stressful day themselves. But by showing interest in the child's life, regardless of the child's age, parents can show the child that he or she is important to them.

The child should be helped to cope with stress by talking with him or her about what may be causing it. Together, parent and the child can come up with a few solutions. Some possibilities are cutting back on after-school activities, spending more time talking with parents or teachers, developing an exercise regimen, or keeping a journal. It should be remembered that some level of stress is normal; and the child should be told that it's OK to feel angry, scared, lonely, or anxious. He/she should be made to realize that other people share his or her feelings.

2. *Developing self-esteem in young children*

Every parent hopes that his or her children are developing a positive sense of self-worth. How the child feels about himself or herself is one of the greatest responsibilities and biggest challenges for the parents. People who have a positive sense of self feel like they have something worthwhile to contribute and a sense of internal worth. They are able to venture out into the world, work toward attaining their goals, and welcome life with anticipation and pleasure.

Children who have self-confidence have a feeling of internal worth that enables them to welcome challenges and work cooperatively with others. When children don't develop self-confidence, they tend to focus on failure instead of success, problems instead of challenges, and difficulties instead of possibilities. There is no single way to enhance self-esteem, but one way is to show children "unconditional positive regard". The children should be made to feel that people care about them, accept them, and approve of them, no matter what. The challenge is to accept the child as a person, even when we do not accept his behaviour. The following parameters if taken care of can help raise the self-esteem of the child:

Honest recognition and praise

Honest recognition and sincere praise come from the heart and draw attention to something specific the child has done. It is always better to be more specific with remarks like "You worked so hard building that block tower!" or "Thank you for helping Rahul pick up the paints."

Self-worth is such a private, internal feeling, the comments of the significant others will have the most impact when they deal with who the child is and how she sees herself from the inside. When we praise children it should be done in a way that heightens their sense of inner satisfaction. Praise is an external source of esteem, which is helpful but not nearly as valuable and effective as internal sources that come from a sense of competence.

Respect

Respect is another key component in reinforcing child's self-worth. There are several ways we can show respect. We can offer them choices when appropriate, then respect and abide by their decisions. Showing confidence in the child's ability to make decisions helps build his self-esteem. Another way to show respect towards children is to explain the reasons behind the rules or adult decisions. Talking about children in front of them should be avoided unless they are included in the conversation.

Competence

The most effective thing that can be done to help the children feel a sense of self-worth is to help them achieve competence or an internal feeling of mastery or control. Every time the child does something well, she feels competent because of what she did, not because of what someone said. Six practical ways to help children gain competence are:

- Encouraging children to make their own choices and be as independent as possible.
- Providing many different experiences and activities for the children to experience success.
- Providing opportunities that are challenging but not too difficult or frustrating. When developing new skills, children need to practice and try things out over and over again.

- Encouraging a diverse range of skills for both girls and boys. Avoid reinforcing stereotypical ideas of what is appropriate play. Pay attention to allowing and encouraging equal access to activities and skills.
- Offering many creative activities where children can explore the process of creation and the expression of their ideas and feelings.

It would be beneficial to provide children as many opportunities as possible for interacting and playing with other children and help them to figure out strategies for getting along with them.

Learning to Deal with Frustration

The process of learning self-control is linked very closely with how a child feels about herself and the frustrations that are part of day-to-day life. Children need help and practice building their frustration tolerance. One of the best ways to make this happen is to provide opportunities for children to make their own choices and decisions. Helping them stick to decisions can be difficult, but it is important for children to experience the consequences of their choices (at least some of the time). Similarly, when we give young child a choice, we have to honour their decision. Of course, not everything can be a choice and not everything is negotiable. Children should not be allowed to hurt themselves or other people (verbally or physically) or to destroy property. They cannot dominate every family or school interaction. Sometimes adults have to say "no."

Physical aggression (biting, pushing, hitting, and throwing) is very common in the early years. Very often, episodes of aggression can be prevented before they begin. Anticipation is always helpful and relieves stress for adults and young children alike. When possible, alert children before transitions, such as the end of playtime, leaving an outing, or the arrival or departure of guests. Rewarding desired behaviour will help children learn what is expected of them. When trouble repeats itself, the situation should be analyzed and changes should be made that get to the root of the problem.

Conclusion

Thus, it can be ultimately concluded that the psychological atmosphere of the school can be made more like that of a congenial home atmosphere. The child ought to be made to feel safe and secure at home and at school. In a way the school is to be considered a projection and enlargement of the psychological values of the well-administered family. It is the child's training ground for communal living. To achieve the utmost from his activities on this training ground, he must be given a sense of belonging to the school community. He must be made to feel a part of it just as he is made to feel his identification with the family group.

A child-friendly school encourages tolerance and equality between boys and girls and different ethnic, religious and social groups. It promotes active involvement and cooperation, avoids the use of physical punishment, and does not tolerate bullying. It is also a supportive and nurturing environment; providing education which responds to the reality of the children's lives. Finally, it helps to establish connections between school and family life, encourages creativity as well as academic abilities, and promotes the self-esteem and self-confidence of children.

References

Abraham, L., "True Love, Time Pass, Bhai-Behen: Heterosexual Relationships among the Youth in a Metropolis", *Paper presented at the workshop on Reproductive Health in India: New Evidence and Issues*, Pune, 2000.

Allen, John J.B., "DSM-IV", in *Encyclopedia of Mental Health,* by Howard S. Friedman (Ed.). San Diego, CA: Academic Press, 1998.

American Psychiatric Association, *Diagnostic and Statistical Manual of Mental Disorders* (DSM- IV), 4th edition, Text Revised (TR), Washington, DC: APA: Washington, 1994 & 2000.

Anderson, C.L., *School Health Practice*, C.V. Mosby Company, 1968.

Andery, Aarons, et al. (Eds.), *Child-to-Child—An Approach to Learning.* Revised and adapted for Indian Schools by the Voluntary Health Association of India, New Delhi.

Bernard, H.W., *Psychology of Learning and Teaching*, McGraw Hill Book Company: New York.

Blum, H.L., *A Working Definition of Health for Planners: Merging Concepts.* University of California School of Public Health, Berkeley, 1971, pp. 22-23.

Brown, B.B., Larson, R.W. and Saraswathi, T.S., *The World's Youth: Adolescence in 8 Regions of the Globe*, Cambridge UK: Cambridge University Press, 2002.

Carrat, F. and Valleron, A.J., *Epidemiological Mapping Using the Kriging Method: Application to an Influenza-like Illness Epidemic in France*, 1992, pp. 1293-1300.

Chek, P., *Scientific Back Training Course*, C.H.E.K. Institute, 1994.

——, *Scientific Core Conditioning Course*, C.H.E.K. Institute, 1998.

Colwell, R.R., *Global Climate and Infectious Disease*, 1996, 274:2025-31.

Crow, L.D. and Crow, A., *Mental Hygiene*, McGraw Hill Book Company: New York.

Dacey, J.S., *Adolescents Today*, Goodyear Publishing Company: California, 1979.

Donnchadha, R., *The Confident Child: A Guide to Fostering Personal Effectiveness in Children*, Newleaf: Dublin, 2003.

Ediger, Marlow and D.B. Rao, *School Organization*, Discovery Publishing House: New Delhi, 2004, pp. 301-25.

Erickson, E.H., *Childhood and Society*, New York: W.W. Norton, 1950.

Field, T., "Infants of Depressed Mothers", *Developmental Psychopathology*, 1992; 4: 49-66.

Fishbein, Morris (Ed.), *The New Medical and Health Encyclopedia*, 4 Volumes, M.D.H.S. Stuttman Co., Inc., Publishers, New York.

Flory, V., *Your Child's Emotional Needs: What They are and How to Meet Them*, MacMillan India Ltd.: New Delhi, 2005.

Ganguly, S.K. and M.L. Gharoti, "Cardiovascular Efficiency before and after Yogic Training", *Yoga Mimansa*, 17, 1, 89-97, 1974.

Gates, A.I. and Others, *Educational Psychology*, Macmillan Company: New York.

Geller, Barbara, "Bipolar Disorder at prospective follow up of Adults who had prepubertal Major Depressive Disorder". *American Journal of Psychiatry*, 158: 125-27, 2001.

Gharote, M.L., "Effect of Yogic Training on Physical Fitness", *Yoga Mimansa*, 31-34, 1973.

Giesecke, J., "Choosing Diseases for Surveillance", *Lancet,* 353(9150): 344, 1999.

Goldsmith, S.B., *The Status of Health Status Indicators*. Health Services Rep 87: 212-20, March 1972.

Gopalakrishnan, N., *Mental Health and You*, Popular Prakashan: Bombay, 1994.

Grout, E. Ruth, "Health Teaching in School", *Journal of School Health*, Vol. 34 (3), p. 148, 1964.

Hadfield, J.A., *Psychology and Mental Health: A Contribution to Developmental Psychology*, Allen and Unwin: London, 1950.

Hall, G.S., *Adolescence,* 2 Volumes, New York: Appleton, 1916.

Health Education for School Age Children—A Framework, Central Health Education Bureau and NCERT: New Delhi.

Health Education Journal, June 1967, 26(2) pp. 97-101.

Hoyman, H., "An Editorial: Health and a Living Faith", *Journal of School Health*, 40(6), 1970, pp. 279-80.

——, "Human Ecology and Health Education", *Journal of School Health,* 41(10), 1971, pp. 538-47.

Hoyman, H., "New Frontiers in Health", *Journal of School Health,* 43(7), 1972, pp. 423-30.

Hoyman, H.S., *Our Modern Concept of Health.* Paper presented at the annual meeting of the American Public Health Association, Detroit, Mich., 1961.

Humphreys, Tony, *Self-Esteem: The Key to Your Child's Future*, Newleaf: Dublin, 2002.

International Classification of Impairments, Disabilities and Handicaps: A Manual of Classification Relating to the Consequences of Disease. Geneva, World Health Organization, 1980.

Jacquelynne, S. Eccles, "The Development of Children Ages 6 to 14", *The Future of Children: When School is Out.* Vol. 9 (2) Fall 1999.

Jahoda, M., *Current Concepts of Positive Mental Health*, Basic Books: Kazdin, A.E & Weisz JN, 2003.

Jussawalla, J.M., *Art of Healthy Living*, Vikas Publishing House: New Delhi, 1995.

Kapur, Malavika, *Mental Health in Indian Schools*, Sage Publications: New Delhi, 1997.

Klein, D.B., *Mental Health: The Psychology of Personal Adjustment*, H. Holt and Company: University of Michigan, 1944.

Kochhar, S.K., *Secondary School Organization*, Sterling Publishers: New Delhi, 1991.

Korchin, Sheldon J., *Modern Clinical Psychology: Principles of Intervention in the Clinic and Community.* CBS Publishers and Distributors: New Delhi, 1999.

Kubie, L.S., "The Fundamental Nature of the Distinction between Normality and Neurosis", *Psychoanalytic Quarterly,* 23: 167-204, 1954.

Kurtz, Z., *Treating Children Well: A Guide to Using the Evidence Base in Commissioning and Managing Services for the Mental Health of Children and Young People.* London: Mental Health Foundation, 1996.

Lindgren, H.C., *Mental Health in Education*, Holt, Rinehart and Winston: New York.

Mayall, B., *Towards Sociology for Childhood,* Buckingham: Open University Press, 2002.

Menninger, K., *The Human Mind,* Oxford, England: Knopf, 1937.

Minaire, P., "Disease, Illness and Health: Theoretical Models of the Disablement Process", *Bulletin of the World Health Organization,* 1992, 70: 373-79.

Moorthy, A.M., "Detraining Effect of Yogic and Non-yogic Exercises on Minimum Muscular Fitness", *Yoga Mimansa*, 21, 3 & 4, 49-54, 1982-83.

Mrazek, P. and Haggerty, R.J., *Reducing Risks for Mental Disorders: Frontiers for Preventive Intervention Research*, Washington DC: National Academy Press, 1994.

Murthy, R.S., "Street Boys' Perception of Sexuality and Sexual Behaviour". Paper presented at the meeting of Tata Management Training Center on Reproductive Health in India, Pune, 1993.

Nash, J.B., *Lecture 2009*, "Developing and Managing High Quality after School Program: A Multidisciplinary Approach", University of Florida, Organized by American Association for Physical Activity and Recreation.

Nixon, F., *An Introduction to Physical Education*, W.B. Saunders, 1947.

Nutrition Atlas, National Institute of Nutrition, Hyderabad.

Oberteuffer, D., *Physical Education: A Textbook of Principles for Professional Students*, Harper & Row, 1970.

Palmer, S., *Toxic Childhood: How the Modern World is Damaging Our Children and What We can do About It*. London Orion, 2006.

Pande, P.K., *New Encyclopedia of Physical Education*, Eight Volumes.

Patrick, D. and Bush, J.W., "Toward an Operational Definition of Health." Paper presented at the annual meeting of the American Public Health Association, Minneapolis, Minn., 1971, p. 7.

Potdar, R.S., Mobilizing Education to Reinforce the Primary Health Care Through School Children as Change Agents and Revitalizing the School Health Program to attain the ultimate goal. "Health for all by A.D. 2000", Unpublished PhD Education, Shreemati Nahibai Damodar Thackersey Woman's University, 1989.

Raju, B., *School Health Program in Selected Middle Schools of Delhi: A Survey*, New Delhi, NCERT, 1970.

Raphael, B., *Scope for Prevention in Mental Health*. Canberra: National Health and Medical Research Council, 1993.

Red, R. and Wattenberg, W.E., *Mental Hygiene in Teaching*, Harcourt, Brace: New York.

Reddy, R.S., *Teaching Health and Nutrition*, Commonwealth Publishers: New Delhi, 2007.

"Report of the Committee on Terminology in School Health Education", *Journal of the American Association for Health, Physical Education and Recreation*, Sept 1951, p. 14.

Report of the Education Commission (1964-66): Education and National Development, 1966, Ministry of Education, Government of India, New Delhi.

Report of the Secondary Education Commission (1952-53), Ministry of Education, Government of India, New Delhi.

Rice, Wayne and David Veerman, *Understanding Your Teenager*, Magna Publishing Company: Mumbai, 2000.

Sanders, M.R., Markie-Dadds C.L. Triple P: "A Multilevel Family Intervention Programme for Children with Disruptive Disorders". In Cotton, P., Jackson, H. (Ed.), *Early Intervention and Prevention in Mental Health*. Melbourne: Australian Psychological Society, 1996: 59-87.

Saraga, E., "Children's Needs Who Decides?" In Mary Langan (Ed.), *Welfare: Needs Rights and Risks*, London: Routledge, 1998.

School Health—A Guide for Primary School Teachers, Directorate General of Health Services, Ministry of Health and Family Welfare, Government of India.

Schwab, N.C., Panettieri, M.J. and Bergren, M.D., *Guidelines for School Nursing Documentation: Standards, Issues and Models,* National Association of School Nurses, 1998.

Shaffer, L.F. and Shoben, E.J., *The Psychology of Adjustment: A Dynamic and Experimental Approach to Personality and Mental Hygiene*. The Riverside Press Cambridge: Boston, 1956.

Shah, A.V., "Integration of Mental Health", *Indian Journal of Psychiatry,* 24, 3-7, 1982.

Sharma, R.N., *Applied Psychology*, S.J. Publications: Meerut, 1997.

Sharma, S.R., *Encyclopedia of Modern Education*, Anmol Publications Pvt. Ltd.: New Delhi.

Sidhu, K.B., *School Organization and Administration*, Sterling Publishers Pvt. Ltd.: New Delhi, 1996.

Sigerist, H.E., *On the Sociology of Medicine*, M.L. Roemer (Ed.), MD Publications, Inc.: New York, 1960, pp. 10-11.

Singh, L.B. and Singh, A.K., "Alienation: A Symptomatic Reaction of Educated Employed Youth in India". *International Journal of Psychology,* 31(2): 101-10, 1996.

Sudarshan, P.V. and Balakrishnaiah, S., *Physical Education Curriculum at Lower Primary Stage—An Evaluation Research Project*, Regional Institute of Education, Mysore, 2003.

Sutton, Carole, *Helping Families with Troubled Children: A Preventive Approach*, John Wiley and Sons: England, 1999.

The Curriculum Guide on Nutrition/Health Education and Environmental Sanitation in Primary Schools, National Council and Education Research and Training (NCERT): New Delhi, 1976.

The National Institute of Mental Health: "Eating Disorders: Facts about Eating Disorders and the Search for Solutions." Accessed Feb. 2002. Netscape: http://www.nimh.nih.gov/publicat/eatingdisorder.cfm.

Thomas, M. et al., A critical appraisal of the quality-of-life measurements. *Journal of the American Medical Association*, 1994, 272: 619-31.

Turner, C.E., Drenckhahn, V.V., and Bates, M.W., *Effectiveness of Radio in Health Education*, A.J.P.H., 25, 5:589 (May), 1935, p. 317.

Weiner, Irving B., *Psychological Disturbance in Adolescence*, John Wiley and Sons: New York, 1970.

Weissman, M., "Depressed Adolescents Grown Up". *Journal of the American Medical Association*, 281, 1707-1713, 1999.

Whitney, Anne L., "School Health Education on the Job: Current Problems and Present Practice". *J. Health & Phys. Ed.*, 6:13-15 (Oct.), 1935.

Williams, J.F. and Shaw, F.V., *Methods and Materials of Health Education*, 1935, p. 2.

Wood, D. Thomas, "Report of the International Higher Education Conference of the World Conference on Education", June 28-July 6, 1923, San Fransisco, California.

World Bank, *World Development Report 1993: Investing in Health*. New York: Oxford University Press, 1993.

World Health Organization: *The First Ten Years of the WHO*, Geneva, 1958, p. 459.

——, *Ottawa Charter for Health Promotion*, Geneva, 1986.

Yearbook of the Association for Supervision and Curriculum Development, "Fostering Mental Health in Our Schools", National Education Association 1201 Sixteenth Street, N.W. Washington 6, D.C., 1950.

Zubrick, S.R., et al., *Western Australian Child Health Survey: Developing Health and Well Being in the Nineties*. ABS cat. No. 4303.5, Perth: Institute for Child Health Research, 1995.

Websites

1. http://www.buzzle.com/articles/wellness-is-not-the-absence-of-illness.html
2. http://www.cdc.gov/nccdphp/aag/pdf/aag_dash2004.pdf
3. http://www.ehow.com/about_6572862_physical-education-curriculum-secondary schools.html#ixzz18w7lTfqY
4. http://www.kamat.com/database/books/kareducation/physical_education.htm
5. http://www.ehow.com/way_5125462_exercises-correcting-posture.html#ixzz0xlknuGFB http://www.ehow.com/about_5052881_causes-poor-posture.html#ixzz17EhFq9cf
6. http://www.allforkidsindia.com/allforkids/Resources/Exercise.aspx
7. http://health.indiamart.com/kidshealth/vaccine/faq-immunization.html

8. http://www.nfhsindia.org/data/india/indch6.pdf
9. http://www.emc.medicines.org.uk.
10. http://www.ehow.com/facts_5410642_childhood-communicable-diseases.html#ixzzlA3gihACy
11. First Aid and CPR Training for Teachers: The Importance of Knowing How to React to School-Related Injuries http://www.suite101.com/content/first-aid-and-cpr-training-for-teachers a129511#ixzz1A24beDIo
12. First Aid and CPR Training for Teachers: The Importance of Knowing How to React to School-Related Injuries:http://www.suite101.com/content/first-aid-and-cpr-training-for-teachers a129511#ixzz1A24q5NcB
13. http://www.sciencedaily.com/releases/2007/12/071217141431.htm
14. Children's Mental Health. What Every Child Needs for Good Mental Health http://www.nmha.org/infoctr/factsheets/72.cfm
15. Vanier Institute of the Family, 2003. Lessons Learned from Canada's Surveys of Children and Youth. Transition Magazine; 33(3). http://www.vifamily.ca/library/transition/333/333.html
16. www.surgeoneneral.gov/library/mentalhealth/home.htm
17. www.nap.edu/openbook.php?record_id
18. en.scientificcommons.org/ruth_e_grout
19. www.bookfinder.com/author/charles-a-bucher

Index